Ever since the First World War, socialists have considered imperialism a calamity: responsible for militarism, economic stagnation, and assaults on democracy in the metropolitan countries, an impediment to economic and cultural development in the Third World. So widespread has this view become that it is shared, in its essentials, not only by Marxists but also by an entire school of liberal development economists. Anti-imperialism has become an article of faith for millions throughout the world. Bill Warren breaks with this traditional outlook, arguing that the theory of imperialism, one of Marxism's most influential concepts, is not only contradicted by the facts but has diluted and distorted Marxism itself. The first part of his book traces the shifting position of the socialist movement on imperialism, from Marx and Engels's favourable view of the British colonization of India to the adoption of an anti-imperialist programme by the Communist International in the late twenties. The pivot of his account is a sustained, comprehensive critique of Lenin's 'Imperialism', demonstrating that the entire theoretical construction was at variance with the actual development of capitalism internationally. In particular Warren disputes the claim that 'monopoly capitalism' represents the ultimate stage of a senile capitalism, and charges that more modern theories of 'underdevelopment' and 'neo-colonialism' are merely postwar versions of Lenin's original thesis, marred by the same defects. The second part of the book sets out to refute the notion that imperialism is a regressive force impeding or distorting economic development in the Third World. It argues that on the contrary direct colonialism powerfully impelled social change in Asia and Africa, laying the foundation for a vibrant indigenous capitalism. Finally, it takes issue with the conventional view that postwar economic performance in the Third World has been disastrous, and presents a powerful empirical case that the gap between rich and poor countries is actually narrowing. Closely argued, clearly written, original, and iconoclastic, 'Imperialism: Pioneer of Capitalism' is a compelling challenge to one of the chief tenets of contemporary socialist politics.

Bill Warren

Verso

Imperialism: Pioneer of Capitalism

Edited by John Sender

British Library
Cataloguing in Publication Data
Warren, Bill

Imperialism: pioneer of capitalism.
1. Underdeveloped. Areas. Economic conditions.
2. Imperialism
3. Marxian economics
1. Title
330.9'172'4   HC 59.7
ISBN 0 86091 035 0
ISBN 0 86091 732 0 Pbk.

This edition first published 1980
© NLB, 1980
NLB and Verso Editions,
15 Greek Street, London W1V 5LF

Second impression 1982

Printed in Great Britain by
The Thetford Press Ltd
Thetford, Norfolk

Contents

List of Tables

Introduction

John Sender

Bill Warren died in January 1978. Notes he made one month before his death make it clear that he regarded the chapters he had completed for this book as first drafts requiring substantiation and detailed revision. He had planned a number of new chapters, but had not yet developed them beyond the barest outlines, simply listing major themes, arguments, and references. Indeed, there is little doubt that the author considered this book only an early draft for the first, and less important, aspect of his principal task, which was to draw explicit political conclusions for working-class strategy in the struggle for socialism in Africa, Asia, and Latin America.

These political conclusions were to have been developed in Part Three of this book, which Warren had tentatively entitled 'The Working Class and Socialist Movements in Third World Capitalism'. His intention was to elaborate an analysis of the rise and characteristics of the working class in the Third World, based on detailed consideration of empirical evidence regarding the social and political role of the proletariat in a number of countries. He had six major themes in mind.

1. The struggle for political liberation from imperialism has tended (both 'naturally' and as a result of political errors) to inculcate the working-class movement of Third World countries with nationalism, for example Peronism in Argentina, Nasserism in Egypt, and the policies of the

Communist Parties in many other countries.[1]

2. The combination of anti-imperialism and state-sector economic development on an impressive scale has led to a Third World ideology of 'socialism' that has misled the working class about the true character of these developing capitalist societies.

3. The resulting domination of the working-class movement by populist nationalism has been immensely reinforced by the petty-bourgeois ideology of 'neo-colonialism', which tends to divert and dampen internal class struggles by channeling mass discontent against external alleged enemies.

4. This combination of circumstances has fostered incorrect theses about the fundamental social forces on which the struggle for socialism can be based, partly because the theory of neo-colonialism underestimates the actual growth of capitalism and therefore of the working class. This underestimation produces what may be termed 'Fanonism', which emphasizes the revolutionary role of the lumpenproletariat and an allegedly undifferentiated peasantry. Underestimation of the pace of proletarianization and the growth of capitalism has also helped to generate the theory that the urban working class constitutes a non-revolutionary labour aristocracy and has encouraged reactionary policies aimed at excluding foreign investment, thereby hampering the development of the productive forces and the working class.

5. All these various trends — Fanonism, adulation of the peasantry, denunciation of the proletariat as a labour aristocracy, and so on — can be shown, both theoretically

1. Warren also intended to write an additional chapter for Part Two, to be inserted after the present chapter 6 and to be called 'Nationalism and Imperialism: A Case of Patricide'. In a half-page outline for this projected chapter, he indicated that he would emphasize that nationalism is the product of imperialism, which it later destroys. He planned to stress the links between nationalism, mass popular aspirations, and industrialization.

and factually, to be ideological reflections of transitory phenomena of the early development of capitalism. They share a reluctance to recognize that capitalism is already developing rapidly in the Third World, and with it the working class, capitalism's grave digger. Indeed, the Russian and Chinese revolutions were able to succeed only because 'neo-colonialism' had created the beginnings of capitalism, and with it an industrial working class.[2]

6. It may be concluded that as Third World capitalism grows, imperialism (as a system of domination by advanced over less-developed capitalist states) declines; as Third World capitalism develops, the working class is destined to play its classic revolutionary role. The sooner this is recognized, and all forms of nationalism and populism rejected, the more successful will be the struggle for socialism.

In view of some of the crude misinterpretations and basic misunderstandings of the political position implied by Bill Warren's earlier published work on imperialism,[3] it must be stated most emphatically that the themes and arguments outlined above in no way suggest a simplistic mechanical correlation between the economic development of capitalism and the prospects for socialism. Warren's major emphasis was that the *fundamental starting-point* for the development of Marxist and working-class strategy must be the recognition that *in general* a progressive position is one that advances the development of the productive forces,

2. A further aim of Part Three would have been to distinguish in more detail between the role of the working class in different types of Third World countries.

3. For example, Warren has been characterized as a 'bourgeois economist', his views stigmatized as typical of 'the diffusionist approach to modernization' and his position as 'representative of a respectable and authoritative club of development experts'. (See A. Hoogvelt, *The Sociology of the Developing Countries,* London, 1974, pp. 78 ff.) More recently, D. Seers, basing his argument on what he admits is an imprecise and subjective interpretation of Warren's position, makes a superficial and crude analogy between a concocted version of vulgar Marxism and the Chicago school of economists. (See D. Seers, 'The Congruence of Marxism and Other Neo-Classical Doctrines', mimeo, July 1978.)

while a reactionary position (Luddism, for example) holds back the development of the productive forces. To interpret this classical Marxist premise mechanically, or to view it through the prism of short-term policy options, would cripple the working-class struggle. On the other hand, however, to ignore the fundamental exigency that the strategy of the proletariat must stand in accordance with the objective forces of economic progress would render the working class incapable of becoming a hegemonic class.

Here Warren's analysis is far from crudely economic or deterministic and stands close to that of Gramsci, who held that political struggle must be based on 'effective reality', on 'the forces which really exist and are operative — basing oneself on the particular force which one believes to be progressive and strengthening it to help it to victory'.[4] Warren's purpose was to argue that in a range of important Third World countries, Marxists must recognize the strategic importance and progressive potential of the existing working class.

The development of capitalism will continue to generate contradictions, and their particular resolution may be reactionary, may drive humanity backwards morally, culturally, and ultimately even materially. Warren explicitly rejected the notion that just because capitalist development opens up new opportunities for human progress, these will automatically become reality. Conscious political intervention is a *sine qua non* of human progress.

The influence of Warren's arguments about the reality of capitalist development in Third World countries and of his critique of dependency theory has not diminished with time. If it is now true that 'the hegemony of dependency theory, which persisted throughout the 1960s and early 1970s, is no more',[5] then the impact of Warren's article on the analyses of

4. Antonio Gramsci, *Selections From the Prison Notebooks,* Lawrence and Wishart, London, 1971, p. 172.
5. *The Insurgent Sociologist,* 'Imperialism and the State', special issue, spring 1977, editorial introduction. This judgement is probably premature,

Marxists working on Africa, Asia, and Latin America,[6] published in *New Left Review* in 1973, must be considered partly responsible for its demise.

On the other hand, to the extent that bourgeois nationalism, utopianism, and modified dependency theories continue to dominate the outlook of social scientists concerned with the Third World, the broader and more detailed critique contained in this book remains apposite. Moreover, its publication may hopefully clarify some aspects of Warren's analysis that seem not to have been properly understood.[7]

The present book has been derived from three sorts of manuscript sources at varying stages of completion at the time of the author's death. First, some typed drafts had been circulated among a small circle of colleagues and subsequently amended and annotated by hand. (Most of

certainly so if we consider the latest textbook on Third World economic development produced by one of the most influential economists on the left. See J. Robinson, *Aspects of Development and Underdevelopment,* Modern Cambridge Economics, Cambridge, 1979.

6. On Africa, for example, see: R. Jeffries, 'Political Radicalism in Africa: "The Second Independence"', *African Affairs,* volume 77, no. 308, July 1978; C. Leys, 'Capital Accumulation, Class Formation and Dependency - The Significance of the Kenyan Case', *The Socialist Register 1978,* London, 1979; N. Swainson, 'State and Economy in Post-Colonial Kenya, 1963-1978', *Canadian Journal of African Studies,* volume XII, no. 3, 1978; M. P. Cowen, 'Capital and Household Production: The Case of Wattle in Kenya's Central Province, 1903-1964', unpublished Ph. D. dissertation, Cambridge University, October 1978. On Asia and Latin America, see B. McFarlane, 'Imperialism in the 1980s', *Journal of Contemporary Asia,* volume 7, no. 4, 1977; R. Lim, 'The Philippines and the "Dependency Debate": A Preliminary Case Study', *Journal of Contemporary Asia,* volume 8, no. 2, 1978; S. Kalmanovitz, 'Théorie de la Dépendance ou Théorie de l'Impérialisme?', *Sociologie du Travail,* January-March 1975; G. Palma, 'Dependency: A Formal Theory of Underdevelopment or a Methodology for the Analysis of Concrete Situations of Underdevelopment?', World Development, volume 6, 1978.

7. For instance, G. Williams has criticized Warren by pointing to this alleged fault in his analysis: 'the failure to realize that the development of capitalism is more than a matter of just increasing manufactured output and establishing a capital goods sector'. (G. Williams, 'Economy and Society', chapter in *Nigeria,* Rex Collings, 1976, p. 44n.) This flawed perception of Warren's position surely cannot be sustained in the light of the discussion in chapter 2 of this book.

chapters 1, 2, 3, and 8 fall into this category.) Second, there were handwritten chapters, one with complete footnote references (chapter 4), the others more preliminary drafts containing many layers of corrections and notes for possible amendments added at varying dates, with indication of points requiring footnotes and references. These did not always provide sufficient details to enable anyone other than the author easily to complete the footnote. (Chapter 7 of this book is based on a handwritten preliminary draft of this kind, as are chapters 5 and 6, although the manuscripts for these chapters were somewhat easier to follow than that of chapter 7.) Finally, portions of previously published articles[8] and sections of the author's correspondence in response to criticism of early drafts of various chapters have been inserted into the main text and footnotes throughout. The two most important insertions are in chapter 7, section 4, which consists almost entirely of portions of the paper 'The Postwar Experience of the Third World', presented by Bill Warren at a conference in Texas in 1977,[9] and chapter 8, section 5.

My guideline in editing these sources was to deviate as little as possible from the author's outlines, notes, and manuscripts, consistent with readability and the flow of argument. I have made no attempt to 'complete' the book by extrapolating from the outline notes for additional chapters, which might have produced a clumsy pastiche of the author's distinctive style and a paraphrase of his views.

There were few substantial editorial contributions. I have added an expanded summary of the main arguments of Part One to chapter 1; some of the sections and sub-headings in chapters 7 and 8 have been re-arranged; and a few paragraphs have been added to strengthen the argument in

8. For example: 'Imperialism and Capitalist Industrialization', *New Left Review,* 1973; *Imperialism and Neo-Colonialism,* British and Irish Communist Organization, March 1977; 'Nations and Corporations', *Times Literary Supplement,* 11 November 1977; 'Poverty and Prosperity', *Times Literary Supplement,* 12 December 1975.

9. This paper, minus the section referred to here, which was transferred to chapter 7, was the basis for chapter 8 of this book.

the second portion of section 4 in chapter 8. About a third of the bibliographic references in the footnotes are additions to the author's manuscript; on occasion, footnotes were transferred into or out of the main text in an attempt to strengthen the impact of an argument or to improve its flow; occasionally, too, footnotes were expanded and tables or statistical data updated, principally in chapters 6, 7, and 8.

Bill Warren specifically wished to thank some of those who had provided help and intellectual stimulus to enable him to complete the work upon which chapter 8 of this book is based. He noted the names of Dr. Shobhana Madhavan, Mike Safier, Peter Ayre, Dr. Richard Jeffries, Biplap Das Gupta, Mrs. Shaziye Kazioglu, and the United Nations Research Institute for Social Development (for materials from their data bank). In editing the manuscripts I have received great help and encouragement from many people, and would like particularly to thank Professor Anthony Hopkins, Roger Owen, and Rose Warren for their detailed and patient assistance.

Edinburgh, April 1980

Part One:
The Development of the Marxist Theory of Imperialism

1
Progressive Imperialism and the Utopian Left

The concept of imperialism has become the dominant political dogma of our era. Together with its offspring, the notion of 'neo-colonialism', it affords the great majority of humanity a common view of the world as a whole. Not only the Marxist-educated masses of the Communist world, but also the millions of urban dwellers of Latin America, the semi-politicized peasants of Asia, and the highly literate professional and working classes of the industrialized capitalist countries, are steeped in this world-view and its ramifications. It represents, of course, not simply a recognition of the existence of modern empires, formal or informal, and of their living heritage. More important, it embodies a set of quite specific (albeit often vaguely articulated) theses about the domination of imperialism in the affairs of the human race as a whole and in particular about the past and present economic, political, and cultural disaster imperialism has allegedly inflicted and continues to inflict on the great majority of mankind.

The powerful grip of this view has, at one stage removed, produced or transformed almost equally widespread and influential secondary ideologies (at least in the West), most notably that encapsulated in the 'Aid Lobby'; its effect has been to contribute towards a transmutation of Western liberalism from a philosophy of forward-looking improvement based upon the past achievements of capitalism to a philosophy of guilt and shame, increasingly forswearing its own heritage and retreating to utopian, static, and backward-looking perspectives. The progressive bourgeois outlook of John Stuart Mill has been increasingly rejected by the Western intelligentsia in favour of the reactionary petty-bourgeois outlook of Proudhon.[1]

The popular dominance of the anti-imperialist world-outlook in the West (admittedly never complete) is a much more recent phenomenon than is commonly realized. Until the Vietnam war in the 1960s, Western concern with imperialism was largely confined to a few academicians and Marxist parties or sects; even for the latter, it was but one of a number of more or less equally important topics. Analytical Marxist works on imperialism after the Second World War (and there were few non-Marxist works on imperialism *qua* imperialism) were most remarkable for their forlorn isolation: Palme Dutt, Baran, and Barrat Brown[2] stood out as lonely as any district commissioner in the outposts of Empire.

All that has since changed. An enormous mass of anti-imperialist literature — analytical and propagandist, academic and political-sectarian, new left and hard-line 'Stalinist', Third World nationalist and radical-liberal — has poured from the press.[3] During the past decade bourgeois publishers have devoted more resources to the topic of anti-imperialism than to any other social, political, or economic theme, with the possible exception of inflation. If to this we add the literature of the masochistic modern version of the White Man's Burden, more or less directly inspired by the view of imperialism as uniformly disastrous, then Marxism can record the greatest publication and propaganda

1. In this context, those liberals who remain within the genuine vibrant liberal tradition are viewed as right-wingers, sometimes even as fascists, by a socialist movement deeply impregnated by the philosophy and superficial propagandism of this intelligentsia.

2. R.P. Dutt, *The Crisis of Britain and the British Empire*, London, 1953; M.B. Brown, *After Imperialism*; P. Baran, *The Political Economy of Growth*. (Full details of these and other references may be found in the bibliography.)

3. The first edition of an expensively produced, two-volume example of this literature was, its author notes, sold out within a year. S. Amin, *Accumulation on a World Scale*, Volume II, p. 589.

triumph of its history. For the great bulk of this literature is self-consciously Marxist in origin or owes much of its intellectual inspiration to Marxist work in the general area, in the sense that it considers itself part of the Marxist tradition of social analysis.[4] In no other field has Marxism succeeded in so influencing — even dominating — the thought of mankind.

1. For a Marxist Re-Evaluation of the Theory of Imperialism

Marxism, in a multitude of guises, has become the principal compass of investigation of imperialism, the penetration and spread of the capitalist system into non-capitalist or primitive capitalist areas of the world.[5] Any reassessment of the relations between the advanced, industrialized capitalist world and the countries of Asia, Africa, and Latin America must therefore entail a reassessment of Marxism as an intellectual current, and vice versa. Ironically, it is at the apogee of Marxism's supreme propaganda achievement, the theory of imperialism, that it has become clear that a re-evaluation of Marxist analysis is not only urgent but long overdue.

Perhaps the least important reason for such a re-evaluation is that the bulk of current Marxist analyses of and propaganda about imperialism actually reverse the views of the founders of Marxism, who held that the expansion of capitalism into pre-capitalist areas of the world was desirable and progressive; moreover, the reversal is generally effected in apparent ignorance of the fact. Indeed, the Marxist movement has become deeply involved in the struggle against imperialism. The theoretical fulcrum of this

4. E.P. Thompson uses the term 'Marxist tradition' to describe his own allegiance, defining this position in 'An Open Letter to Leszek Kolakowski', in *The Socialist Register 1973*, London, 1974, pp. 24 ff.
5. This definition will be used throughout this work. Other definitions will be considered later.

reversal of the Marxist view is the theory of the advent of a new and degenerate stage of capitalism (monopoly capitalism) that can no longer perform any positive social function, even in those societies Marx and Engels regarded as backward compared with the capitalist West during the nineteenth century and most of which, by the same criteria, are still backward today. The practical, political foundation for this reversal was the quest by Marxists, especially the Bolsheviks, for allies against the powerful centres of capitalist state power. This quest became particularly important in efforts to neutralize the threat such centres presented to the precarious Soviet state.

But — and here we submit to the more crucial exigencies dictating re-evaluation — the new, reactionary stage of capitalism turned out to have immeasurably greater economic vigour and capacity for technological innovation than its nineteenth-century predecessor. Ultimately, it proved able to extend the realm of political democracy far wider than previously. In itself, this should not have been surprising, since the major and most famous Marxist theoretical work to elaborate the diagnosis of capitalism's senility, Lenin's *Imperialism: The Highest Stage of Capitalism*, ignored the major analytical achievements of Marxist economics in favour of a crude under-consumptionism buttressed by superficial observations by the bourgeois-liberal propagandist Hobson. Nor did the guidance provided by the political requirements of the Russian revolution prove adequate, in the long run, to the broader needs of the socialist movement in assessing imperialism and in directing its policies accordingly. The 'world revolution' against imperialism — a fusion of the movement of the working class against its bourgeois rulers in the West and the revolt of the colonial and semi-colonial peoples against the major imperialist powers — turned out to be not a world revolution against capitalism *as such*, but rather (to the extent that it was a world revolution at all[6]) only a struggle

6. It was such a world revolution only *temporarily, patchily, and superficially*, the two movements achieving such limited links and

against particular capitalist countries. More precisely, the struggle against imperialism, which Marxism expected would be synonymous with the struggle against capitalism, actually confused two quite distinct movements: the socialist working-class movement in the industrialized capitalist countries and the intrinsically bourgeois movement of Third World nationalism, the one striking at the state system of Europe and North America in order to establish socialism, the other striking at the same target in order to promote the faster and further growth of industrial capitalism. The struggle for socialism and the struggle for a wider expansion of capitalism were thereby combined in the notion of an anti-imperialist movement. That the inherent logic of anti-imperialist nationalism was the more rapid and extensive development of capitalism throughout the world was not necessarily or always understood by the nationalists themselves, let alone the Marxists. It was implicit in Lenin's own characterization of nationalism and the progressive role of the bourgeois nation-state[7] that the Third World would undergo vigorous capitalist development concurrent with rising nationalism and national liberation. But it is only now, decades after the Second World War, that the inadequacies of a theory of imperialism that involves the working-class movement in a bourgeois movement — incorrectly characterized as socialist because anti-imperialist — can be clearly seen. Marxism's involvement in and theoretical characterization of the anti-imperialist movement has disarmed the working classes of much of Asia,

---

coordination as they did by dint of the orchestration of the Russian revolution and the Comintern. The shadowy existence of the 'world revolution' was a direct reflection of the contradictory but real substance of the Soviet revolution, which itself fused a socialist and a national revolution (not to mention a proto-bourgeois peasant revolution).

7. 'But there is no disputing the fact that, having awakened Asia, capitalism has called forth national movements everywhere in that continent too, that the tendency is towards the creation of national states in Asia; that precisely this style of state ensures the best conditions for the development of capitalism.' V.I. Lenin, 'The Right of Nations to Self-Determination' in *The National Liberation Movement in the East*, Moscow, 1962.

Africa, and Latin America in the struggle for their political and cultural independence of the bourgeoisie, and especially of bourgeois nationalism; it has strengthened the mechanical economistic strain in Marxism that views the advent of socialism in the West as the product not of conscious political action, but of economic crisis or stagnation;[8] and it has occasionally led Marxism into the morass of a subjectivist voluntarism according to which socialism can be achieved almost irrespective of objective economic or cultural conditions, provided anti-imperialist fervour remains white-hot. Above all, Marxism itself has acquired a dual social character: it has become the philosophy simultaneously of socialism, of working-class hegemony in a technologically and culturally advanced industrial society, and of modernizing nationalism, whose basic historical function is pre-socialist and, for much of humanity, specifically bourgeois.

The consequent intellectual dilution of Marxism may well have been necessary for its survival and spread, and thus for its future intellectual renewal.[9] Moreover, outside the industrialized capitalist heartland in the twentieth century, Marxism was certainly a more suitable industrializing ideology than the ideologies of eighteenth- and nineteenth-century capitalist industrialization which, for various reasons, were no longer entirely appropriate.

But whatever the gains of Marxism's profound involvement in the anti-imperialist movement, the reassertion of its role as the philosophy of socialism and the working class requires re-examination of this involvement and of its theoretical and historical foundations.

8. The prosperity of the West and the allegedly non-revolutionary character of its working classes being the result, on this view, of imperialist robbery of the colonies and semi-colonies.

9. As indeed Gramsci argued in a more global context: *The Modern Prince*, in *Selections from the Prison Notebooks of Antonio Gramsci*, p. 164.

2. Schematic Outline of the Arguments

The argument that follows is divided into two parts. The first sketches the development of Marxist theory on imperialism, analysing the intellectual and social-historical dimensions of the reversal of Marx's own view of the progressive character of imperialism. Some of my major contentions may be summarized as follows.

1. The unique achievements of capitalism, both cultural and material, must not be overlooked, particularly the fact that capitalism released individual creativity and organized co-operation in production. This emphasis on the role of capitalism in human progress forms the basis of a critique of anti-capitalist romanticism and of the separation for propagandistic purposes of the material and cultural aspects of capitalism's success. The important distinction between anti-capitalist and socialist ideology — between a moral, a-historical and a socialist critique of capitalism — is firmly established.

2. There is an important connection between capitalism and parliamentary (bourgeois) democracy; the latter provides the best political environment for the socialist movement and creates conditions that favour a genuine learning process by the working class. In fact, the view that capitalism serves as a bridge to socialism must be upheld. The fact that the first successful socialist revolution took place in a country at the early stages of capitalist industrialization is by no means as destructive of the traditional Marxist view as is frequently maintained. Lenin's polemics against the Narodniks, his understanding and development of the concept of the *progressiveness* of capitalism, were central to the elaboration of a successful revolutionary strategy.

3. But it was Lenin himself, in his *Imperialism: The Highest Stage of Capitalism*, who initiated the ideological process

through which the view that capitalism could be an instrument of social advance in pre-capitalist societies was erased from Marxism. The detailed critique of this pamphlet presented here includes an examination of the abundant evidence inconsistent with the theory that imperialism is rooted primarily in an internal excess of capital in imperialist countries. I will also argue that Lenin was wrong about the alleged economically retrogressive effect in the industrialized countries of monopolization between 1870 and 1914 (or between 1900 and 1914). Indeed, this period was marked by rising overall growth rates, significant agricultural advances, higher living standards, and the emergence of a new phase of technological progress.

4. The Marxist analysis of imperialism was sacrificed to the requirements of bourgeois anti-imperialist propaganda and, indirectly, to what were thought to be the security requirements of the encircled Soviet state. The surrender of the classical position was formally completed at the Sixth Congress of the Communist International in 1928. I will examine the logic and the immediate historical background of the Comintern's rejection of even the token deference Lenin's *Imperialism* had paid to Marx's position on these matters, together with the claim that imperialism retarded industrialization and the development of the productive forces in the Third World.

5. The more recent theories of 'underdevelopment' are best regarded as postwar versions of Lenin's *Imperialism*, the theory of 'neo-colonialism' having provided a vehicle for the wholesale transfer of Lenin's theory into the period of independence. Powerful new social and political forces may be identified — principally burgeoning Third World nationalism after the Second World War — that provide a reasonable explanation for the ideological dominance of the underdevelopment fiction, since the Leninist theory of imperialism, with its emphasis on parasitism and the pillage of the Third World, was perfectly

suited to the psychological needs and political requirements
of Third World nationalists.

The second part of the book is devoted to a polemic against
widely accepted views that imperialism (and subsequently
neo-colonialism) is and has been a socially retrogressive
force preventing or distorting economic development and
thereby creating relationships of mounting subordination
and dependence between rich and poor countries. The major
theses of this section may be schematized as follows.

1. Contrary to current Marxist views, empirical evidence
suggests that the prospects for successful capitalist development in many underdeveloped countries are quite favourable. This implies both substantial industrialization and the
capitalist transformation of traditional agriculture.

2. Empirical evidence further shows that substantial
advances along these lines have already been achieved,
especially in industrialization, while capitalist agriculture is
developing more slowly (although here too there has been
significant progress). More specifically, the period since the
end of the Second World War has witnessed a major surge in
capitalist social relations and productive forces in the Third
World.

3. Direct colonialism, far from having retarded or distorted
indigenous capitalist development that might otherwise
have occurred, acted as a powerful engine of progressive
social change, advancing capitalist development far more
rapidly than was conceivable in any other way, both by its
destructive effects on pre-capitalist social systems and by its
implantation of elements of capitalism. Indeed, although
introduced into the Third World externally, capitalism has
struck deep roots there and developed its own increasingly
vigorous internal dynamic.

4. Insofar as there are obstacles to this development, they originate not in current relationships between imperialism and the Third World, but in the internal contradictions of the Third World itself.

5. The overall, net effect of the policy of 'imperialist' countries and the general economic relationships of these countries with the underdeveloped countries actually favours the industrialization and general economic development of the latter.

6. Within a context of growing economic interdependence, the ties of *'dependence'* (or subordination) binding the Third World and the imperialist world have been and are being markedly loosened with the rise of indigenous capitalisms; the distribution of political-economic power within the capitalist world is thereby growing less uneven. Consequently, although one dimension of imperialism is the domination and exploitation of the non-communist world by a handful of major advanced capitalist countries (the United States, West Germany, Britain, France, Japan, etc.), we are nevertheless in an era of declining imperialism and advancing capitalism.

2
Capitalism and Historical Progress

The bourgeoisie cannot exist without constantly revolutionizing the instruments of production, and thereby the relations of production, and with them the whole relations of society. Conservation of the old modes of production in unaltered form, was, on the contrary, the first condition of existence for all earlier industrial classes. Constant revolutionizing of production, uninterrupted disturbance of all social conditions, everlasting uncertainty and agitation distinguish the bourgeois epoch from all earlier ones. All fixed, fast-frozen relations, with their train of ancient and venerable prejudices and opinions, are swept away, all new-formed ones become antiquated before they can ossify. All that is solid melts into air, all that is holy is profaned, and man is at last compelled to face with sober senses his real conditions of life, and his relations with his kind.

Manifesto of the Communist Party

1. Capitalism and Material Progress

The idea of progress, of a constant tendency towards the continuous improvement of human life, whether material, moral, or cultural, is an extremely recent one in history, the direct outcome of the rise of capitalism. The Renaissance was predicated upon conditions of rapid and accelerating changes in trade, the practical arts, financial institutions, and the organization of production brought about by the emergent bourgeoisie.[1] Before the Renaissance, any such outlook would have run counter to accepted views and would have been largely incomprehensible to society at large and to any social group within it.

The pre-Renaissance incomprehensibility of any notion of progress was rooted in the extreme slowness of technological change relative to the lifetime of the individual,[2] which both precluded an outlook that would relate moral and cultural to material progress and obscured the existence of any such progress. That material progress in the development and application of new techniques should not appear as a constant element in society was to be expected in a context in which such economic improvement as was visible possessed only a limited self-sustaining character, tending to be swamped by subsequent population increases and lacking the kind of institutional and technological environment that would make specific technological innovations catalysts for inter-related production processes and institutions.

It is the self-sustaining momentum and rapid pace of technical change[3] under capitalism, and especially industrial capitalism, that distinguish it from *all* earlier societies. This cumulative and continuous character of change can be analysed into a social and a technological aspect. Socioeconomically, what was crucial was not any particular advance in the social division of labour, however substantial, but rather the character of the mechanism that brought about the more complex social division of labour: the market. The increasing development of production for the market under feudalism begat the familiar processes whereby rising

1. S. Pollard, *The Idea of Progress: History and Society*, chapter 1.
2. Ibid., p. 16.
3. That is, technological change actually embodied in operational processes.

competition led to a polarization into the less and the more successful and a consequent relative and absolute realloca- tion of resources. A capitalist class producing entirely for the market and owning the means of production arose, while the mass of the population were deprived of access to these same means of production and forced to sell their labour-power as a commodity on the market.[4] Two aspects here were crucial to the new cumulative character of economic development. First, paradoxically, under the logic of the market economy production was not tethered by the limits of existing effective demand (or indeed of any specific market); second, the double social conditions of deprivation of the direct producers of ownership and/or control of the product in a market economy (as opposed to a slave economy) created the technical basis and forms required for factory and eventually machine industry.

Whatever its origins, the logic of the domination of production by the exchange relationship was to make market success, and thus accumulation, the spur to productive effort in the operational productive unit.[5] Production for the market became production for profit so as

4. It is clear from his marginal notes on the draft manuscript that at this point and elsewhere in the chapter the author intended revising his argument in order to give slightly less emphasis to the role of the market in the development of capitalism. *Editor's note.*

5. To characterize profit-maximization as the motive of capitalist production is meaningless without specifying a time horizon (short-term profit maximization might be at the cost of establishing a secure long-run position in a particular market). Empirical studies show that capitalist firms aim primarily at maintenance or expansion of market shares rather than maximum return on capital or maximum profit margins. Central emphasis on market shares is much more directly related to accumulation than to any variety of profit maximization, the characterization of which in any case dissolves into tautology when considered statically and becomes impossible if considered in the dynamic context of a growing firm. Motivation in terms of market shares must involve changing time-horizons, so that even specification of profit targets with specified time-horizons can have only the most limited value. The normal method of modern firms is to set a minimum profit rate and then aim for maximum turnover. As firms become larger and time-horizons for specific invest- ments are lengthened, the gulf between short-term profit maximization and market success widens.

further to expand market shares. Under capitalism, to stand still is to perish; to fail to reinvest profit, or to do so at a rate of interest less than the average, is likewise to court disaster. Success is an even greater stimulus to renewed effort than failure, since it demands greater efforts to invest the greater surplus profitably.

There is no reason why the continuously expanding productive power of the system should find itself more than temporarily restrained by the limits of existing purchasing power. In the period when capitalism had not yet established domination over the entire economy, its very development was a self-sustaining process in that the separation of the direct producers from their means of production and the increased specialization that accompanied the expansion of the competitive market automatically increased the range of use-values, which previously had been produced within the primary production unit[6] or were subject to non-market forms of exchange, and had now to be increasingly purchased on the market. Once the economy had been more or less entirely dominated by capitalist production relations, competition continued to create markets to justify the expanded production capacity for which it was itself responsible.[7] Above all, competition in the given technical conditions of machine production meant constant innovations in both consumer and producer goods, which constantly renewed the market on a basis of higher productivity; once one entrepreneur had introduced a successful innovation, no competitor could afford to ignore the new situation. Competition through innovation thus constantly created new markets, the negative effect of 'premature' obsolescence on the profit rates of the backward firms being more than offset by the success of the innovating firms. Innovation in the producer-goods sector is perhaps

6. Certain types of village or small tribal communities may legitimately be regarded as production units.
7. This aspect of the operation of the capitalist economy has received a limited and one-sided recognition by the left in the more or less absurd concept of 'consumerism'.

the major force in secular market expansion, tending to drag the consumer-goods sector along by creating expanding employment incomes, even if real wages remain stable. If trade unions tend (as they do) to raise real wages irrespective of supply/demand conditions in the labour market at roughly the rate of productivity increase, then a powerful reinforcing factor in the secular expansion of the market is present.[8] Capitalism's problem could (and indeed to a large extent has) become not the lack of effective demand to purchase the output of existing capacity, but the scarcity of capacity to satisfy competing effective claims on resources.

Once a free labour force had been created, its combination with a production system with no finite market horizon[9] brought about the factory system, capable of utilizing the labour force under more effective supervision, discipline, and organization than was possible in the putting-out system, itself able to operate at lower costs than the guild system. The cooperation and rationalization of labour permitted by the factory system provided both the incentive and the conditions for three inter-connected developments: replacement of human skills by machinery; replacement of human and animal by inanimate power, especially steam; origin of the specialized entrepreneurial function[10] to coordinate the increasingly complex inter-relationships between production processes in the same factory. Production ceased to be limited by individual human skills and

8. Besides the direct effects of the rise in real wages on demand, the pace of investment in newer vintage machines in the producer-goods sector is accelerated. As more productive machines are introduced, the more dynamic firms gain from the rise in profit margins as costs decline relative to existing price levels. The faster the trade unions then push wages up in the most productive firms and set the pattern for wage rates in the firms employing older-vintage machinery, the faster will innovation expand the market as other firms are forced to follow the innovators.

9. In pre-capitalist modes of production market horizons would, for example, be set by population, territorial limits, resources, and relatively static technologies.

10. The entrepreneurial function was of course co-existent with manufacture from the start, but the dual impact of machinery and inanimate power transformed it from a relatively passive overseer operation to an endeavour of active organization and innovation.

16

power, and eventually technology and science acquired a life
of their own and became an autonomous force in economic
advance.[11] Once power-driven machinery, in a competitive
framework, became the heart of productive life, its
technological characteristics — i.e., the technological inter-
relatedness of markets, materials, products, and processes
— were such that improvements in any one area created both
the incentives (often the necessity) and the possibilities for
yet newer innovations elsewhere.[12] Even Landes's analogy
of ever-widening ripples from a stone thrown into water is
inadequate to describe the dynamism of this process, since

11. In Landes's words '... one of the primary stimuli of modern
technology is free-ranging imagination; the increasing autonomy of pure
science and the accumulation of a pool of untapped knowledge, in
combination with the ramifying stock of established techniques, have
given ever wider scope to the inventive vision.' David S. Landes, *The
Unbound Prometheus: Technological Change and Industrial Development
in Western Europe from 1750 to the Present.*
12. 'In all of this diversity of technological improvement, the unity of the
movement is apparent: change begat change. For one thing, many
technical improvements were feasible only after advances in associated
fields. The steam engine is a classic example of this technological inter-
relatedness; it was impossible to produce an effective condensing engine
until better methods of metal working could turn out accurate cylinders. For
another, the gains in productivity and output of a given innovation
inevitably exerted pressure on related industrial operations. The demand
for coal pushed mines deeper until water seepage became a serious hazard:
the answer was the creation of a more efficient pump, the atmospheric
steam engine. A cheap supply of coal proved a godsend to the iron industry,
which was stifling for lack of fuel. In the meantime, the invention and
diffusion of machinery in the textile manufacture and other industries
created a new demand for energy, hence for coal and steam engines, and
these engines and the machines themselves had a voracious appetite for
iron, which called for further coal and power. Steam also made possible the
factory city, which used unheard-of quantities of iron (hence coal) in its
many-storied mills and its water sewage systems. At the same time, the
processing of the flow of manufactured commodities required great
amounts of chemical substances: alkalis, acids, and dyes, many of them
consuming mountains of fuel in the making. And all of these products –
iron, textiles, chemicals – depended on large-scale movement of goods on
land and sea, from the sources of the raw materials into the factories and out
again to near and distant markets. The opportunity thus created and the
possibilities of the new technology combined to produce the railroad and
steamship, which of course added to the demand for iron and fuel while
expanding the market for factory products, and so on, in ever-widening
circles.' Ibid., pp. 2-3.

at any moment points of the peripheral ripples may become new and more vigorous centres of further ripples. In sum, the epic achievement of capitalism was to release both the forces of individualism, of individual creative initiative, that pre-capitalist societies had stifled,[13] and the economic potential of large-scale productive cooperation in the factory system. The complementarity of the two was the necessary condition for the cumulative character of economic and technological change ushered in by the industrial revolution.[14] Market stimuli and technical complexity lent the process its dynamism. Neither organized cooperation in production nor individual (competitive) economic initiative were new, but their explosive fusion in the capitalist factory system launched an unprecedented continuous momentum. Marx saw no contradiction between the increasing socialization of labour (in the direct productive process) and the develop-ment of individualism, despite the penchant of many of his followers to counterpose the two.[15] Their fundamental complementarity was obscured by their apparent opposition at the dawn of industrial capitalism, individualism taking the form of competitive rivalry (seemingly the leading element in the ideology of capital), socialization seeming to represent the core of the ideology of labour. This paradox was the result of the fact that the conditions of human society prior to the advent of capitalism had exerted far greater pressure on individual initiative than on social

13. By comparison, that is, with the potentialities capitalism was to reveal.

14. 'Division of labour in manufacture thus presupposes a certain degree of development of the social division of labour: on the other hand it develops the latter further . . . . For all that, there is always this difference between social division of labour and division of labour in manufacture, that the former necessarily produces *commodities*, whereas in the latter the detail worker does *not* produce commodities. Hence concentration and organiza-tion in the latter, scattering and disorder of competition in the former.' F. Engels, *On Marx's 'Capital'*, Moscow, 1972, p. 85.

15. This often takes the form of a contradiction between competition and cooperation. Naturally, competition cannot be equated with individualism. Nevertheless, they arose together as integral features of capitalism, and each stimulated the growth of the other. Socialists have, by association, thus tended to frown upon individualism.

cooperation, reflecting mankind's closeness to nature and limited control over it. The decisive advance in man's mastery over nature wrought by industrial capitalism thus required the domination of the cooperative dimension of factory production by the competitive, individualistic decision-making of the businessman. The objective conditions that required this predominance of individualism in a coercive form were historically specific and did not imply a timeless superiority of private enterprise over public ownership, or competition over planning.[16] These conditions were, in the most basic sense, those of limited culture, including low levels of technique and the need for many centres of creativity when the organizational and technological interconnections of society were still relatively undeveloped. These conditions still pertain in much of the Third World. The view that capitalism can no longer fulfil any positive function in these countries therefore has no prima facie justification.

2. Capitalism and Cultural Progress

It is, of course, a commonplace for Marxists that capitalism was economically progressive at least until the end of the nineteenth century.[17] But it has become customary for many contemporary Marxists to qualify this fact so heavily that it tends to fade from view beneath a plethora of caveats. Recognition of the immense material achievements of capitalism is generally accompanied by emphasis on the tremendous cost in human suffering associated with that progress, especially in its early stages,[18] and by a related emphasis on the uneven character and temporary reversals

16. There are, of course, many different forms of individualism, some of which may be regarded as having a negative impact - from a socialist viewpoint.

17. After which Leninism holds that the relations of production under monopoly capitalism became a fetter upon the forces of production.

18. Cf. Christopher Hill, *Reformation to Industrial Revolution*, London, 1967. Characteristic of the stultifying effect this emphasis has had on

of the advances.[19] The costs are itemized in some detail: the decline of craftmanship; the aesthetic and moral destruction of pre-capitalist communities (generally implied or even stated to be superior to acquisitive capitalism); the depersonalization of human relations by the cash nexus.[20] Someone who had only dabbled a bit in Marxist literature could be forgiven for acquiring the impression that modern Marxism regards capitalism as an unfortunate aberration in human history, whose economic advances could have been achieved and deficiencies avoided if only enough people had been converted to socialism a little earlier.

Nevertheless, the emphasis on unevenness, imbalance, regional deprivation, suffering, costs, and so on takes second place in the denigratory arsenal to the separation of the moral and cultural features of capitalist society from its economic achievements, the latter gaining positive, if

---

Marxist analysis is the fact that for many the acid test of whether one had adopted the Marxist approach to historical study became whether one believed that the British working class had suffered a decline in its living standards during the industrial revolution. There could, of course, be no Marxist analytical presumption either way prior to empirical investigation, and the spirit of the controversy was moralistic, not scientific. Naturally, the debate turned out to be largely barren. The principal contributions to the discussion have been brought together in a volume edited by Christopher Hill.

19. This strand of what may be called denigratory historiography has recently been given a curious twist by a Marxist criticism that Marxism itself has gone to excessive lengths in ignoring the contradictory and uneven character of human progress since the Enlightenment. (Tom Nairn, 'The Modern Janus', in *The Break-Up of Britain*.) Nothing could be further from the truth.

20. E.g. by Walter Rodney, *How Europe Underdeveloped Africa*, Bougle L'Ouverture and Tanzania Publishing House, 1972, and by K.B. Griffen, *Underdevelopment in Spanish America*, London, 1969. Such attitudes and analyses have a very long tradition. The work of nineteenth-century Russian populists shows a remarkable similarity to more recently fashionable approaches. 'They were deeply impressed by (Marx's) exposition of the cruelties of capitalist development – so deeply that they could not accept his thesis that the rise of capitalism was, all the cruelties none the less, the greatest progress in human history. Their image of capitalism was, on the whole, non-Marxist since they saw capitalist development as an essentially retrogressive process.' A. Walicki, *The Controversy over Capitalism: Studies in the Social Philosophy of the Russian Populists*, p. 137.

reluctant, recognition, the former censure. The relationship between cultural and material progress under capitalism cannot be fully explored here, but a few brief remarks are necessary. To start with, anti-capitalist ideology is not the same as socialist ideology;[21] correspondingly, a moral critique of capitalism need not coincide with a socialist critique.[22] Danger looms when the socialist movement confuses itself by the indiscriminate adoption of anti-capitalist ideologies. Second, the moral and cultural standards by which capitalism is frequently adversely judged are themselves the direct product of capitalism. An anti-capitalist critique may be a-historical, judging capitalist society, especially its early stages, on the basis of the most advanced moral and cultural achievements of that same society.[23] Alternatively, an anti-capitalist critique of capitalism may adopt pre-capitalist or petty-bourgeois

21. *Ideology* here is used in its literal sense and does not mean false consciousness.

22. An anti-capitalist ideology can be backward-looking, reactionary, or both. In principle a socialist ideology can only be forward-looking in that it builds on and does not attempt to negate the achievements of capitalism. The confusion of reformist ideals and the specific analysis of capitalist development has been recognized as a common failing. Cf. F.H. Cardoso, *The Originality of the Copy: ECLA and the Idea of Development*, mimeo, n.d.

23. Lenin criticized the Narodniks for what amounted to an anti-capitalist but non-socialist and a-historical critique of capitalist economic progress in Russia: 'As to whether the development of capitalism in Russia is slow or rapid, it all depends on what we compare this development with. If we compare the pre-capitalist epoch in Russia with the capitalist (and that is the comparison of the situation which is needed so as to arrive at a correct solution of the problem) the development of social economy under capitalism must be considered extremely rapid. If, however, we compare the present rapidity of development with that which could be achieved with the modern level of technique and culture as it is in general, the present rate of development of capitalism must be considered slow.' (*The Development of Capitalism in Russia*, p. 659). 'Culture as it is in general' refers, as the context makes clear, to the culture of the advanced capitalist societies of the West. This brief statement by Lenin epitomizes the differences between a socialist, historical critique of capitalism and a romantic a-historical critique, between a forward-looking and a backward-looking critique. The elementary point that whether social (or economic) development is fast or slow depends on what one is comparing it with is too often ignored by utopian critics of Third World capitalism.

criteria, most often some form of backward-looking romanticism entirely alien to the rugged realism and forward-driving thrust of Marxism, and indeed to the spirit of the Renaissance of which Marxism is the scion.

It should be emphasized, moreover, that the standards to which I refer — equality, justice, generosity, independence of spirit and mind, the spirit of inquiry and adventure, opposition to cruelty, not to mention political democracy — are not late-comers to capitalism, the product of an experienced working class and the foretastes of the coming of socialism. They emerge early in the cultural history of capitalism, well before the working class becomes an independent political and cultural force. Indeed, these standards are either ushered in by capitalism or achieve a relative dominance within capitalist culture unequalled by any major earlier or contemporaneous cultures.[24] The humanistic side of capitalist culture emerged very early in the development of capitalism in the first industrial society, Britain, and profoundly affected the workings of the capitalist productive apparatus from the beginning.[25] The period of cruellest exploitation in the history of English industrial capitalism is also the period of maximum national freedom from restraint, legal or customary, and is remarkable as much for its brevity as for its cruelty.[26]

Third, the possibility of genuine moral choice, while never absent from human history, increases to the extent that people (and individual persons) can consciously control their own destiny; and this capacity itself depends in the first place on the extent to which they free themselves from the leaden weight of nature. Increasing mastery of nature

24. We exclude here small, primitive societies, on the ground that for several centuries the problem of mankind has centred around how to organize big societies in which life is highly regarded so that sophisticated technology develops to the purpose, directly or indirectly, of saving and lengthening life; society thus necessarily ceases to be primitive.

25. The process is outlined in K. Polanyi, *The Great Transformation: the Political and Social Origins of Our Time.*

26. This period was approximately the period of the industrial revolution, from 1780 to 1840. After 1840 the Factory Acts were introduced and substantial improvements were effected.

obviously provides no guarantee that moral choices will be superior, by whatever standards. But it does guarantee that they will increasingly be *choices*. For that very reason we may expect that the era of highly industrialized societies — which has yet to arrive for the majority of humanity — will be one of moral confusion and exploration rather than confident strides forward.[27]

Fourth, although it is a modern bromide that the mere accumulation of things does not imply cultural or moral improvement, it is commonly overlooked that the ever-increasing production of new kinds of things forever involves the acquisition of new skills, activities, relationships, pleasures, challenges, social explorations, etc.[28] The desire for change for its own sake may be regarded as a 'divine spark' or as a sign of superficial folly, but if both the ability to make more effective choices and the option constantly to explore new worlds are regarded as desirable, then the fundamentally progressive moral and cultural character of capitalism cannot be doubted.

Fifth, since the most evident moral criticism of capitalism is its lack of humanity in the broadest sense, it is pertinent to note that if the technical advances of capitalism have brought the world horrors on an unprecedented scale, this is essentially a technical by-product,[29] whereas the striving for sympathetic relations between people is far more the deliberate product of conscious effort. Furthermore, the horrors of the twentieth century — the slaughter of the First

27. The notorious moral complacency of Victorian England was even shorter lived than the period of industrial laissez-faire.

28. Consider the enrichment of working-class life (not to mention that of other human beings) resulting from bicycles, the cinema, refrigerators, record players, and gas cookers, to mention a few 'consumerist' items at random.

29. In one sense the all-encompassing character of the two world wars was a symptom of the strains brought about by the ramifying unity of mankind stemming from the spread of the capitalist world market. Capitalism was the first great civilization to create *mankind*, as distinct from individual relatively distinct communities and civilizations. This was a physical creation as distinct from the abstract creations of the great monotheistic religions. As such it created the material basis for a further advance of that morality based on a conception of human unity.

World War, the Nazi concentration camps, the Vietnam War
— although obviously unprecedented in terms of the
absolute numbers killed, are relatively equivalent in their
impact to the enormities and brutalities of earlier centuries,
the ravages of the Golden Horde or the Thirty Years War. It
is instructive that so many should feel that the atrocities of
the Nazis and the staggering numbers of civilians they
killed were uniquely horrible, and therefore characteristic of
twentieth-century capitalism in particular. In fact, the
horrific atrocities, the propensity to large-scale indiscriminate slaughter, and the racism of Nazism were not at all
unprecedented in history. What *was* unique (apart from the
huge absolute numbers killed and the modern techniques
used) was the sense of moral outrage felt by a large
proportion of that section of humanity culturally closest to
the Germans: the rest of Western Europe, North America,
and Australasia. This moral outrage stemmed from the
feeling that Germany had betrayed the Western heritage,
reverting to earlier barbaric centuries.[30] It is this very feeling
of moral outrage and betrayal that permits the twentieth
century to be falsely regarded as the repository of the moral
breakdown of the human species.

If capitalism has at the least paid the tribute vice pays to
virtue by enthroning a morality that condemns it to make a
continuous show of moral endeavour (and it ought to be
obvious that this is an excessively grudging estimate), it is a
telling criticism of the modern socialist movement that it
cannot live up to that morality, to the nineteenth-century
liberal morality exemplified, for instance, by John Stuart
Mill's rationality and humanism.[31] In retrospect, the
historical tendency of the socialist movement to draw a
sharp dividing line between bourgeois and socialist morality

30. The First World War came to be regarded as senseless rather than
shameful. Moreover, it was principally soldier killing soldier, probably no
more brutally than it had ever been done previously.

31. The difference between the revanchist, inward-looking, and backward character of the modern 'radical' women's liberation movement and
Mill's humanist and progressive tract on The Rights of Women symbolizes
the point, and is not at all the special case it might at first sight appear.

and culture has obscured more than it has clarified. It is rather the case that the cultural and moral differences between modern industrial societies and pre-industrial societies and cultures are far more fundamental than those between industrial societies themselves. And conversely, it is likely to be the case that the element of cultural continuity between Western liberal capitalist societies and the socialist societies hypothetically to follow will turn out to be greater than ever envisaged by the 'socialist versus capitalist' schema.

In such a historical perspective, it may appear that the morality of unrestrained competition, the law of the jungle, is no more than the early, temporary, and transitional appearance of the more fundamental morality of the fullest development of the capacities of the individual, possible only under an advanced stage of mastery over nature, itself the product, above all, of the techno-economic achievements and momentum created by bourgeois society. In Marx's words: 'The ancient conception, in which man always appears (in however narrowly national, religious or political a definition) as the aim of production, seems very much more exalted than the modern world, in which production is the aim of man and wealth the aim of production. In fact, however, when the narrow bourgeois form has been peeled away, what is wealth, if not the universality of needs, capacities, enjoyments, productive powers, etc., of individuals produced in universal exchange? What if not the full development of human control over the forces of nature — those of his own nature as well as those of so-called "nature"? What, if not the absolute elaboration of his creative dispositions, without any preconditions other than antecedent historical evolution which makes the totality of this evolution — i.e., the evolution of all human powers as such, unmeasured by any *previously established* yard-stick — an end in itself? What is this, if not a situation where man does not reproduce himself in any determined form but produces his own totality? Where he does not seek to remain something formed by the past, but is in the absolute moment of becoming? In bourgeois political economy — and in the epoch of production to which it corresponds — this complete elaboration of what lies within man appears as the total alienation and the destruction of all fixed one-sided purposes as sacrifice of the end in itself to a wholly external compulsion.'[32]

In the light of this penetrating estimation, the separation of the material from the cultural achievements of capitalism for petty propagandistic purposes shrivels to nothing. There is certainly no simple unilinear relationship between economic and moral progress, but the mere complexity of that relationship cannot nullify its positive character.

3. Capitalism as the Bridge to Socialism

The most favourable light in which Marxism has viewed capitalism has been, of course, as the progenitor of socialism. In this traditional (or classic) view, socialism was the system of organization of society appropriate to technologically advanced, large-scale machine industry, the historic function of industrial capitalism having been to build up to this level of development from the feudal environment.[33] A central aspect of this function was capitalism's creation not only of the objective conditions for socialism, but also of the subjective instrument for its achievement, the proletariat. It was not the mere existence of the working class as the principal exploited class of capitalism that made it the historic instrument of socialism, but the specific social and cultural characteristics, and political experience, that the conditions of capitalism tended

32. Karl Marx, *Pre-Capitalist Economic Formations*, pp. 84-85. Eric Hobsbawn, in his introduction, fittingly describes this as 'a passage full of hope and splendour'.

33. The fact that Russia was successfully industrialized under a Marxist regime seriously undermined this particular traditional view. It need not logically have done so, since the cost of a socialist movement's assuming a bourgeois function has been at least a partial loss of its socialist character. This does not, however, imply a negative view of the Soviet achievement.

to give it. Most notably, these were the increased independence of the individual workers from customary personal relationships of servitude and the collective organization encouraged by their aggregation in large factories. Furthermore, parliamentary democracy was considered the characteristic political form of bourgeois rule and, up to the Russian revolution, was regarded as both the best political environment for the functioning of the socialist movement and the necessary training ground for the working class to acquire the skills required to run a socialist society.[34] This view of bourgeois democracy as providing the conditions conducive to a learning process for the working class was not predicated solely on the 'passive' grounds that political democracy provided room for manoeuvre for the developing socialist movement.[35] It was also held that democracy would provide positive ('active') political training for the proletariat, developing its ability through a democratic public clash of ideas, policies, and outlooks in order to evolve appropriate solutions for the problems of society's advance, oppose incorrect or reactionary solutions, win backward sectors of society for the correct solutions, etc. Bourgeois political democracy would provide the working class the best conditions in which to acquire the cultural depth required to

34. G. D. H. Cole, *The Second International,* London, 1956.
35. As opposed, for example, to the recurrently fashionable view (which goes back at least to Sorel) that the best conditions for socialist activity are under a dictatorial bourgeois regime, since this would expose the underlying authoritarian character of bourgeois civil society. It followed that provocative acts of violence, often bearing no moral relationship to the alleged cause, would force the bourgeoisie to revert to authoritarian rule and thus enhance the prospects for socialism. This strategic perspective ignores the fact that the working class itself has struggled hard for the democratic achievements from which it has gained so much and is unlikely to look favourably upon a socialist movement that aims to destroy hard-won gains for an abstract utopia. Moreover, in modern circumstances struggle under an authoritarian regime would inevitably become a struggle for the restoration of political democracy rather than a struggle for socialism. Nor is there any reason why the struggle for the restoration of democracy should immediately be transformed into a successful socialist upsurge. On the contrary, as Portugal and Greece have recently shown us. Finally, it is also relevant that bourgeois society and ideology, contrary to the mythology of the women's liberation movement, are fundamentally anti-authoritarian.

become a ruling class.[36] Indeed, this view was one of the most important constituents of the belief, held by all Russian Marxists prior to the October Revolution and for some time after it, that no Russian revolution could long succeed without a socialist revolution in the West. Socialist success in the civilized West was cr nsidered the condition for socialist success in the barbaric East.[37] This outlook was reversed by the Comintern after 1917, in what appears to have been a rationalization of the specific needs and character of the Soviet revolution.[38]

On the basis of the experience of the 1930s and of many, if not most, of the underdeveloped capitalist countries today, a widespread view has arisen that parliamentary democracy is not the typical political form of capitalism, or that it is no more than a passing phase which tends, with the growth of monopoly and the sharpening of class contradictions, to develop into fascism, or perhaps into some form of corporate

36. Cf. K. Kautsky: 'Democracy is indispensable as a means of ripening the proletariat for the social revolution.' *The Social Revolution*, First ed. 1902, Second ed. 1907, cited in V. I. Lenin, *Marxism on the State: Preparatory material for the book 'The State and Revolution'*, Progress Publishers, Moscow, 1972, p. 68. Implicit in this whole outlook was a contrast between the working class as ruling class (Gramsci's hegemonic class) and a situation in which society is ruled by an elite acting for the working class but uncontrolled by it.

37. This was on the understanding that the building of socialism involved considerably more than the overthrow of capitalist state power. The traditional Marxist distinction between a political and a social revolution (cf. Fernando Claudin *The Communist Movement: From Comintern to Cominform*) does not exactly fit the case, since even if the Russian revolution has not succeeded in establishing a socialist society, it certainly achieved a social revolution.

38. The new emphasis on anti-imperialism was, of course, important here, as we shall see in Chapter 4. Lucio Colletti has correctly described this reversal as a change that proved decisive for the subsequent course of world history: 'The failure of the western revolution destroyed the strategy which had hitherto underpinned the practice of the Bolsheviks. The possibility of gradually bridging the gulf between Russian backwardness and a socialist programme, through the industrial and cultural support afforded by the resources of a socialist Europe, was now unpredictably severed. Almost at once the party found itself no longer on solid ground . . . the old Slavophile, anti-enlightenment tendencies soon gained an unexpected new lease of life.' 'The Question of Stalin', in R. Blackburn (ed.) *Revolution and Class Struggle, A Reader in Marxist Politics*, pp. 178-9.

state.[39] It now appears, however, that the fascist experience was an interlude that arose not from fundamental characteristics of capitalism as such (e.g. monopolization and the growing threat of working-class power) but from specific conditions in particular states.[40]

Capitalism and democracy are, I would argue, linked virtually as Siamese twins.[41] It was precisely those characteristics of feudalism that permitted and encouraged the rise of capitalism that also permitted and encouraged the rise of political democracy. Similarly, the growth of capitalism and political democracy were interrelated, each fructifying the other. Crucial for both was the development of towns as independent polities within the interstices of feudal authority, which independence arose from the fragmented character of that authority. Since feudal exploitation (command over the surplus) was achieved not through the market but by the direct social coercion of custom, law, and force, the feudal nobility necessarily exercised many of the powers that would normally be exercised by the state in a bourgeois society. Nevertheless, a state was necessary (to look to the overall interests of the feudal nobility). The

39. A conceivable alternative form of this argument might be that political democracy as it exists under capitalism is not inherent in the nature of the capitalist social formation as such, but is a specific product of the working class. But apart from the fact that the working class is itself a product of capitalism, the growth of political democracy and the rise of the bourgeoisie have a common source in the development of the towns as semi-independent polities in the interstices of feudalism. The growth of the institutions of democracy was essential to the growth of the bourgeoisie, and vice versa. Cf. Barrington Moore, *Social Origins of Dictatorship and Democracy: Lord and Peasant in the Making of the Modern World*, chapter VII; and Perry Anderson, *Passages from Antiquity to Feudalism*, Part Two, chapter 1. Moreover, as is implied in the above comments, the development of bourgeois democracy began centuries before the working class had emerged onto the political scene as an organized force.

40. See N. Poulantzas, '. . . fascism can only be explained by reference to the *concrete situation* of the class struggle, as it cannot be reduced to any inevitable need of the "economic" development of capitalism.' (*Fascism and Dictatorship: The Third International and the Problem of Fascism*, p. 39.)

41. The discussion of this point is based principally upon the work of Barrington Moore, Perry Anderson, and Landes. It relates specifically to Western Europe.

consequence was a never-ending conflict of authority between monarchy and nobility producing the fragmentation of sovereignty that enabled the towns to develop their own political rights. This was essential for the full realization of their economic potential, permitting them to take advantage of the shift of long-distance trade to the Atlantic and to undermine the feudal character of the rural economy. The result was a further strengthening of political democracy, which although not always brought about by the bourgeoisie directly,[42] did always accord with its secular economic interests.

Directly connected to the independent status of the towns under feudalism was not only political democracy but also the permeation of West European society by the sanctity of individual property irrespective of rank,[43] and thus by a cultural climate conducive to maximum scope for private enterprise. Supplementing this was the rule of non-arbitrary law, which permitted and encouraged the development of contracts, implying agreement between persons of equal rights and not depending upon relations of force between economic transactors. The more force declined in economic life, the greater was the weight of rationality in resource *allocation*. The role of independent towns, generally in alliance with the monarchy, was crucial in the rise of the rule of law in Western Europe. Once a certain threshold had been passed in the development of capitalist enterprise and political democracy, the floodgates were opened and the spread of democracy became cumulative. Urbanization, the printing press, growing literacy, the development of bourgeois ideology itself, the constant change and mobility of a rapidly expanding economy, the rising self-consciousness of the workers as a class — all these factors combined to ensure that political democracy for the bourgeoisie would have to be democracy for everybody.

42. Notably not in the case of the French revolution.
43. This was, of course, partly the heritage of classical Rome, since Roman law had developed the concept of absolute property for the use of a slave society.

But if the achievement of capitalist industrialization was linked inherently to the achievement of parliamentary democracy,[44] may this not have been merely a necessary initial phase, in part occasioned by the need to mobilize subordinate classes against the aristocratic or royal foe? It seems impossible to sustain such a thesis, in the light of the integral connection between the growth of bourgeois hegemony (both political and economic) on the one hand and political democracy on the other. This connection was maintained and developed over several centuries and has been successfully reinforced, despite the social weakness of the bourgeoisie, since the Second World War, with the further extension of democracy under a more planned capitalism.[45] In Western Europe and North America, Australia and Japan there can be no doubt that parliamentary democracy today has more meaning for the individual citizen and gives more scope for the working classes to influence social life than ever before in history. The process of expanding parliamentary democracy, initiated by the bourgeoisie, has been given powerful new impetus by the proletariat and has thus far proved to have a powerful and irresistible momentum *within capitalism.*

4. Progressive Capitalism and the Bolshevik Revolution

It was in backward Russia that the political dimensions of the Marxist view of the progressive character of capitalism were most single-mindedly developed, ironically enough by Lenin. That the first successful socialist revolution should

44. Parliamentary democracy is here referred to in the broadest sense of the development of parliament as a representative and legislative body, not in the narrower sense of universal popular suffrage, etc.

45. The period since the war has witnessed the steady advance of working-class parties, both Social Democratic and Communist. The development of the mass media has also created remarkable new democratic opportunities, which, left-wing myth to the contrary, have not been cleverly manipulated by the 'establishment', but have produced considerably more open societies. Furthermore, political democracy has

take place in a country that had not long commenced its capitalist industrialization was in fact consistent with a reasonable application of the classical Marxist approach to capitalist countries at an early stage of their industrialization.[46] Precisely because Lenin adopted and developed the classical Marxist approach, his first polemics were against the Narodniks, who upheld theoretical and political positions closely resembling those of many modern Marxists and liberals oriented to the Third World.[47] The Narodniks argued that capitalism in Russia could not develop beyond a certain point, because the very conditions created by its initial development — stratification within the peasantry and impoverishment of the great majority (both artisans and peasants) — caused a contraction of the home market that set insuperable limits to capitalist progress. Moreover, to the extent that capitalism did develop, it produced a rootless, amoral population lacking the social solidarity and cherished values of small-scale production in the traditional Russian village.[48] It was, they maintained,

---

now been thoroughly established in Germany, and fascist regimes have been overthrown in Portugal and Greece. Full bourgeois political democracy has yet to develop in these two countries (and in Italy), but immense steps forward have been taken; Spain is moving rapidly in the same direction.

46. This does not imply that classical Marxism correctly predicted where the first socialist revolution would occur. But specific predictions or informed speculations can be wrong without impairing the validity of the general outlook on which they are based. This is particularly likely when, as in this case, the descent from certain general principles to highly specific situations is made without adequate mediating steps.

47. Bob Sutcliffe was one of the first to note this point in his essay 'Imperialism and Industrialization in the Third World', in R. Owen and B. Sutcliffe (eds.), *Studies in the Theory of Imperialism*.

48. Lenin cites the following disapproving Narodnik-type description of the village of Kataski and its increasingly modern type of factory hand. 'A certain patriarchal manner, a simplicity in the relations between masters and workmen, which, however, is not so noticeable at first sight and is unfortunately (?) disappearing increasingly every year . . . testifies to the kustar (small-scale industry, above the level of handicrafts and producing for the market) character of the industries (?). It is only recently that the factory character both of the industries and of the population has begun to be observed under the influence, in particular, of the town, intercourse with

precisely by building upon the village community that the evils of capitalism could be avoided and an original and humane path to socialism achieved. They therefore pinned their faith on the peasantry as the revolutionary class. Lenin, on the contrary, argued not only that capitalism was already developing vigorously in Russia, but also that the very conditions the Narodniks claimed retarded the expansion of the home market, namely the separation of peasants and artisans from their means of production, while certainly causing impoverishment in one sense,[49] none the less expanded the sphere of monetary commerce by forcing the mass of former producers to seek their necessities of life

---

which has been facilitated by the inauguration of the steamboat service. Today, the village looks like a regular industrial township: there is no sign of agriculture whatever; the houses are built close together as in the towns; fine brick houses of the rich, and alongside of them the miserable hovels of the poor; the long wooden and brick buildings of the factories crowded in the middle of the village — all this sharply distinguishes Kataski from the neighbouring villages and clearly points to the industrial character of the local population. The inhabitants themselves possess features of a character that also call to mind the type of "factory hand" who has already taken shape in Russia: a certain showiness in house furniture, in clothes and manners, spendthrift habits of life in most cases, and little care for the morrow, a forwardness and often affectation in speech, a certain superciliousness towards the country yokel — all these features are possessed by them in common with all Russian factory people.' (*Development of Capitalism in Russia*, pp. 437-8.) These remarks are cited by Lenin from the *Transactions of the Commission of Investigation of Kustar Industry*, IX, p. 2567, and relate to the year 1880. The question marks are Lenin's. Similarly, in the *Statistical Returns for Moscow Gubernia* (Vol. VII, Pt. III, Moscow 1883, p. 58) it is disapprovingly noted that 'the factory hand is a moralist, a "smart alec" '. (*Development of Capitalism in Russia*, p. 600.)

49. The sense in which it was a process of impoverishment was that the direct producers were deprived of their tools (including land) and therefore of their independent means of livelihood. It is, of course, entirely possible that millions suffered impoverishment in the sense also that their consumption of basic articles like food and clothing was reduced, at least until they acquired reasonably paid employment. This implied, however, no necessary shrinkage of the market for capitalism, since even if such a reduction in consumption did take place, it would be accompanied by an absolute rise in *monetary demand* as the very process that led to impoverishment was forcing the former peasants and artisans to acquire on the market what they had previously acquired by other means. Cf. V. I. Lenin, *On the So-Called Market Question* (written in 1893).

by selling their labour-power. Increased destitution of the masses was entirely compatible with the expansion of the market, Lenin held; indeed, it was the condition for it.

Moreover, the long-term dynamic of the system, based on the production of surplus-value and the imperative need to reinvest it, created a self-reinforcing momentum of economic growth regardless of the limitations of the market.[50] Capitalism tends to create a market where none has existed before.[51] Capitalism was already implanted in Russia, and as a superior mode of production, it bore within it the class of the future, the working class. The development of capitalism necessarily increased the cohesion, numbers, organization, culture, and social power of the proletariat, whereas its effect on the peasantry was to promote disintegration, to stratify it between those who became successful (commercial farmers) and those who were deprived of their means of production.[52]

Lenin, therefore, adopted the classic Marxist view, despite the apparently bleak prospect it offered in a country with so low a proportion of the work force employed for wages in

50. 'On the problem of interest to us, that of the home market, the main conclusion is the following: capitalist production, and consequently, the home market, grow not so much on account of means of consumption as on account of means of production.' (*Development of Capitalism in Russia*, p. 31.) This is, of course, the result of the competitive spur to firms in a market economy which forces investment of profits, i.e. accumulation of producer goods, *ahead* of existing markets, thereby creating ever-expanding new markets. Lenin at times wrongly attributed this trend to the alleged tendency, theoretically unjustifiable and practically unproven, for the organic composition of capital to rise over time.

51. This is not to say that the market cannot set limits to economic development at any particular time. On the contrary. But what Lenin was emphasizing was that the drive to accumulate and expand market shares in a competitive environment constantly tended to push those limits outward such that the market could not be said to be an independent obstacle to capitalist development, except in a very restricted sense.

52. The only sense, indeed, in which the peasantry could be regarded as a cohesive class at all was the sense in which it found itself opposed to a landlord class. Furthermore, while the peasantry might under certain circumstances be a revolutionary class against landlordism or the landlord state, its very conditions of life tended to make any revolution based on it a semi- or proto-bourgeois movement, for private property and market relations.

modern factories;[53] despite the misgivings of Marx himself as to whether the road to socialism in Russia really had to lead through capitalist development;[54] and finally, despite the communal characteristics of the Russian peasantry, which had led the Narodniks to pin their faith on it as the revolutionary class that could inaugurate socialism. With the development of capitalism and therefore of the working class, the social base was created for a genuinely socialist revolution: the class that was to provide the direct social lever for the transfer of power and was to consolidate and maintain that power in fierce social struggles. Furthermore, it was the clarity of Lenin's perception of the progressive function of developing capitalism in backward Russia that enabled him to assess correctly the potential role of the peasantry as a revolutionary force which could, as a result of its increasingly bourgeois and petty-bourgeois character, help weaken and smash the landlord state that had placed so many restrictions on its bourgeois ambitions.[55] *On the other hand, while the penetration of capitalism into the countryside intensified the unity of the peasantry against*

53. 'The proportion of the Russian population actively occupied in manufacturing and mechanical industries on the eve of World War I, though twice as high as in 1860, was still extremely low, with less than two industrial workers per 100 persons in the total population. At about this time in the United States there were 11.6 gainfully occupied persons in manufacturing and mechanical industries (per 100 persons in the total population).' F. Lorimer, *The Population of the Soviet Union*, League of Nations, 1946, p. 2, cited in Andrew Rothstein, *A History of the USSR*, p.15.

54. 'I have arrived at this conclusion: if Russia continues to pursue the path she has followed since 1861, she will lose the finest chance ever offered to a people and undergo all the fatal vicissitudes of the capitalist regime.' Marx to the editors of *Otechestvennye Zapiski*, November 1877, in *Karl Marx on Colonialism and Modernization*, p. 468. See also Umberto Melotti, *Marx and the Third World*, chapter 20.

55. Although Russian economy and society were becoming rapidly bourgeoisified, the Tsarist state remained a feudal absolutist state, defending the feudal modes of exploitation still predominant in the Russian countryside. See P. Anderson, *Lineages of the Absolutist State*, chapter 6, where it is argued that Lenin's later judgement (1912) was that capitalist relations were overshadowed by feudal relations in the Russian countryside. Lenin had earlier emphasized the degree to which capitalism was steadily developing in Russia.

the landowners and the Tsarist state,[56] *it simultaneously tended to divide it along socio-economic lines* as market relations became more and more important, thus creating the conditions for neutralizing its potential menace to the *socialist* revolution as a basically bourgeois or petty-bourgeois class.

This dual politico-economic result of the penetration of capitalism into the Russian countryside (and Lenin's clear understanding of it and perception of its progressive character) was crucial to the success of the October Revolution. Although the February Revolution would undoubtedly have occurred even if the Bolsheviks had never existed, their correct policy before February created the basis for the later worker-*poor* peasant alliance, for it was their consistency on this question that earned the Bolsheviks the trust, at least for certain crucial periods, of significant sections of the peasantry and their political representative, the Socialist Revolutionaries. The Bolsheviks' undeviating demand for confiscation of the landlords' estates won maximum peasant unity against the Tsarist state and prepared the neutralization of the middle peasants when the revolution took a socialist direction. After February, however, Lenin's emphasis was less on the unity of the peasantry than on their class differences, corresponding to the difference between the two aspects of capitalist penetration of the countryside.

The Bolsheviks' analysis and tactics were in no way decisive for the February Revolution, except insofar as they placed them in a stronger *future* position with respect to the peasantry. But it was quite otherwise with the October Revolution, for here the Bolshevik slogan of a dictatorship of the proletariat in alliance with the *poor* peasantry proved decisive in practice. The Bolshevik alliance with the Left Socialist Revolutionaries proved critical at a crucial

56. 'Conflicts with the nobility, with the towns, and with the state . . . acted as powerful external pressures evoking peasant solidarity.' T. Shanin, *The Awkward Class, Political Sociology of Peasantry in a Developing Society: Russia 1910-1925,* p. 141.

moment in the socialist overturn.[57] Had the Socialist Revolutionaries remained united, had the peasantry been a homogeneous class, had the Bolsheviks not taken advantage of their divisions, there would have been no socialist revolution.

Having recognized that the most rapid development of rural capitalism would strengthen both these aspects of the progressive (revolutionary) potential of the peasantry, Lenin always fiercely opposed sentimental attitudes towards or political support for the semi-communal *mir*, or village community. 'The reality (small production) which the Narodniks want to raise to a higher level, by-passing capitalism, already contains capitalism with its antagonism of classes and clashes between them — only the antagonism is in its worst form, a form which hampers the independent activity of the producer. By ignoring the social antagonisms which have already arisen and by dreaming about "different paths for the fatherland" the Narodniks became Utopian revolutionaries, because large-scale capitalism only develops, purges, and clarifies the content of these antagonisms, which exist all over Russia.'[58] Lenin thus read the character of the peasantry's socio-economic aspirations far more accurately than either the Narodniks (and their successors, the Socialist Revolutionaries) or the Mensheviks.

The further penetration of capitalism into agriculture would create more rural proletarian or semi-proletarian allies for the factory working class, while aggravating tensions between the peasantry as a whole and the landlords. In the event, the Bolshevik success in October 1917 must be attributed in large measure to the specific perceptions of Lenin's perspective that capitalist development was progressive, both in society at large and in agriculture. This perspicacity was one of the reasons why the Bolsheviks, beginning from a position of extreme

57. E. H. Carr, *The Bolshevik Revolution 1917-1923*, Volume I, chapter 4.
58. V.I. Lenin *The Economic Content of Narodism and the Criticism of it in Mr. Struve's Book* (1894).

numerical inferiority in February 1917, won out against a range of capable opponents.[59] The outlook that underlay this success was cogently summarized in one sentence in one of Lenin's earliest works: 'In respect not only of Russia, but also of the West, our Narodniks are incapable of understanding how one can fight capitalism by speeding up its development, and not by "holding it up", not by pulling it back, but by pushing it forward, not in reactionary but in progressive fashion.'[60]

Nor was Lenin's tolerance of capitalist development as a necessary bridge to socialism at all reluctant or half-hearted. He praised the productive superiority of large-scale industry over small, and of small over handicrafts. He was keenly appreciative of the labour mobility in agriculture resulting from the deprivation of the direct producers of their land and tools;[61] of the high degree of social and economic instability caused by the fluctuations in the fortunes of large-scale machine-industry;[62] of the breakdown of community

59. Especially capable were the Socialist Revolutionaries, who proved no mean opponents, even during those periods when they were a minority.

60. *The Economic Content of Narodism,* p. 353.

61. 'We assert, the Narodnik theory notwithstanding, that the "peregrination" of the workers not only yields "purely economic" advantages to the workers themselves, but in general should be regarded as a progressive thing; that public attention should be directed, not towards replanning migrational industries by local "occupations at hand", but on the contrary, towards removing all the obstacles in the way of migration, towards facilitating it in every way, towards cheapening and improving all the conditions of the movement of the workers, etc. The grounds for our assertion are as follows. 1) "Purely economic" advantage accrues to the workers from "peregrination" because they go to places where wages are higher, where their position as seekers of employment is a more advantageous one.... 2) "Peregrination" destroys bonded forms of hire and the *Otrabotki.* . . . 3) "Peregrination" means creating mobility of the population. Peregrinations are one of the most important factors preventing the peasants from "gathering moss", of which more than enough has been fastened on them by history. Unless the population becomes mobile, it cannot develop, and it would be naive to imagine that a village school can teach people what they can learn from an independent acquaintance with the different relations and orders of things in the South and in the North, in agriculture and in industry, in the capital and in the backwoods.' *The Development of Capitalism in Russia,* pp. 259-262.

62. 'The "instability" of large-scale machine industry has always evoked and continues to evoke reactionary complaints from individuals who

values[63] — all attitudes that contrast strangely with modern Marxist emphases. Nor was there the slightest hypocrisy or 'inhumanity' in all this. These conditions of violent disruption, uncertainty, and change, conjoined with the formation of a factory-employed working-class in a growing industrial sector,[64] were exactly those required to create independent-minded individuals able to organize themselves collectively.[65] Again, these conditions were not simply the physical ones that promoted organization or the negative ones that broke the chains of personal dependence. Capitalism (especially large-scale machine capitalism) required a high level of culture from its direct producers: education, literacy, versatility, curiosity, punctuality, personal organization, etc.[66]

In summary, that a socialist revolution first occurred in a predominantly peasant society that had not yet achieved

---

continue to look at things through the eyes of the small producer and who forget that it is this "instability" alone that replaced the former stagnation by the rapid transformation of methods of production and of all social relationships.' Ibid., p. 599.

63. 'The "corruption" of the town workers scares the petty bourgeois who prefers the "family hearth" (with its immorality and club rule), "settled life" and does not understand that the awakening of the man in "the beast of burden", an awakening of such enormous and epoch-making significance that all sacrifices made to achieve it are legitimate, cannot but assume tempestuous forms under capitalist conditions in general and in Russia in particular.' *The Economic Content of Narodism,* pp. 386-7.

64. The combination was important since disruption alone would have imprisoned the 'freed' labourer in the cultural fringes of the patriarchal backwardness from which he was physically separate.

65. Again, there was nothing hypocritical about Lenin's violent denunciation of the misery that capitalism brought the masses. He was sensitive to both facets of capitalist development; such a dual sensitivity was required if the working class was to acquire an independent status as a conscious historical actor. But the inherent ambiguity of an independent working-class movement in the early stages of capitalist development was bound to lend a utopian emphasis to politics by implying an impossible might-have-been (that an existent alternative agent for carrying out capitalism's functions could have been found) or an equally impossible immediate future.

66. Lenin considered that the higher cultural standards of the workers required by large-scale machine industry were themselves an element in the expansion of the domestic market, requiring as they did the purchase of new products, e.g. books, newspapers, pens, clocks, etc.

more than limited industrialization was not a refutation of
classical Marxism, but very much the result of its successful
application, the product of the conscious adaptation of
classical Marxism to Russia's specific circumstances
and the dynamic trends in Russian society. The paradox lay
not in the advent of a socialist regime in a peasant society,
but in the presence of a highly sophisticated political
leadership for the working class at such an early stage of its
(relative) numerical and cultural development. But it should
be remembered that if the wedge of capitalist large-scale
machine industry driven into the Tsarist economy was the
decisive factor permitting the establishment of a socialist
state, it was the narrowness of this wedge — and indeed the
all too recent character of its appearance — that ultimately
prevented the socialist state from presiding over the
development of a socialist civil society incorporating any
substantial measure of political freedom, independent
working-class activity, or a more advanced development of
individualism. The Russian revolution of October 1917 fully
justified, in its contradictory outcome, classical Marxism's
view of the historical role of capitalism as the bridge to
socialism.

5. The Imperialist Mission of Capitalism

Since Marx and Engels considered the role of capitalism in
precapitalist societies progressive, it was entirely logical
that they should have welcomed the extension of capitalism
to non-European societies.[67] That this extension was
externally initiated and generally imposed by force did not
annul, or even qualify, their judgement. Violence did not
necessarily mean retrogressive disruption or greater suffering than peaceful reaction.[68] The exogenous introduction of
capitalism does not imply a static dualism or sterile

67. Whether or not Marx and Engels's views on colonialism were justified
will be discussed in a subsequent chapter.
68. This is one of the themes of Barrington Moore.

compound of the newly-entered capitalist mode of production with precapitalist modes of production within the same polity, for the devastatingly superior productivity and cultural attributes of capitalism[69] are bound in the end to subordinate all other modes of production and eventually eliminate them entirely.

Marx accordingly recognized the historically progressive role of British imperialism in no uncertain terms, indeed in words of poetic vision.

'These small stereotype forms of social organism', he wrote, referring to Indian villages, 'have been to the greater part dissolved, and are disappearing, not so much through the brutal interference of the British tax-gatherer and the British soldier, as through the working of English steam and English free trade. Those family communities were based on domestic industry, in that particular combination of hand-weaving, hand-spinning and hand-tilling agriculture which gave them self-supporting power. English interference having placed the spinner in Lancashire and the weaver in Bengal, or sweeping away both Hindoo spinner and weaver, dissolved these small semi-barbarian communities, by blowing up their economical basis, and thus produced the greatest, and, to speak the truth, the only *social* revolution ever heard of in Asia.

'Now, sickening as it must be to human feeling to witness these myriads of industrious patriarchal and inoffensive social organizations disorganized and dissolved into their units, thrown into a sea of woes, and their individual members losing at the same time their ancient form of civilization and their hereditary means of subsistence, we must not forget that these idyllic village communities, inoffensive though they may appear, had always been the solid foundation of Oriental despotism, that they restrained the human mind within the smallest possible compass, making it the unresisting tool of superstition, enslaving it beneath traditional rules, depriving it of all grandeur and

69. Above all, the permeation of capitalist culture by the twin ideas of progress and individualism.

historical energies. We must not forget the barbarian egotism which, concentrating on some miserable patch of land, had quietly witnessed the ruin of empires, the perpetration of unspeakable cruelties, the massacre of the population of large towns, with no other consideration bestowed upon them than on natural events, itself the helpless prey of any aggressor who deigned to notice it at all. We must not forget that this undignified, stagnatory and vegetative life, that this passive sort of existence, evoked on the other part, in contradistinction, wild, aimless, unfounded forces of destruction, and rendered murder itself a religious rite in Hindostan. We must not forget that these little communities were contaminated by distinctions of caste and by slavery, that they subjugated man to external circumstances instead of elevating man to be the sovereign of circumstances, that they transformed a self-developing social state into never changing natural destiny, and thus brought about a brutalizing worship of nature, exhibiting its degradation in the fact that man, the sovereign of nature, fell down on his knees in adoration of Hanuman the monkey and Sabbala the cow.

'England, it is true, in causing a social revolution in Hindostan, was actuated only by the vilest interests, and was stupid in her manner of enforcing them. But that is not the question. The question is, can mankind fulfil its destiny without a fundamental revolution in the social state of Asia? If not, whatever may have been the crimes of England, she was the unconscious tool of history in bringing about the revolution.'[70]

Moving on to the more directly political and economic aspects of British rule, Marx wrote as follows in a famous dispatch to the *New York Daily Tribune*, published 8 August 1853.[71]

'England has to fulfil a double mission in India: one

---

70. K. Marx, 'The British Role in India' (*New York Daily Tribune*, 25 June 1853), in S. Avineri (ed.), *Karl Marx on Colonialism and Modernization*, pp. 93-94.
71. 'The Future Results of British Rule in India', ibid., pp. 132-137.

destructive, the other regenerating – the annihilation of old Asiatic society, and the laying of the material foundations of Western society in Asia.

'. . . The British were the first conquerors superior, and therefore inaccessible to, Hindoo civilization. They destroyed it by breaking up the native communities, by uprooting the native community, and by levelling all that was great and elevated in the native society. The historic pages of their rule in India report hardly anything beyond that destruction. The work of regeneration hardly transpires through a heap of ruins. Nevertheless it has begun.

'The political unity of India, more consolidated, and extending further than it ever did under the Great Moguls, was the first condition of its regeneration. That unity, imposed by the British sword, will now be strengthened and perpetuated by the electric telegraph. The native army, organized and trained by the British drill-sergeant, was the *sine qua non* of Indian self-emancipation, and of India ceasing to be the prey of the first foreign intruder. The free press, introduced for the first time into Asiatic society, and managed principally by the common offspring of Hindoos and Europeans, is a new and powerful agent of reconstruction. The Zemindaree and Ryotwar themselves, abominable as they are, involve two distinct forms of private property in land — the great desideratum of Asiatic society. From the Indian natives, reluctantly and sparingly educated at Calcutta, under English superintendence, a fresh class is springing up, endowed with the requirements for government and imbued with European science. Steam has brought India into regular and graphic communication with Europe, has connected its chief ports with those of the whole south-eastern ocean, and has revindicated it from the isolated position which was the prime law of its stagnation . . . .

'The ruling classes of Great Britain have had, till now, but an accidental, transitory and exceptional interest in the progress of India. The aristocracy wanted to conquer it, the moneyocracy to plunder it, and the millocracy to undersell it.

But now the tables are turned. The millocracy have discovered that the transformation of India into a reproductive country has a vital importance to them, and that, to that end, it is necessary, above all, to gift her with means of irrigation and of internal communication. They intend now drawing a set of railroads over India. And they will do it . . .

'We know that the municipal organization and the economical basis of the village communities have been broken up, but their worst feature, the dissolution of society into stereotype and disconnected atoms, has survived their vitality. The village isolation produced the absence of roads in India, and the absence of roads perpetuated the village isolation. On this plan a community existed with a given scale of low conveniences, almost without intercourse with other villages, without the desires and efforts indispensable to social advance. The British having broken up this self-sufficient inertia of the villages, railways will provide the new want of communication and intercourse . . . .

'I know that the English millocracy intend to endow India with railways with the exclusive view of extracting at diminished expenses the cotton and other raw materials for their manufacturers. But when you have introduced machinery into the locomotion of a country, which possesses iron and coal, you are unable to withhold it from its fabrication. You cannot maintain a net of railways over an immense country without introducing all those industrial processes necessary to meet the immediate and current wants of railway locomotion, and out of which there must grow the application of machinery to those branches of industry not immediately connected with railways. The railway system will therefore become, in India, truly the forerunner of modern industry.

'Modern industry, resulting from the railway system, will dissolve the hereditary divisions of labour, upon which rests the Indian castes, those decisive impediments to Indian progress and Indian power.

'The Indians will not reap the fruits of the new elements of society scattered among them by the British bourgeoisie till in Great Britain itself the now ruling classes shall have been supplanted by the industrial proletariat, or till the Hindoos themselves shall have grown strong enough to throw off the English yoke altogether. At all events, we may safely expect to see, at a more or less remote period, the regeneration of that great and interesting country.'[72]

Engels not only welcomed the French conquest of Algeria as a 'fortunate fact for the progress of civilization,'[73] but also considered a positive socialist colonial policy a likely necessity. In a letter to Kautsky, 12 September 1882, he wrote, 'In my opinion the colonies proper, i.e., the countries occupied by a European population — Canada, the Cape, Australia — will all become independent; on the other hand, the countries inhabited by a native population, which are simply subjugated — India, Algeria, the Dutch, Portuguese, and Spanish possessions — must be taken over for the time being by the proletariat and led as rapidly as possible towards independence.'[74]

In the same tradition, Lenin certainly never would have

72. For similar reasons, Marx favourably viewed the annexation of Mexican territory by the United States. Hobsbawm, *The Age of Revolution, 1789-1849.*

73. '. . . The conquest of Algeria is an important and fortunate fact for the progress of civilization . . . the conquest of Algeria has already forced the Beys of Tunis and Tripoli, and even the Emperor of Morocco, to enter upon the road of civilization. They were obliged to find other employment for their people than piracy and other means of filling their exchequers than tributes paid to them by the smaller states of Europe. And if we may regret that the liberty of the Bedouins of the desert has been destroyed, we must not forget that these same Bedouins were a nation of robbers, whose principal means of living consisted of making excursions either upon each other, or upon the settled villagers, taking what they found, slaughtering all those who resisted, and selling the remaining prisoners as slaves. All these nations of free barbarians look very proud, noble and glorious at a distance, but only come near them and you will find that they, as well as the more civilized nations, are ruled by the lust of gain, and only employ ruder and more cruel means. And, after all, the modern *bourgeois*, with civilization, including order and at least relative enlightenment following him, is preferable to the feudal lord or to the marauding robber, with the barbarian state of society to which they belong.' F. Engels, 'French Rule in Algeria', article in *The Northern Star,* 22 January 1848, in Avineri, *Karl Marx on Colonialism and Modernization,* pp. 47-48.

74. Avineri, *Karl Marx on Colonialism and Modernization,* p. 473.

considered denouncing the foreign powers and businessmen for their prominent role in the generation of industrial capitalism in Russia, a role that nowadays would be called neo-colonialist and condemned by the liberal left. Indeed, the imperialist spur to Russian industrialization was decisive for the success of the Russian revolution. The Russian industrial sector, with large-scale and technologically advanced enterprises, trebled in real terms in the two decades before 1914, one of the fastest growth rates in Europe.[75] Just prior to the First World War, Russia was the fourth-largest steel producer in the world, ranking higher than France. In absolute terms the industrial sector was the fifth biggest in the world, and accounted for 20 per cent of total national income (excluding railways.)[76] Here was implanted the combative, revolutionary, and forward-looking proletariat, vastly outnumbered in a sea of peasants. *And this industrial sector was primarily the product of foreign loans and direct foreign investment. State promotion of industrial development*[77] *was financed mainly by loans from the French money market.*[78] Direct investment by foreign firms also played a crucial role:[79] 'Foreign capital

75. T. H. Von Lane, *Serge Witte and the Industrialization of Russia,* New York, 1963, p. 269, cited in Anderson, *Lineages*, p. 353.

76. R. Goldsmith, 'The Economic Growth of Tsarist Russia 1860-1913', *Economic Development and Cultural Change*, (April 1961), pp. 442, 444, 470-1, cited in Anderson, *Lineages*, p. 353.

77. 'The great industrial upswing came when, from the middle of the eighties on, the railroad building of the state assumed unprecedented proportions and became the main lever of a rapid industrialization policy. Through multifarious devices such as preferential orders to domestic producers of railroad materials, high prices, subsidies, credits and profit guarantees to new industrial enterprises, the government succeeded in maintaining a high and, in fact, increasing rate of growth until the end of the century. Concomitantly, the Russian taxation system was reorganized, and the financing of industrialization policies was thus provided for (to repay foreign loans), while the stabilization of the rouble and the introduction of the gold standard assured foreign participation in the development of Russian industry.' Alexander Gerschenkron, *Economic Backwardness in Historical Perspective*, p. 19.

78. A. Rothstein, *A History of the USSR*, p. 14.

79. The important role of direct foreign investment in Tsarist industrialization is ignored in Perry Anderson's account, which also tends to minimize

imports began to flow into the coal, oil, iron and steel industries, attracted by vastly higher profits (25 - 50%) than it could earn at home. Between 1896 and 1900 a quarter of all new companies formed were foreign, and by 1900 foreign capital accounted for 28% of the total. By 1914 the proportion had risen to 33%. Foreign capital controlled 45% of Russia's oil output, 54% of her iron output, 50% of her chemical industry, 74% of her coal output. More than half the capital of the six leading banks of the country — themselves controlling nearly 60% of all banking capital and nearly half of all bank deposits — was foreign.'[80]

6. Progressive Capitalism and Reactionary Imperialism

Marx, Engels, and Lenin, who considered capitalism historically far more advanced than any earlier civilization, logically welcomed its extension to non-capitalist regions, whether by means of direct colonialism (India) or 'neo-colonialism' (Russia). Soon, however, a strange paradox emerged in Marxist thought. Imperialism, conceived by Marx and Engels as the historical process of capitalist expansion into the non-capitalist world,[81] and regarded as

the actuality and prospects of the capitalist transformation of Russian agriculture — especially by judging the Stolypin policy to have failed (or at least not succeeded) within an impossibly brief time span, whereas the figures he quotes show remarkable progress in this respect, given the brevity of the time lapse. His point that taxation of the peasantry to repay foreign loans for industrialization 'blocked the expansion of the internal market' is a misunderstanding, since what was involved was the development of the internal market *along different lines* than would otherwise have been the case. Indeed, but for the First World War, the industrialization so financed would have been likely ultimately to speed up the expansion of the domestic market through various linkage effects. The burden of Anderson's bias here appears to be to minimize the possibility of Tsarism's promoting a successful capitalist development along Prussian lines. (Perry Anderson, *Lineages*, pp. 348-360).

80. Rothstein, *A History of the USSR*, p. 14, citing Alexinsky, *Russia and Europe*, 1917.

81. Marx and Engels did not use the term 'imperialism' as such, but the

progressive precisely because of their analysis of capitalism as the most advanced social system hitherto achieved, came to be regarded as the characteristic of capitalism that nullified its previously progressive features. The tail wags the dog. It is now not the character of capitalism that determines the progressiveness (or otherwise) of imperialism, but the character of imperialism that determines the reactionary character of capitalism.

This paradox is not a matter of semantics depending on the definitions of terms: capitalism and imperialism, progressive and reactionary. Nor do its origin and solution lie in the ancient texts. Its most fundamental source is a contradiction in Marxist thinking itself, which in turn reflected (in a distorted form) particular contradictory aspects of social reality, which had created a situation such that Marxists could act effectively only by closing their eyes to some extent to the reality on which they had previously been on such amicable terms. The shift was polemically accomplished for the world communist movement by Lenin in his *Imperialism: The Highest Stage of Capitalism* (1917). Lenin's essay reversed Marxist doctrine on the progressive character of imperialist expansion and, by an irresistible ideological process, erased from Marxism any trace of the view that capitalism could henceforth represent an instrument of social or economic advance, even in precapitalist societies. The historic mission of capitalism was declared ended.

---

expression adequately sums up their general frame of reference in discussing specific imperialist phenomena. It is also the author's frame of reference and fundamental definition, although others will be used according to the context.

3
About-Turn: Lenin's 'Imperialism'

The traditional Marxist view of imperialism as progressive was reversed primarily by Lenin (implicitly breaking with his earlier theoretical approaches[1]) in his *Imperialism: The Highest Stage of Capitalism*. In effectively overturning Marx and Engels's view of the character of imperialist expansion, Lenin set in motion an ideological process that erased from Marxism any trace of the view that capitalism could be an instrument of social progress even in precapitalist societies, although this shift was not logically necessary to his central thesis. But the proposition that imperialism was reactionary, in Marxist terms, could be sustained only by clouding the issues in ambiguity, by distorting history and rejecting some fundamental precepts of Marxist economics.

1. Problems of Social Progress in the Developed and Underdeveloped World

In his work on imperialism, Lenin paid little attention to the effects of imperialism on the underdeveloped countries, for he was almost entirely concerned with its sources and repercussions in the advanced capitalist world. *Imperialism: The Highest Stage of Capitalism* was written in 1916 at

1. Notably, he broke with his previous views on under-consumptionism, and implicitly with his assertion that foreign capital plays a progressive role in industrialization.

the height of the First World War, when the working classes of Europe were slaughtering one another by the million in the name of patriotism; the Second International had split, major sectors of it abandoning the internationalist principles on which it had been founded and supporting the nationalist carnage. The major aim of Lenin's argument was twofold: to explain the origins of the war and to account for the abandonment of internationalism by the majority of the working classes, who were following the opportunists in their support of the war. As we shall see, although his results were logically and analytically lamentable, Lenin did score Marxism's glittering propaganda success of the twentieth century, for the pamphlet was able neatly to explain *both* the causes of the war *and* the reasons for the opportunist, nationalist proletarian support for it by one and the same phenomenon: imperialism.[2]

But Lenin went even further. He tried to identify the sources of imperialism in an underlying transformation of the capitalist economies leading to a new stage of capitalism, in his view the final one. Indeed, Lenin frequently spoke of imperialism not simply as an aspect of capitalism but as equivalent to monopoly capitalism. Current popular usage has tended to equate modern imperialism with the prevailing relationships of domination and exploitation between advanced capitalist and underdeveloped economies. This tendency was in part encouraged by Lenin's own emphasis on the export of capital to the underdeveloped countries. This has led to a somewhat schizophrenic approach to the question on the left, such that one Marxist authority on imperialism, Tom Kemp, can produce a book on industrialization in nineteenth-century Europe without mentioning imperialism, while another, Ernest Mandel, can write a book on the 'contradictions of imperialism' without discussing the underdeveloped world.[3]

2. There is, of course, no reason why these two phenomena should necessarily have the same causes. That Lenin's argument did advance a simultaneous explanation added to its psychological force.
3. Tom Kemp, *Theories of Imperialism*, London, 1967, and *Industrial-*

This schizophrenic approach has tended to blur the distinction between the problems of social progress in the developed and the underdeveloped world, such that if advanced capitalism is considered to have become an outright brake on human progress, this is regarded as characteristic of capitalism all over the world. The concept of the world revolution (of the oppressed rural masses of Asia, Africa, and Latin America, plus the revolutionary proletariat of the imperialist world) against the advanced capitalist countries is thus confused with the world revolution against capitalism as such. Lenin's *Imperialism* succeeded in blurring this distinction and turning the alleged socially reactionary character of *advanced* capitalism into the last stage of capitalism *in general*, thereby precluding a priori any progressive role for capitalism in the colonial and semi-colonial world.[4]

2. Lenin's Basic Arguments

The crux of Lenin's argument was that the advent of monopoly capitalism marked the end of those progressive aspects of capitalism that Marx and Engels had proclaimed in the *Communist Manifesto*. Capitalism had become 'over-ripe'. His thesis was that competition under industrial capitalism led inevitably to concentration of capital and thus to monopoly, trade combines, cartels, etc., whose control of the domestic markets of the advanced capitalist world was so firm that the vigorous competitive incentive to

isation in 19th Century Europe, London, 1969. Ernest Mandel, *Europe Versus America,* London, 1970. Recognizing the problem of a multiplicity of usages, Giovanni Arrighi notes that '. . . major events and trends since the end of the Second World War constitute *macroscopic anomalies* with regard to Lenin's theory of imperialism; and . . . the inability of Marxists to grasp them as such is perhaps the principal cause of the ambiguities and misunderstandings on which the theoretical debate of the sixties and seventies has run aground'. (*The Geometry of Imperialism,* p. 16.)

4. The corollary of the proposition that capitalism in the Third World was not progressive was that as a social system it was not only nasty, but also doomed to endless failure.

innovate had vanished, the living standards of the masses could no longer rise, and above all, the expanded profits of the monopolists would eventually find all profitable spheres of domestic investment exhausted. This latter circumstance led in turn to rivalry for profitable outlets abroad, generating a struggle for the division and redivision of the world among the leading imperialist states. Stagnation at home meant imperialism abroad. The international wave of imperialist expansion in the late nineteenth and early twentieth century was thus to be explained by the stage of monopoly capitalism that had been reached in the major industrial countries, which forced them into territorial rivalry for investment outlets, especially in the colonial or semi-colonial countries, where labour, land, and raw materials were cheap and capital scarce.

This summary is a faithful representation of the underlying logic of Lenin's theory and therefore ignores various discrepancies, minor contradictions, and elaborations in his presentation.[5] I have therefore omitted Lenin's

5. Lenin's own summary of his theory ran as follows: 'If it were necessary to give the briefest possible definition of imperialism, we should have to say that imperialism is the monopoly stage of capitalism. Such a definition would include what is most important, for, on the one hand, finance capital is the bank capital of a few big monopolist combines of manufacturers; and, on the other, the division of the world is the transition from a colonial policy which has extended without hindrance to territories unoccupied by any capitalist power to a colonial policy of monopolistic possession of the territory of the world which has been completely divided up.

'But very brief definitions, although convenient, for they sum up the main points, are nevertheless inadequate, because very important features of the phenomenon that has to be defined have to be especially deduced. And so, without forgetting the conditional and relative value of all definitions, which can never include all the concatenations of a phenomenon in its complete development, we must give a definition of imperialism which will embrace the following five essential features:

'1. The concentration of production and capital developed to such a high stage that it created monopolies which play a decisive role in economic life.

'2. The merging of bank capital with industrial capital, and the creation, on the basis of this "finance capital", of a financial oligarchy.

'3. The export of capital, which has become extremely important as distinguished from the export of commodities.

'4. The formation of international capitalist monopolies which share the world among themselves.

emphasis on the rise of 'finance capital' (the second feature of his own definition), since it is inessential to the basic logic of the theory and even tends to weaken the argument. Also omitted is Lenin's emphasis on the division of the world among international capitalist monopolies (the fourth feature of his definition), which, unless it is regarded merely as the basis for inter-state rivalry, is in implicit contradiction with the territorial division of the world among imperialist states. The causal links between the five essential features of Lenin's description are brought more directly into the definition than in Lenin's version.[6]

This theory of capitalist imperialism has been attacked on various grounds. The attacks may be divided into three broad categories: those criticisms concerned to advance an alternative explanation, generally of a sociological character, of which Schumpeter's social atavism is the most famous;[7] those criticisms concerned to demonstrate that political-strategic rather than economic factors have played the major role in imperialist acquisitions and rivalries;[8] those criticisms concerned to dispute the economic basis of Lenin's argument, particularly its underlying logic, together

---

'5. The territorial division of the world among the greatest capitalist powers is completed.

'Imperialism is capitalism in the stage of development in which the dominance of monopolies and finance capital has established itself, in which the export of capital has acquired pronounced importance, in which the division of the world among the international trusts has begun, in which the division of all territories of the globe among the great capitalist powers has been completed.' (Imperialism: The Highest Stage of Capitalism, pp. 108-109).

6. The remaining comments in this section are drawn largely from my 'New Introduction' to George Padmore's Africa and World Peace.

7. J. Schumpeter, Imperialism; Social Classes, Meridian Books, New York, 1960. Schumpeter argued that capitalism absorbs men's energies in peaceful economic activities to an extent unknown in earlier societies. Insofar as imperialism still existed, it was related directly to the incomplete penetration of society by capitalist institutions, psychology, etc. Imperialism thus represents the expenditure of human energies in atavistic forms that no longer correspond to any specific national objective as such.

8. For example, R. E. Robinson and J. E. Gallagher, with Alice Denny, Africa and the Victorians; D. K. Fieldhouse, The Theory of Capitalist Imperialism, Part 5.

with the empirical evidence he marshals with regard to capital flows and the dominance of monopoly and finance capital.

Schumpeter's theory of imperialism as social atavism is marred by circular reasoning that permits him to disregard a wide range of relevant phenomena as not requiring explanation, most notably in the case of the United States.[9] His argument is also unable to account for the burst of imperialist activity from the 1880s to 1919, known as the second phase of imperialist expansion, particularly since the rapid industrialization of Western Europe, North America, and Japan (and Russia to a lesser extent) during the preceding period had afforded plentiful alternative outlets for the surplus psychic energy the absorption of which was imperialism's function, according to this theory. As Hannah Arendt has so brilliantly argued, it was precisely the industrial bourgeoisie[10] that resolved the

9. Relevant in the sense of what is conventionally regarded as the factual data to be explained by the theory. Schumpeter could have made clear that his theory purported to explain a different, more limited, set of phenomena, but he did not do so. 'Among all capitalist economies', he writes, 'that of the United States is least burdened with pre-capitalist elements, survivals, reminiscences and power factors ... we can conjecture that among all countries the United States is likely to exhibit the weakest imperialist trend. This turns out to be the truth'. (*Imperialism,* p. 72). It should, of course, be kept in mind that Schumpeter was writing in 1921. But the United States had shown its expansionist character in the 1850s, and expansion was resumed soon after the Civil War. The United States became one of the major participants in the 'new imperialism' of the late nineteenth century, acquiring first the Hawaiian Islands, which effectively became an American protectorate in 1875. Pearl Harbour became an American naval base in 1887. In 1898 the United States took formal possession of the Hawaiian Republic, declared war on Spain, seized Puerto Rico, Guam, the Philippines, and the Mariana Islands, and also established a protectorate over Cuba. We have here an almost pure example of capitalist imperialism. For a variation of the social atavism theory, see V.G. Kiernan, 'State and Nation in Western Europe', in *Past and Present,* No. 31, July 1965, p. 38.

10. H. Arendt, *The Origins of Totalitarianism,* chapter 5. The role of the bourgeoisie in bringing about the second phase of imperialist expansion may have been direct or indirect. Thus in both Russia and Germany, where the bourgeoisie had little or no political power and where precapitalist elements might be expected to be of decisive importance (according to Schumpeter's view), it was the existence and achievements of an industrial bourgeoisie that precipitated these countries most decisively into the

contradiction between the culturally homogeneous, consensual, and thus constraining, basis of the nation state and the untrammelled, infinite expansionism of capitalist production. This was done by promoting the imperialist outburst of the late nineteenth and early twentieth centuries as a specifically violent and aggressive phenomenon.[11]

More recently, the political-strategic criticisms of Lenin exemplified in the works of Robinson and Gallagher, Fieldhouse, and others have become popular. The substance of their approach is strictly to separate economic, political, and strategic considerations, to analyse each major historical episode concerning imperialism in the light of this division, to stress the complexity of events, and to suggest that economic factors have been significantly less important than Lenin argued.[12] Barraclough has commented appropriately on the simplistic methodological procedure that thus isolates economic and political processes: 'When we are told that the new imperialism was "a specifically political phenomenon in origin" (D.K. Fieldhouse, 'Imperial-

---

imperialist rivalry of the late nineteenth century. Bismarck's intervention in Africa was determined to a large extent by the achievements of German industrialization after 1871, which had created internal demand for external markets and contributed to a world economic situation in which imperialism appeared the only means of responding to this demand and of guaranteeing Germany's power as a nation-state. As for Russia, specifically capitalist economic motives became decisive in Tsarist foreign policy from 1893 onwards — as symbolized by Witte's trans-Siberian railway, promoted to revolutionize world trade, supersede the Suez Canal as the principal Western link with China, and enable Russia to saturate the Chinese market with Russian textile and metal goods. Cf. Barraclough, *An Introduction to Contemporary History*, pp. 51 and 54-55.

11. It should be recalled that the climax of nation-state formation in the advanced world occurred in the late nineteenth century, with the unification of Germany and Italy.

12. Lenin did not regard imperialism as a purely economic phenomenon, contrary to a common misrepresentation. Thus, after advancing the definition cited above, he added: 'Imperialism can and must be defined differently if consideration is to be given not only to the basic, purely economic factors to which the above definition is limited, but also to the historical place of this stage of capitalism in general, or to the two main trends in the working-class movement.' (*Imperialism*, p. 109.) And: 'politically, imperialism is in general a striving towards violence and reaction'. (Ibid., p. 110.)

ism: An Historiographical Revision', *Economic Review,* Vol. XIV, p. 208), the short answer is that in such a context the distinction between politics and economics is unreal.'[13] The political, strategic, and economic dimensions of the trade routes to India form a seamless whole that exemplifies Barraclough's argument, recognition of which is essential for understanding Britain's imperial policies in Africa from Cape to Coast.

Although Lenin was innocent of such crude approaches, there remains a sense in which he explained too much. Imperialism, he argued, arose from the export of capital, which in his view had become the typical feature of capitalism as a result of the superabundance of capital accumulated in the advanced countries (*Imperialism*, pp. 16-17). It was *also* the consequence of the fact that capitalism had already wholly divided the world into colonies and spheres of influence controlled by the principal capitalist powers (*Imperialism*, chapter 6). The problem here is that there is no immediately apparent reason why internal 'over-ripeness' of the individual capitalist economies (dominated by monopolies and finance capital with excess capital spilling out of the capital-saturated domestic economy) should necessarily coincide with the stage of nearly complete territorial division of the world among the great imperialist powers,[14] especially if foreign investment was a feature of industrial economies from the outset (and even more especially if uneven development is an irreducible feature of capitalist economic progress).

This problem is easily resolved through the remaining variety of criticism of Lenin's *Imperialism*. It will be shown below that the valid elements of this third variety of criticism[15] all serve seriously to undermine the over-ripe, capital-export theory of imperialism.

13. *An Introduction to Contemporary History*, p. 51.
14. There is clear historical evidence that in fact there was no such coincidence.
15. Many of the directly economic criticisms of Lenin, of course, are invalid, either incorrect or irrelevant. Thus, it is frequently pointed out that the greatest proportion of foreign investment from Britain and other

Positive evidence that trade rivalries[16] and tariff barriers in the newly industrialized or industrializing capitalist countries of the nineteenth century played a role in provoking imperialist reactions, and the apparent dependence of Britain's economic success on its early-acquired empire, suggest that Lenin's alternative, largely implicit, emphasis should be adopted. This identified the primary causal factors underlying modern imperialism as the trade-induced trend towards the territorial division of the world

---

developed countries went to Europe, North America, and Australia rather than the colonies or underdeveloped countries. (Cf. Barrat Brown, *Essays on Imperialism*, p. 36 and Fieldhouse, *Theory of Capitalist Imperialism*, p. 89.) Lenin was undoubtedly misleading on this point. He included Canada, and presumably Australia and New Zealand, among Britain's 'colonies' (*Imperialism*, p. 79), whereas previously he had implied that foreign investment went mainly to 'backward countries' (p. 77). And his figures blurred the distinction between the capitalist and precapitalist world. But this is no way blunts his explanation of the new imperialism in terms of rivalry induced by capital export, particularly since much territorial acquisition occurred for pre-emptive reasons, as Lenin clearly recognized (p. 102). Nor does this criticism invalidate Lenin's explanation of the territorial rivalry to acquire backward countries. The common criticism that the export of capital returned large profits and thus could not reduce the surplus of capital (Barrat Brown, *Essays on Imperialism*, p. 35) in no way undermines the conjecture that the reduction of domestic capital surplus was the *motivation* of capital export. The criticism that the source of funds for capital export was often not the profits of monopolistic firms but rather loans to governments or government-guaranteed subsidiaries (Barrat Brown, *Essays on Imperialism*, p. 35) is beside the point if the necessity for capital to go abroad (whatever its source) resulted from a dearth of investment opportunities at home consequent to monopolization. Criticisms that ignore the underlying logical structure of Lenin's work are legion, and it would be tedious to go on. It is worth noting, however, that accusations of dishonesty distilled from an inspection of faults in logic take no account of Lenin's well-known integrity and the horrifying slaughter in the midst of which he was writing. The situation appeared to require great urgency of publication, so that the working class would learn the lessons that would enable them to overthrow the system responsible for the war. *Imperialism* ought therefore to be considered a draft and not the product of mature reflection on the subject. A scrutiny of Lenin's *Development of Capitalism in Russia* clearly demonstrates his intellectual scrupulousness and care in a work that went through many revisions.

16. D.C.M. Platt, *Finance, Trade and British Foreign Policy, 1815-1914;* W.L. Langer, *The Diplomacy of Imperialism, 1890-1902,* p. 72; W.A. Williams, *The Tragedy of American Diplomacy,* chapter 1; D.S. Landes, *The Unbound Prometheus,* chapter 5.

among the imperialist powers and the uneven development of the major capitalist countries.

3. The Export of Capital

The export of capital was central to Lenin's theory, both as a proof of the over-ripeness of capitalism and as a specific link between this phenomenon and the scramble for territories in the late nineteenth century. But it cannot be shown either that capital export was characteristic of a specific (later) stage of capitalism or that it was decisively connected with the scramble for territories.

In principle there is no reason why export of capital should be presumed the result of 'pressure' due to the disappearance or reduction of profitable investment outlets in the metropolitan countries. It may just as well result from the development of preferable (or what were thought to be preferable) investment opportunities abroad.[17] Indeed, foreign investment may be the direct result of booming domestic investment, and vice versa.[18] Booming domestic investment not only creates the profits that *can* be invested both at home and abroad, but also and more importantly stimulates (and incorporates in new equipment) technological advances that in turn open new *opportunities* for investment abroad. An outstanding instance of this process may be seen in the development of railways. More than 40 per cent of the capital exported from Britain in the hundred

17. This is not to say that foreign investment *never* took place because of an absolute lack of investment opportunities at home, however temporary. This may well have been the case in Britain in the 1880s. See Aldcroft and Richardson, *The British Economy*, pp. 119-121.

18. The fact that foreign investment may stimulate domestic investment through export expansion and consequent multiplier-accelerator effects does not support the Leninist thesis that foreign investment can alleviate monopoly-produced domestic under-consumption, since according to Lenin, capital export alleviates this problem *only* by exploiting new markets abroad and not by feedback effects on expanding domestic production or the forces of production, which are supposedly still held in the stranglehold of monopoly.

years before 1914 was used to finance railway investment overseas,[19] and British-financed railway construction abroad was not only the *result* of booming conditions at home[20] (especially from the 1840s to the 1870s), but also the *cause* of further domestic expansion. As railways were built abroad by British contractors, engineers, skilled labourers, and often navvies, they provided a direct and expanding market for British exports of steel, iron, and coal, as well as the products of the engineering industries, which had themselves received further impetus from the coming of the railways. Even if direct links between export of money capital and export of commodities cannot be demonstrated in every case, it is clear that world economic expansion in the nineteenth century — contingent on the spread of railways in every continent, largely financed and often built by the British — contributed immensely to the overall dynamism of the markets in which Britain sold and vastly cheapened the supplies purchased.[21] Indeed, short-term fluctuations in British domestic economic activity have been closely correlated with fluctuations in export demand, not only in the nineteenth century, but up to the Second World War.[22] Because of the central role of British finance in developing world markets in the nineteenth century, export-demand fluctuations may in turn be correlated with fluctuations in

19. P. Mathias, preface to *The Export of Capital From Britain, 1870-1914*, p. vii.

20. It is significant that the early development of the British railway system in the 1830s and 1840s did *not* reflect any pressing need for improved transport by industrial society. Rather, it resulted from the search for investment outlets for the surpluses accumulated during the prosperity of the textile phase of the industrial revolution, a useful illustration of the general relationship, positive in the long run, between domestic economic progress and foreign lending during the nineteenth century. E.J. Hobsbawm gives an excellent succinct survey of how the railway boom acted as the driving force of the second phase of the industrial revolution, from the 1840s to the great depression of 1873-1896, in his *Industry and Empire*, chapter 6.

21. Hobsbawm, chapter 6, and A.R. Hall, editors' introduction in *The Export of Capital From Britain, 1870-1914*.

22. F.R. Paish, 'British Economic Fluctuations', *Lloyd's Bank Review*, July 1970.

British lending abroad.[23] In other words, the more Britain lent abroad, the greater was the short-term, as well as long-term, stimulus to domestic activity and investment, for the trade cycle was thereby tilted upwards.[24] Furthermore, although the vicissitudes of prospective profits on the domestic market, together with the domestic availability of funds, would certainly affect the flow of capital abroad, it does not appear to have been the case that capital export in the nineteenth century as a whole was the result of stagnant domestic investment opportunities. If anything, domestic prosperity and correspondingly high investment levels promoted foreign investment[25] continuously and in a self-reinforcing manner. Domestic prosperity and high investment rates did not durably exhaust future domestic investment opportunities.

In a sympathetic review W.H.B. Court has concisely summarized the criticisms that may validly be made of this dimension of Lenin's theory: 'Experience shows that the wealthy countries of the West have lent money throughout the world. It does not follow that such capital would have continued accumulating in these countries if it had never been lent. Foreign lendings were not born necessarily of

23. A. G. Ford, 'Overseas Lending and Internal Fluctuations, 1870-1914', in *The Export of Capital From Britain, 1870-1914.*

24. Ford (pp. 84-96) detects twenty-year cycles of home and foreign investment in the nineteenth century, which he analyses as due largely to the fact that foreign investment was made at the expense of domestic investment and consumption. But the wider ramifications of British foreign investment in developing the whole world economy are such as to confute any view that the growth of the British economy during the nineteenth century was slowed by foreign investment on the whole. On the other hand, it seems likely that its growth *relative to its industrial competitors* may have been slowed.

25. Between 1815 and 1875 British investors exported a capital surplus amounting to about 500 million pounds sterling. The greatest export occurred between 1850 and 1873, when prices were rising and prosperity reached a nineteenth-century peak. Foreign investment frequently rose when business prospects at home were encouraging. (Lelend H. Jenks, *The Migration of British Capital to 1875*, p. 333.) This suggests that the twenty-year cycle alternating between domestic and foreign investment noted by Ford was the result of 'pull' rather than 'push' factors, insofar as such a distinction is useful.

monopoly or accumulation, which would in any case have gone on. Great Britain in the last century lent enormously, long before her industry or her credit system showed the least tendency in the world towards monopoly; but had there been no openings abroad for her capital, much of that capital would never have been saved at all. She had so much to lend, because she lent indefatigably; only the economic developments abroad made possible by her loans brought about the further increase in her wealth out of which new loans were raised. And she lent chiefly when she was herself making full calls upon her capital for home development, not – as some suppose – when development at home drooped unprofitably.'[26]

Lenin's thesis is equally undermined by the fact that capital export, far from being a symptom of a particular (degenerate) stage of capitalism, has been a significant feature of industrial capitalism from its inception. British foreign investment was considerable from the 1820s onwards, French from the 1850s.[27] It is important to note that Britain was far the largest foreign lender throughout the nineteenth century. By 1913 Britain owned approximately £4,000 million of investments abroad, compared with £5,500 million for France, Germany, Belgium, Holland, and the United States combined.[28] In 1915 British foreign investments at least equalled, probably exceeded, the combined total of those of the rest of Europe; British overseas holdings were twice those of France and nearly three times those of Germany.[29] Until the First World War, Britain, France, and Germany were the three largest foreign lenders.[30] For the chief foreign lender, Britain, foreign investment was

26. W.H.B. Court, 'The Communist Doctrines of Empire', in W.K. Hancock's *Survey of British Commonwealth Affairs*, p. 300.

27. S. Kuznets, *Modern Economic Growth: Rate, Structure and Spread*, p. 327. Capital exports probably exceeded imports from Britain as early as the end of the eighteenth century. Cf. Hobsbawm, *Industry and Empire*, p. 91.

28. Hobsbawm, *Industry and Empire*, p. 125.

29. William Woodruff, *Impact of Western Man: A Study of Europe's Role in the World Economy 1750-1960*, p. 117.

30. Kuznets, *Modern Economic Growth*, p. 326.

concurrent with industrial capitalism from the beginning. Moreover — and this counts even more seriously against Lenin's thesis — there is no discernible point at which foreign investment showed a significant upward acceleration or a markedly increased importance in economic operations. There were certainly no such shifts in the 1870s, 1880s, or 1900s (the various decades at which Lenin dates the opening of the new phase of imperialism).[31] More generally, there is no real break in the trend towards the end of the nineteenth century. The two leading capital-exporting countries, Britain and France, were already quite active in this field as early as the 1820s and the 1850s respectively. Reliable figures go back farthest for Britain, and these show no sharp acceleration in the rate of foreign investment towards the end of the century. (See Table 1.) Kuznets's authoritative study shows similar trends. He comments: 'the rate of growth of cumulated foreign capital between the 1820s and the 1870s was probably even higher than that between the 1870s and World War I.'[32] This is precisely the opposite of what would be anticipated from the link Lenin posits between capital export and the rise of monopoly capitalism. (It is also inconsistent with his dating of the opening of the boom in colonial annexations: after the 1870s.)

31. Lenin dated the domination of monopoly capitalism from the beginning of the twentieth century (*Imperialism*, pp. 57, 26). The rise of its elements, the growth of monopolies and the development of finance capital, he also placed in the early twentieth century (p. 74), along with the export of capital, which 'reached formidable dimensions only in the beginning of the twentieth century' (p. 78). The imperialist division of the world into colonies and spheres of influence 'is closely associated with the latest stage in the development of capitalism' (p. 94), and specifically with the necessity for capital export. But Lenin had to recognize that the partition of the world by the large capitalist powers occurred mainly *before* the twentieth century. He generally dates this process from the 1870s (p. 95), and says that it accelerated in the 1880s (p. 96). But in the case of Britain, far the greatest colonial power of all, 'the period of the enormous expansion of colonial conquests is that between 1860 and 1880' (p. 95). How, in Hancock's words, can 'the political consequences of an economic process precede the process itself'? (W.K. Hancock, *Wealth of Colonies*, p. 12.)

32. Kuznets, *Modern Economic Growth*, p. 327 and Table c.5. B, pp. 322-323.

Table 1

Growth of Capital Investment of United Kingdom,
France, and Germany 1825-1915
(in millions of US$ to the nearest $100 million)

	1825	1840	1855	1870	1885	1900	1915
United Kingdom	500	700	2,300	4,900	7,800	12,000	19,500
France	100	300	1,000	2,500	3,300	5,200	8,600
Germany	100	300	1,000	2,500	1,900	4,800	6,700

Foreign investment is defined as the total of outstanding investment in other countries, public or private, made on a long-term basis.

Source: Woodruff, *Impact of Western Man*, Table IV/1, p. 150.

This discrepancy cannot be explained by reference to the relatively small initial stock of accumulated foreign capital, since foreign investment was already contributing substantially to the British balance of payments by the late 1850s[33] and constituted nearly one-third of total net capital formation in the decade 1855-64, a figure exceeding that of the decades 1875-84 and 1895-1904. (See Table 2.) Moreover, the figures of Table 1 record the cumulative total stock of foreign capital invested.

Table 2

Germany and United Kingdom: Foreign Investments as
Percentage of Total Net Capital Formation, 1855-64 to 1905-14

United Kingdom		Germany	
1855-64	— 29.1	1851/5-1861/5	— 2.2
1865-74	— 40.1	1861/5-1871/5	— 12.9
1875-84	— 28.9	1871/5-1881/5	— 14.1
1885-94	— 51.2	1881/5-1891/5	— 19.9
1895-1904	— 20.7	1891/5-1901/5	— 9.7
1905-1914	— 52.9	1901/5-1911/13	— 5.7

Source: Landes, *The Unbound Prometheus*, p. 331

The volume of annual flows, of course, rose considerably more slowly and showed no marked tendency to increase

33. D. H. Aldcroft and Harry W. Richardson, *The British Economy, 1870-1939*, pp. 84-86.

over the four decades covered by Kuznets's data.[34]

Of the three major capital-exporting nations, only Germany evinced capital flows whose timing bore even an approximate relation to the development of monopoly capitalism (Table 1), and this was scarcely a case of surplus capital seeking outlets abroad that were unavailable at home. So great was the internal demand for capital, with extremely rapid growth of net domestic product in a context of rapidly advancing technical progress, that interest rates in Germany were consistently higher than in Britain or France, and foreign investment faced serious competition for funds from domestic capital needs. Moreover, the German government long discouraged capital export on the grounds that domestic needs were pressing and should take priority.[35] The general point is sufficiently dramatized by one datum: 78 per cent of securities newly issued in France between 1906 and 1911 had foreign debtors, whereas in Germany the figure was only 11 per cent.[36] Furthermore, a significant proportion of such foreign lending as was made was directly tied to financing German exports, especially of heavy industrial goods, the close link between industry and the banks facilitating this phenomenon.[37] This fact in itself refutes Lenin's emphasis on capital as opposed to commodity export as one of the distinguishing features of the new imperialism, at least in the case of Germany.

More generally, Lenin's theory held that the 'over-ripe', capital-saturated economies that were acquiring territories should evince a *net outflow* of capital, but during the period from the 1880s to the outbreak of the First World War several imperialist countries (the United States, Japan, Russia,

34. Kuznets, *Modern Economic Growth*, pp. 322, 326.

35. Herbert Feis, *Europe, The World's Banker, 1870-1914*, chapter IV.

36. Knut Borchardt, 'The Industrial Revolution in Germany, 1700-1914', in Carlo M. Cipolla, ed., *The Fontana Economic History of Europe: The Emergence of Industrial Societies — 1*, p. 142.

37. We may also note that the relative importance of foreign investment in total German investment declined steadily from the 1880s to 1914 (Table 2), a fact inconsistent with the 'spill over' and 'monopoly capital' dimensions of Lenin's theory, insofar as they can be treated separately.

Italy, Portugal, and Spain) were net capital importers,[38] and all engaged to varying degrees in the heightened territorial rivalry of the period.[39] Moreover, as we have seen, Germany was almost as little to be regarded as capital-saturated as were the net capital importers, and its ambitions were indeed a crucial factor in the colonial contest.

If it is argued that even the larger of these powers — the United States, Germany, Russia, and Japan — were relatively unimportant as capital exporters and colonial powers compared with Britain and France and must therefore be considered marginal with respect to Lenin's analysis, then any reasonable explanation for the massive upsurge in territorial rivalry between the 1880s and 1914 vanishes. For the significant aspect of the outburst of territorial acquisition was that it did *not* originate from Britain, the predominant, established, industrial imperial power (and only to a small extent from France[40]), but

38. Fieldhouse, *The Theory of Capitalist Imperialism*, p. 190; Woodruff, *Impact of Western Man*, chapter IV; Kuznets, *Modern Economic Growth*, chapter VI. By 1914 the United States was a considerable net debtor in absolute terms. The value of European investments in the United States ($6,500 million) represented 14 per cent of international indebtedness at that date. (Woodruff, p. 120.)

39. The United States in the Pacific, Cuba, and North Africa; Japan in the Far East, and also Russia; Italy in East and North Africa; Portugal in East and West Africa; Spain in West and North Africa.

40. France had colonies (Algeria and Senegal) before 1870, and was the leading industrial power on the continent in the early nineteenth century. Although starting industrialization earlier, France was subsequently outstripped by Germany, the United States, Russia, and Japan. By the second half of the nineteenth century, Germany had become the continent's leading industrial power. (See E.J. Hobsbawm, *The Age of Revolution, 1789-1849*, chapter 9; Claude Fohlen, 'The Industrial Revolution in France, 1700-1914', in *The Fontana Economic History of Europe: The Emergence of Industrial Societies — 1*; Sidney Pollard and Colin Holmes, eds., *Documents of European History*, Volume 2, *Industrial Power and National Rivalry, 1870-1914*, London, 1972, chapter 2.) Nevertheless, French industrialization did accelerate during the 1890s. (Pollard and Holmes.) France was therefore both challenger and challenged in the battle for markets and territories. But the superior economic dynamism of the United States and Germany, the relatively smaller size of the French empire, and various political factors predisposed France to an emphasis on territorial acquisition that severely threatened British interests in any area it took over. Eventually, this made France the second-largest colonial power.

precisely from the challengers to that power — from the vigorous young industrial powers, primarily the United States, Japan, and Germany, which were just emerging onto the world market and either viewed Britain's industrial power as the result of the empire or regarded the empire as an obstacle to their own economic expansion.[41]

Turning to the remaining dimension of Lenin's theory, the empirical evidence does not support the contention that monopolization was the causal link between the 'over-ripeness' of capitalism, capital exports, and the new imperialism. The partition of the world among the imperialist powers had been largely completed before the end of the nineteenth century, by which time one-fifth of the land surface of the globe and one-tenth of the world's population were under the direct control of European powers. By 1900, some 90 per cent of Africa had been subjected to Europe, and most of that part of Asia that was ever to be directly colonized. But as Lenin himself recognized, the domination of the major economies by industrial combinations took hold no earlier than the first decade of the twentieth century.[42] Even this is too early for Britain,[43] which had far the largest empire and exported the greatest volumes of capital. Indeed, at the end of the nineteenth century the greatest imperial powers, Britain and France, possessed the least and most recently concentrated industrial structures of all the major powers; both countries achieved their imperial status well before an oligopolistic and centralized industrial structure took root. Even more to the point, their periods of highest capital export significantly preceded the rise of monopoly. On the other hand, the most capital-hungry great powers before 1914 — the United States, Germany, Russia, and Japan —

41. Barraclough, *Introduction to Contemporary History*, p. 50.
42. Hancock, *Wealth of Colonies*, pp. 11-12.
43. The emergence of monopolistic firms in Britain was slow before the ₁920s. (Barrat Brown, *Essays on Imperialism*, p. 35.) France was not dominated by monopoly capitalism before the First World War. (Fieldhouse, *The Theory of Capitalist Imperialism*, p. 189.)

were those whose industries were earliest dominated by large corporations.[44]

After 1914, however, it was clearly a different tale in the capitalist world as a whole. Oligopoly[45] was the order of the day. France and Britain still lagged behind, but the industrial structure was radically more concentrated, and tariff protection much higher, than in the nineteenth century. Yet the capital export of the advanced industrial countries never recovered its pre-1914 relative importance. Indeed, average annual capital flows between the world wars ($110-170 million, in 1913 prices) were but a small proportion, *in absolute terms*, of the 1900-1913 figure ($1,100 million).[46] Although the average yearly volume was about $2,000 million in 1951-55 and $3,000 million in 1956-61 (again in 1913 prices), two or three times the 1900-1913 level,[47] this growth was just about in line with the rise of total output,[48] and it rose slower than total gross domestic investment in the principal industrialized countries.[49] Moreover, whereas the bulk of pre-1914 exported capital was essentially (although by no means exclusively) market-orientated,[50] in the 1950s and 1960s more than a third of the

44. William Appleman Williams, *The Contours of American History*, pp. 346-356; Pollard and Holmes, *Industrial Power and National Rivalry*, pp. 75-76; H. Rosovsky, *Capital Formation in Japan, 1868-1940*.

45. Oligopoly is defined as the situation in which the share of output of any given industry accounted for by a relatively small number of large firms is such that these firms can, by their individual action, significantly affect the general price and output levels of the industry as a whole.

46. It can reasonably be argued that the depth and duration of the depression of the 1930s was in large part the result of the growth of monopoly, as Maurice Dobb does in *Studies in the Development of Capitalism*, chapter 8. Since the depression itself was a major factor in generating negative flows from creditor countries during the period 1930-1938 (Kuznets, *Modern Economic Growth*, p. 323), this would reverse Lenin's causal link between the rise of monopoly and the export of capital.

47. Kuznets, *Modern Economic Growth*, p. 529.

48. Angus Maddison, *Economic Growth in the West: Comparative Experience in Europe and North America*, Appendix A, pp. 194-204.

49. Ibid., p. 76.

50. Political considerations were of special importance in influencing the direction of French and German foreign investment, but this investment was expected to pay for itself directly, as well as indirectly. (Feis, *Europe: The World's Banker*.) Concessional financing was negligible.

exported funds took the form of official donations, and another fifth were issued by governments or international agencies at concessionary rates, such that in the 1950s only about 45 per cent of the total was accounted for by private capital flows. If an approximate comparison is made between private capital flows in 1951-61 and total foreign capital flows in 1900-1914, the annual volume for the latter would be $1,100 million, the former not more than $1,200 million (both at 1913 prices); this modest rise is practically negligible when compared with the growth in real output and domestic investment during the same period.[51] This comparison of basically-market-oriented capital flows is clearly the more relevant for the theory of monopolization and capital export. Indeed, it drives the final nail into the coffin of that theory. Lenin's *Imperialism* was obsolete even before it was translated into English, indeed as soon as it appeared. The great age of capital export was over by 1914.

We have seen that a number of dramatic economic criticisms of Lenin's theory may validly be advanced: the non-domination of the imperialist economies by monopolistic firms; the fact that a number of challenging imperialist powers were themselves net capital importers between 1870 and 1914; the fact that capital export was *always* a significant feature of industrial capitalism, showed no sudden acceleration in the late nineteenth century, and cannot be related to a specific period of maturity. Each of these criticisms serves seriously to undermine the theory that the new imperialism of the late nineteenth and early twentieth centuries was due to the pressure towards capital exports consequent to the monopolization and 'over-ripeness' of the capitalist economies. This brings us to the most crucial feature of Lenin's explanation of the new imperialism: it was effectively the reverse of the truth. Imperialism, far from being the product of a senile, decaying capitalism compelled to invest abroad the capital it no longer had the 'vigour' to absorb at home, was on the contrary the product of young and vigorous capitalist economies

51. Kuznets, *Modern Economic Growth*, p. 329.

newly emerging onto the international arena to challenge their rivals in *trade*. The expansion of trade, rather than of foreign investment, was the logical conclusion of the accelerated industrialization of the nineteenth century, along with the mounting interdependence of national economies as the result of massive improvements in communications.[52]

The historical documentation of the period clearly demonstrates that during the pre-1914 rivalries the states-men of every major imperialist country were primarily concerned with trade and strategic considerations, which were, of course, closely related and mutually reinforcing. Spheres for foreign investment, or the protection of the interests of bond-holders, were generally not considered economic interests worthy of very emphatic distinction from overseas economic interests in general, and *these* interests were frequently summarized simply as 'trade', while the former were frequently and logically considered primarily means for the promotion of exports (especially, but not only, by Germany and France).[53]

This primary emphasis on trade in the new imperialist expansion is evident for the United States, Germany, Britain, France, and Japan.[54] This was indeed entirely

---

52. Cf. the comments of Landes, *Unbound Prometheus*, p. 248: 'Marxist students of history have been wont to see the international rivalries that preceded the First World War as the thrashing of a system in process of decline and dissolution. The fact is that these were growing pains of a system in process of germination.'

53. Feis, *Europe: The World's Banker*.

54. This is conclusively demonstrated for the United States by Williams, *The Contours of American History*, chapters I-IV of Part 3; for Britain by D.C.M. Platt, *Finance, Trade and British Foreign Policy, 1815-1914*; for Japan by G.C. Allen, *A Short Economic History of Modern Japan: 1867-1937*; for Germany by W.O. Henderson, *The Industrial Revolution on the Continent: Germany, France, Russia 1800-1914*; and J. H. Clapham, *The Economic Development of France and Germany, 1815-1914*. More general discussions establish the point in a wider perspective, e.g. Landes, *The Unbound Prometheus*, chapter VI; W.L. Langer, *The Diplomacy of Imperialism, 1890-1902, 1915*, p. 75; Pollard and Holmes, *Industrial Power and National Rivalry 1870-1914*, introduction to chapter 3; Barraclough, *Introduction to Contemporary History*, chapter 2.

logical, since contrary to Lenin's categorical statement — 'Under the old capitalism, when free competition prevailed, the export of *goods* was the typical feature. Under modern capitalism, when monopolies prevail, the export of capital has become the typical feature' (*Imperialism*, p. 76) — the real shift was from capital to commodity export. In fact, between 1874 and 1914 foreign trade became relatively more important than foreign investment for the three major creditor countries, Germany, France, and Britain, where capital outflows ranged between $500 million and $1,100 million per year (in 1913 prices); during approximately the same period (1885-86 to 1913) annual volumes of foreign trade (again at 1913 prices) ranged between $6,000 million and $13,000 million. Allowing for a movement of services of about one-fifth, the average outflow of foreign capital investment would amount to less than one-tenth of the foreign-trade volume (summing both imports and exports).[55] Moreover, *the rise of foreign capital flows was markedly more moderate than that of trade flows* during this period.[56] British commodity exports to Latin America, Asia, and Africa far exceeded investment in those continents,[57] and Britain's foreign investment and trade flows were always oriented towards the underdeveloped world to a greater extent than those of other creditor countries.

To sum up, empirical evidence refutes Lenin's theory that imperialism was rooted primarily in an excess of capital in the imperialist countries seeking outlets abroad. There is no evidence of any relationship between territorial acquisition and 'superabundance' of capital, nor indeed that a stage of superabundance had been reached by any of the imperialist

55. Or approximately one-fifth of the value if exports alone are considered the relevant comparison.
56. Kuznets, *Modern Economic Growth*, p. 326. For the separate British figures, see Aldcroft and Richardson, *The British Economy, 1870-1939*, which show the same picture as the aggregate figures, which are in any case dominated by Britain but are worth noting inasmuch as Britain was the principal capital exporter.
57. See the figures in Woodruff, *Impact of Western Man*, p. 276 and Table 14; Kuznets, *Modern Economic Growth*, Table 6.5.A.

powers. On the contrary, net capital inflows were a feature of some of these powers during the imperialist period, and gross outflows were generally characteristic of the early stages of capitalist industrialization. 'Monopolization', which Lenin took to be the link between 'over-ripeness' and capital export, was of no great importance in any imperialist state (with the possible exception of Germany), especially in the two most important, Britain and France, until well after the territorial scramble.

Furthermore, Lenin's assertion that the export of capital became more important than that of commodities for the capitalist countries in the imperialist epoch was incorrect, as the statistical evidence on trade and foreign investment shows. The historical documentation also conclusively demonstrates that trade considerations were of decisively greater importance in the motivations of policy-makers than the interests of bond-holders, insofar as the two were separable.

Quite apart from the empirical weakness of Lenin's case, however, the explicatory power of his theory was rather feeble, depending as it did on a double coincidence. He assumed that the stage of monopolization and over-ripeness is reached almost simultaneously by all the major capitalist countries, such that an international scramble is bound to result. This notion must be difficult for Marxists to accept, when Lenin's own emphasis on the uneven development of capitalism is recalled. Further, why should this coincidence in turn coincide with the point at which the world just happens to be completely, or almost completely, divided up?

4. The Phase of Economic Regression in the Advanced Capitalist Countries

Monopolistic (or more correctly, oligopolistic) capitalism did come in the twentieth century. Throughout this century, the Marxist movement has looked upon it as the cause and symbol of an economically retrogressive phase of capitalism compared with the previous period of competitive capital-ism.[58] This view, together with the conceptual identification of imperialism and monopoly capitalism, has had a profound influence in shaping the left's view that the expansion of capitalism into Africa, Asia, and Latin America could have only reactionary implications. It is outside the scope of this book to explore in detail the question of the sense in and extent to which monopoly capitalism was economically retrogressive in the advanced capitalist world. A few brief points must, however, be made.

To start with, Lenin's view in 1916 was that monopoly capitalism *had already* shown itself to be in decay. This was demonstrated, he believed, by a trend towards technical stagnation,[59] by failure to raise the living standards of the masses, by failure to develop agriculture,[60] and by a generally slower rate of economic growth.

58. As noted earlier, Lenin also considered monopoly capitalism to be characterized by *political* reaction, presumably in comparison with earlier, non-monopoly capitalism.

59. In chapter VIII of *Imperialism*, entitled 'The Parasitism and Decay of Capitalism', Lenin wrote: 'Like all monopoly, this capitalist monopoly inevitably gives rise to a *tendency* to stagnation and decay. As monopoly prices become fixed, even temporarily, so the stimulus to technical and, consequently, to all progress, disappears to a certain extent, and to that extent also, the economic possibility of deliberately retarding economic progress. . . . Certainly, monopoly under capitalism can never completely, and for a long period of time, eliminate competition in the world market. Certainly, the possibility of reducing the cost of production and increasing profits by introducing technical improvements operates in the direction of change. Nevertheless, the *tendency* to stagnation and decay, which is the feature of monopoly, continues, and in certain branches of industry, in certain countries for certain periods of time, it becomes predominant' (pp. 120-121). Here and elsewhere in the pamphlet, statements about techno-logical stagnation are so heavily qualified that they are almost meaningless logically. The intent, however, seems clear enough: to suggest a change for the worse in this respect in comparison with the era of competitive capitalism.

60. 'It goes without saying that if capitalism could develop agriculture, which today lags far behind industry everywhere, if it could raise the standard of living for the masses, who are everywhere still poverty-stricken and underfed, in spite of the amazing advance in technical knowledge, there could be no talk of a superabundance of capital . . . But if capitalism did these things, it would not be capitalism . . . as long as capitalism remains what it is, surplus capital will never be utilized for the purpose of raising the

All these points are demonstrably incorrect. Overall growth rates (of both total output and output per capita) for the period 1870-1913 were both positive and high relative to the period 1913-1950 (Table 3),[61] although lower than in the 1950s and 1960s.[62] Comparison of the 1870-1913 growth rates with the pre-1870 period, although more crucial for Lenin's theory, is more difficult for statistical reasons. Nevertheless, the evidence summarized by Blackaby, Freund, and Paige[63] for Japan, the United States, Canada, Sweden, Denmark, Norway, Germany, Italy, and Britain (Table 4) permits neither refutation nor corroboration of the view that the period 1870-1913 experienced slower growth consequent to the alleged onset of monopolization.[64] Nor is

---

standard of living of the masses in a given country, for this would mean a decline in profits for the capitalists; it will be used for the purpose of increasing those profits by exporting capital to the backward countries.' (*Imperialism*, p. 77.)

61. The rise in total and per capita output was positive in Japan, too, during this period; in fact, it was quite rapid. See D.C. Paige, F. Blackaby, and S. Freund, 'Economic Growth: The Last Hundred Years', *National Institute Economic Review*, No. 16, July 1961, chapter 1, pp. 26-27, 30-31.

62. UNCTAD, *Handbook of International Trade and Development Statistics*, 1972.

63. See note 61.

64. Their two alternative output series for France (Table 8, p. 39), although somewhat contradictory, suggest a remarkably steady growth rate from the mid-1850s to 1913. Commenting on their findings, the authors themselves explain why the figures are unlikely to give us a clear answer: 'The averages for the whole period before 1913 must be treated cautiously, because they cover very different periods for different countries — periods ranging from 30 to 60 years. But it is not sensible — as it is for 1913-1959 — to compare common chronological sub-periods for these countries; for whereas from 1913 onwards two world wars and a great depression dominated the economic trend in all the countries considered here, before 1913 each country's economic development was largely determined by its domestic circumstances. For instance, the United Kingdom and Sweden, which had been the fastest growing countries in the late 'sixties and early 'seventies, were stagnating in the later 'seventies. This was the time when Germany and the United States were growing very fast indeed — Germany after the achievement of political unity and the United States after the American Civil War. Or again, from 1898 to 1913 Britain and Germany were both growing slowly; but it was a prosperous period of rapid economic growth for some of the other countries' (pp. 34-35). See also Chart 1 in the same article, which shows much the same picture for the changes in total output.

the picture made less equivocal if we adopt the period 1900-1913 instead (Table 4, and chart 1 of Blackaby, Paige, and Freund). Thus, the period from which Lenin dates monopolization in the major capitalist countries (either 1870-1914 or 1900-1914) witnessed rapid growth in output, productivity, and per capita product in nearly all the countries concerned, faster than during the subsequent period, until the postwar boom of the fifties and early sixties.

Table 3

Annual Growth Rates of Total Output and Output per Head, 1870-1960

(a) = Growth rates of total output			(b) = Growth rates of output per head		
	1870-1913		1913-1950		1950-1960
	(a)	(b)	(a)	(b)	(a)	(b)
Belgium	2.7	1.7	1.0	0.7	2.9	2.3
Denmark	3.2	2.1	2.1	1.1	3.3	2.6
France	1.6	1.4	0.7	0.7	4.4	3.5
Germany	2.9	1.8	1.2	0.4	7.6	6.5
Italy	1.4	0.7	1.3	0.6	5.9	5.3
Netherlands	2.2	0.8	2.1	0.7	4.9	3.6
Norway	2.2	1.4	2.7	1.9	3.5	2.6
Sweden	3.0	2.3	2.2	1.6	3.3	2.6
Switzerland	2.4	1.3	2.0	1.5	5.1	3.7
United Kingdom	2.3	1.3	1.7	1.3	2.6	2.2
Canada	3.8	2.0	2.8	1.3	3.9	1.2
United States	4.3	2.2	2.9	1.7	3.2	1.6
Average	2.7	1.6	1.9	1.1	4.2	3.1

Source: Maddison, *Economic Growth in the West*, pp. 28 and 30.

Lenin's emphasis on the failure of monopoly capitalism to develop agriculture is not borne out by the evidence either. The average rise in productivity in agriculture seems more or less to have kept pace with that of industry throughout the nineteenth century. The most rapid growth of agricultural productivity took place after 1913,[65] largely as a result of

65. Blackaby, Paige, and Freund, 'Economic Growth: The Last Hundred Years', p. 39.

Table 4

Rapid Rates of Growth of National Product Per Man-Year Before 1913 (annual percent increases)

	Long-term Average Growth Rate to 1913		Fastest 8-year Periods of Growth		Periods During Which Growth Exceeded			
					2% a year		3% a year	
	Starting Year	Rate	Period	Rate	Period	No. of Years	Period	No. of Years
Japan	1880	3.4	1891-99	4.7	1880-1911	31	1880-1911	31
			1880-88	4.5				
Sweden	1863	2.4	1866-74	4.6	1866-98	32	1863-75	12
			1890-98	2.9	1900-11	11	1891-98	7
			1900-08	2.8			1903-08	5
US	1871	2.2	1872-80	5.2	1871-1907	36	1871-89	18
			1896-04	3.1			1896-1905	9
Denmark	1872	2.1	1877-85	2.4	1877-84	7	1878-82	4
			1888-96	2.4	1887-93	6	1887-90	3
					1895-99	4		
Canada	1872	1.9	1875-83	4.1	1874-90	16	1874-86	12
			1895-1903	2.2	1899-1904	5		
UK	1857	1.6	1867-75	2.7	1859-73	14	1867-73	6
			1881-89	2.5	1881-89	8		
Germany	1853	1.5	1874-82	3.5	1873-93	20	1873-86	13
			1882-90	2.0				
Norway	1865	1.3	1905-13	2.7	1905-13	8	1909-13	4
			1871-77	2.4				
Italy	1863	0.7	1897-1905	2.3	1898-1902	4	—	—
					1904-07			

Source: Blackaby, Paige and Freund, NIER, July 1961, Table 5, p. 34.

changes that had got well under way in the later decades of the nineteenth century.[66] Before the First World War relative agricultural prices rose faster than relative agricultural incomes, which suggests that agricultural productivity was not keeping pace with agricultural incomes.[67] Nevertheless, considerable progress was made during the years before 1913; most important, the ground was laid for even more substantial improvement subsequently. Gross output per farm worker in the United States is estimated to have risen 45 per cent between 1870 and 1900, while national product per man-year rose about 110 per cent in the same period. In Denmark, agricultural output per worker increased by 60 per cent, and that of all other sectors by just over 100 per cent, between the periods 1870-1879 and 1905-14; in Canada between 1870 and 1910, output per man-year in agriculture increased 83 per cent, in manufacturing by 50 per cent, while GNP rose 67 per cent.[68] (In these countries, however, agriculture probably developed faster than elsewhere.) In Germany, agricultural stagnation, or relatively slow growth, was the rule in the 1870s and 1880s but gave way to rapid advances after 1890, a result of notable technical advances.[69] In Italy between 1897 and 1913, a period of rapid industrialization, agricultural production was buoyant and more than kept pace with the expanded demand.[70] British agricultural performance in responding to changes in the world market in this period was generally poorer than other countries, and poorer, therefore, than during the earlier part of the century.[71]

More generally, European agriculture suffered a drastic crisis during the 1870s and 1880s, owing to cheap food imports from Russia, North America, and Argentina, the

66. Landes, *The Unbound Prometheus*, pp. 242-243.
67. Blackaby, Paige, and Freund, p. 39.
68. Ibid., pp. 39-40.
69. Borchardt, pp. 126-128.
70. Luciana Cafagna, 'The Industrial Revolution in Italy, 1830-1914', in Cipolla, ed., *The Fontana Economic History of Europe: The Emergence of Industrial Societies — 1*, pp. 300-302.
71. Hobsbawm, *Industry and Empire*, pp. 166-168.

result of major innovations in cultivation techniques (dry farming of open plains), transport (the opening of the great plains by railways and greater efficiency of marine transport, especially the steamer), and new methods of food conservation (canning and refrigeration).[72] Part of the response of European agriculture was to seek tariff protection, successfully on the whole (although not in the case of Britain); but the more fundamental answer was major technological and organizational improvement.[73] In Denmark cooperation was extended to take advantage of the revolutions in processing, storage, marketing, and credit. Similar measures were taken in many countries.[74] In Russia the Stolypin reforms were a major attempt to commercialize agriculture. In France a Ministry of Agriculture was established and agricultural education promoted (as elsewhere in Europe), in addition to government-sponsored attempts at cooperation.[75] Increased agricultural specialization (pork and bacon in Denmark, cheese in Switzerland and France), more extensive use of fertilizers (new mineral and artificial varieties and imported organic fertilizers such as Peruvian guano), increased mechanization (especially in Germany), and the large-scale development of market-gardening around the great cities all contributed to the highest food consumption levels Europe had ever known, besides meeting the foreign challenge.[76] Lenin's denunciations of the inability of monopoly capitalism to develop agriculture could scarcely have been more misguided.[77]

Nor was Lenin any more correct in supposing that capitalism could not raise the living standards of the masses. Between 1870 and 1910 the population of Europe

72. Ibid.,

73. Pollard and Holmes, *Industrial Power and National Rivalry, 1870-1914*, pp. 2-3; Landes, *The Unbound Prometheus*, p. 242.

74. Hobsbawm, *Industry and Empire*, p. 168.

75. Pollard and Holmes, *Industrial Power and National Rivalry, 1870-1914*, pp. 2-3.

76. Landes, *The Unbound Prometheus*, pp. 242-243.

77. In this context, monopoly capitalism referred to the character of the economy as a whole, and not necessarily to the organization of agriculture.

rose from 290 to 435 million, while national incomes doubled or tripled. The steady increase of per capita income spread downwards to the lowest income groups, permitting greater proportions of income to be spent on manufactures.[78] Real wages rose significantly, in Britain by one-third between 1870 and 1900,[79] stagnating thereafter until the First World War, although the improvement in social amenities which had set in earlier continued,[80] as reflected in the continuing decline of the death rate. In Germany real wages doubled between 1870 and 1913.[81] In Italy real wages had risen by about 25 per cent between 1897 and 1913.[82] In France working-class living standards rose between 1870 and 1906,[83] and probably subsequently. In fact, in all the advanced countries, with the possible exceptions of Russia and Japan, the living standards and social amenities of the lower-income groups were significantly higher in 1913 than in 1870 — and in most cases higher than in 1900. Moreover, the variety and quality of available consumer goods had improved immensely for the lower classes over this period.[84]

Let us now turn to Lenin's final point, the supposed retardation of technical progress by monopoly capitalism. In reality, it was precisely the 1890s that opened a new phase of technology and its economic applications, alongside a revolution in industrial management.[85] The basis of the technological economic revolution was the systematic and institutionalized application of science to industry, a

78. Landes, *The Unbound Prometheus*, pp. 241-242.

79. J. Kuczynski, *Die Geschichte der Lage der Arbeiter in England von 1640 bis in die Gegenwart*, Volume IV, Part 3; cited in Landes, *The Unbound Prometheus*, p. 242.

80. Hobsbawm, *Industry and Empire*, chapter 8.

81. Borchardt, p. 116.

82. Cafagna, 'The Industrial Revolution in Italy', p. 302.

83. E. Levasseur, *Questions ouvrières et industrielles en France sous la troisième République*, Paris, 1907, pp. 630-663; cited in Pollard and Holmes, *Industrial Power and National Rivalry*, pp. 475-476.

84. Hobsbawm, *Industry and Empire*, chapter 8; Walter Minchington, 'Patterns of Demand, 1750-1914', in Cipolla, *The Fontana Economic History of Europe: The Industrial Revolution*, second impression, 1975.

85. Hobsbawm, *Industry and Empire*, p. 107.

fundamental new development. The major growth sectors of this phase were the electrical and chemical industries; the immense ramifications of these industries, as well as of the development of the internal combustion engine, are now obvious.[86]

It thus seems evident that Lenin was wrong about the supposedly retrogressive effect of monopolization during the period he was considering, whether 1870 to 1914 or 1900 to 1914, as regards overall growth, the progress of agriculture, the rising living standards of the masses, and the application of technical advances to the economy. The Western economies have since become still more monopolistic, but the trends noted above have continued nevertheless. The years since 1914 have witnessed enormous improvements in the living standards of the masses in the monopoly capitalist countries, even more rapid increases in agricultural productivity than during 1870-1914 (to the extent that European and North American agricultures have consistently produced surpluses for export or have been subsidized to limit production),[87] and a breathtaking number of technical innovations, even the most important of which it would take tediously long to enumerate. These achievements have been most striking since the Second World War, but important progress in all these fields was also registered in the intervening period. The massive unemployment of the inter-war years did not prevent a continuing rise in living standards of the great majority of workers who remained employed (although the psychological effects of insecurity in the working classes as a whole left deep scars), and unemployment did not prevent the development of new mass-production industries producing durable consumer goods that were previously unavailable. This period also

86. Ibid., p. 145.
87. For a full discussion, see Landes, *The Unbound Prometheus*, chapter 5. In the United States agricultural output per unit of land area under cultivation rose on average by 80% between 1941-5 and 1971-5. During the same period wheat yields increased by 90% and the corn yield increased 280%. W. Leontieff et al., *The Future of The World Economy, A United Nations Study*, New York, 1977, p. 4.

saw the rise of radio and the cinema and the development of the aircraft industry. Overall growth rates were by no means negligible; although they were less than after the Second World War, it is by no means clear that they were generally below growth rates in the 1870-1913 period.[88]

The reasons why Lenin's thesis that monopoly capitalism was parasitic and decadent is invalid are not difficult to enumerate. The rise of oligopolistic market structures — or monopolistic firms, as they are popularly called — has not reduced competition but on the contrary has intensified it. The development of oligopoly and various forms of association and combination (in individual economies) has been associated with the disappearance of monopoly on a world scale and its replacement by competition — the disappearance, that is, of the British world monopoly of manufacturing with the rise of vigorous competitors towards the end of the nineteenth century. These two phenomena — growth of monopolistic, cartellized firms and industries nationally, and intensification of competition internationally — were closely connected; indeed, it was the latter that generated the former (along with technical factors, themselves connected to increased competition, which tended to increase the size of the individual unit). The development of large monopolistic firms also permitted major advances in efficiency, primarily through economies of scale and the systematic application of science and new organizational methods to production.

The effects within the national economies of the internationalization of competition and the integration of the major industrial economies after the 1870s have far outweighed any domestic trends towards the restriction of competition by the rise of monopoly internally. Moreover, it is doubtful that even the internal effects of the rise of

88. Compare the figures in Table 4, Blackaby, Paige, and Freund, for the growth of total product between 1922 and 1938, with those of Maddison (p. 28), which, excluding Japan (for which Maddison does not give figures), show half the ten developed economies growing *faster* in the inter-war period than in the period from 1870 to 1913.

'monopoly' were really destructive of competition. It seems more likely that the rise of large-scale and more efficient oligopolistic firms expanded competition *nationally*, replacing the relatively local and limited competition of the earlier smaller-scale firms. In effect, the *only* aspect of competition that oligopoly tended to reduce was strict *price* competition, because of the increased importance of overhead costs, the inflexibility of wages, and the domination of the market by a relatively small number of firms. Competition over *sales*, quality, and, most important, technology (in both products and methods) have proved far more effective in impelling economic progress. The negative aspects of an oligopolistic economy, so strongly emphasized by economists in the 1930s, were based upon a static analysis which only Schumpeter broke through in his panegyric to the capitalist 'process of creative destruction'[89] — an analysis far more Marxist than any produced since Marx himself and the Lenin of *The Development of Capitalism in Russia*.[90]

Contrary to myths about the promotion of 'consumerism' by the advertising industry, which allegedly creates artificial needs, this competitive dynamic, together with the expansion of the market as a result of rising real incomes of the working class, has made monopoly capitalism far more responsive to the needs of the masses than nineteenth-century capitalism ever was. If the development of new products and markets has often occurred in anticipation of as yet non-existent demand, only those who are already well-off will disparage such achievements, which historically have immensely improved the quality of life of the working classes.

Nor can we fail to dismiss the fairy tale that rising public squalor has accompanied increased private affluence. In

89. Joseph A. Schumpeter, *Capitalism, Socialism, and Democracy*, chapters VII and VIII.
90. For a recent argument that 'the capitalist mode of production has become far *more* competitive through two hundred years of development', see: J.A. Clifton, 'Competition and the Evaluation of the Capitalist Mode of Production', *Cambridge Journal of Economics*, Volume I, No. 2, June 1977.

any reasonable historical perspective, capitalism has steadily devoted greater and greater proportions of its resources to public goods and amenities, with reasonably positive effects on the whole. That new problems now exist is no more than a reflection of the fact that new problems and needs arise in every sphere as human societies develop.

5. Backward Capitalism in the Third World

In *Imperialism* Lenin scarcely touched on the effects of imperialism in the exploited colonies and semi-colonies. He alluded to the fact that these countries had been drawn into international capitalist intercourse. With the construction of railways, he noted, 'the elementary conditions for industrial development have been created'. This, he held, had created conditions permitting the export of capital to these countries. More positively, he also wrote: 'The export of capital greatly affects and accelerates the development of capitalism in those countries to which it is exported. While, therefore, the export of capital may tend to a certain extent to arrest development in the countries exporting capital, it can only do so by expanding and deepening the further development of capitalism throughout the world.'[91]

Further on, he noted that 'in the colonies, capitalism is only beginning to develop' (p. 116), and that it 'is growing with the greatest rapidity in the colonies and in overseas countries' (p. 118). And: 'Thanks to her colonies, Great Britain has increased the length of "her" railways by 100,000 kilometres, four times as much as Germany' (p. 119). This revealing remark was a reference to the growth of railways in the British Empire between 1890 and 1913, which Lenin contrasted to Germany's domestic increase.

91. *Imperialism*, p. 79. In his discussion of the need for colonies in order to supply raw materials, Lenin gives a brief account of how capital export may promote development of the mineral and agricultural sectors (p. 102).

His point was to show that in 'sharing out this "booty", an exceptionally large part goes to countries which, as far as the development of productive forces is concerned, do not always stand at the top of the list' (p. 118). Germany is characterized as having experienced a superior development of the productive forces (p. 119).

Now, Lenin has here turned the colonies into the cause of the expansion in Britain's railways; the reality was that Britain was responsible for increasing the length of the colonies' railways. (Compare Marx's treatment of British rule in India.) This inversion of causal links is characteristic of the entire pamphlet. At the time Lenin wrote, the Marxist movement as a whole was theoretically committed to the view that imperialism would industrialize the non-capitalist world; and on the few occasions that he referred explicitly to this world, Lenin unequivocally endorsed this view (at least formally). Yet the general thrust of his argument — that monopoly capitalism was parasitic, decadent, and stagnant compared with competitive capitalism — was bound to give the impression that the relationship between imperialist countries and colonies and semi-colonies was one of simple robbery ('booty') rather than a dynamic process of two-sided capitalist development, the typical combination of exploitation and expansion of the productive forces. There are constant references to finance (monopoly) capital's garnering profits by coupon clipping, financial swindles, and manipulation. The following is typical: 'The development of capitalism has arrived at a stage when, although commodity production still "reigns" and continues to be regarded as the basis of economic life, it has in reality been undermined and the big profits go to the "geniuses" of financial manipulation' (p. 34). Moreover, the relationship of the imperialist countries to the colonies and semi-colonies is frequently described as parasitic. For example: 'the capitalist parasitism of a handful of wealthy states' (p.78); or 'in one way or another, nearly the whole world is more or less the debtor and tributary of these four international banker countries' (p. 75).[92]

The inevitable result of this entire approach was that the traditional view that imperialism would industrialize the non-capitalist world was reduced to formal obeisance to the sacred texts. Imperialism came increasingly to be regarded as the *major* obstacle to industrialization in the Third World. Capitalism was thus declared to be devoid of positive social functions anywhere. These conclusions were implicit in Lenin's *Imperialism*, but they were not to be fully and explicitly drawn until the 1928 Congress of the Communist International.

92. For similar statements, see also pp. 73 and 67. The underlying assumption is that capital export is a matter of lending money. Taking the capitalist world as a whole, however, capital export must have a counterpart in increased exports of commodities to the countries concerned. The assumption of stagnation in the imperialist economies is not consistent with the industrialization of the rest of the world by capital export.

4
The Theory of Imperialism in the International Communist Movement

1. The Nation-State and the Theory of Imperialism

Marx and Engels could hardly have had a theory of imperialism, at least as the term has come to be used by liberal and socialist thinkers, since it was only towards the end of the nineteenth century that capitalist industrialization had developed over a wide enough range of countries for the phenomenon to be observable. Their scattered comments on the subject, especially Marx's notes on the effects of British rule in India, however, leave no room for doubt that they held that the overall effect of imperialism, taking account of long-term and indirect results (not necessarily less important for their indirectness), would be to accelerate the creation of a world market and thereby not only to unite humanity but also to bring the backward societies the material and cultural benefits of Western civilization.

When Marxist theories of imperialism were elaborated in the first two decades of the twentieth century — by Kautsky, Hilferding, Luxemburg, Bauer, Bukharin, and Lenin — all shared the thesis that imperialism would develop the productive forces in backward areas, and in particular would promote modern industry.[1] They thereby maintained Marx's views in this respect.

But the thesis adopted by the Sixth Congress of the Communist International in 1928 on 'The Revolutionary Movement in the Colonies and Semi-Colonies', which formally reversed this view, arguing that imperialism retarded the industrial development of the colonies, merely registered a point of view that had gradually become dominant within the Communist movement as a whole (although the two Communist parties most experienced in colonial affairs, the British and the Indian, opposed the thesis on the grounds that a process of 'decolonization' was under way, Britain collaborating with the Indian bourgeoisie to industrialize the subcontinent). The position expressed in the 1928 Comintern thesis remains the dominant view of the world Communist movement today; it was one of the earliest statements of the underdevelopment outlook that was to become the stock in trade of liberal development-economists after the Second World War.

The key figure in the change was Lenin, in whose hands the theory of imperialism became the instrument of a search for the appropriate strategy and tactics of 'world revolution'. The mediating theoretical link was the corpus of Marxist theory on the national question. Lenin's wholehearted acceptance of the priority of Europe for the socialist revolution, together with his own geographical location at the hinge linking Europe and Asia, impelled him to develop a Russian strategy within the context of his conception of world revolution. The Russo-Japanese War of 1905, the associated Russian revolution, and the consequent explosion of national movements in the East had briefly but vividly dramatized the interconnection between imperialist rivalries and revolutionary movements, as mediated by Eastern nationalism. As it happened, nationalism in Europe and Marxist and liberal thinking on the matter after 1871

1. Kautsky was an exception. See *Socialism and Colonial Policy: An Analysis*, 1907. Kautsky did, however, allow that colonies of European settlement (which he called 'work colonies' as opposed to 'exploitation colonies') were likely to witness the development of advanced productive forces (pp. 17-20).

were to develop in such a way as to undermine any possibility of a serious extension of Marx and Engels's outlook on 'progressive imperialism'.

Marx and Engels had generally regarded the formation of (preferably large and centralized) nation-states as conducive to cultural progress and the advance of the productive forces. On the whole, they had supported movements for the formation of such states (whether through secession or coalescence), regarding such processes as an extension of the principles of individual liberty and political democracy of the French revolution, as the assertion of popular against dynastic power. The organization of communities on the basis of strong nation-states was regarded as a preliminary step towards their organization on an international basis.

During the first two-thirds of the nineteenth century it was not obvious that nationalism might come into conflict with individual liberties, political democracy, and international-ism rather than represent their logical extension or complement, except in special cases.[2] But by the 1890s, with the growth of protectionism, colonialism, and militarism, the transmutation of traditional national into imperialist rivalries, and the fusion of imperialist ideologies and popular nationalism, it became difficult for Social Demo-cracy to avoid the realization that the kind of world upon which the steady advance of the workers' movement through utilization of the institutions of liberal democracy had been premised was menaced by strange new forces, presaging the break-up of the old order based on parliamentarism and free trade.

Marx had been a firm believer in free trade, its association with democracy, and its capacity to expand the scope of economic progress. He had expected that the sphere of free trade would grow ever wider and that the barriers between

2. Usually cases of small nations looking to Russian help to achieve their self-determination, e.g. the Czechs. See also the case of Germany, where the causes of democracy and nationalism began to diverge after 1848, as the business classes increasingly threw their weight behind absolutist Russia, although this did not become readily apparent until the 1860s; even then it could plausibly be regarded as temporary.

nations would become correspondingly weaker as capitalism developed. In fact, however, the rise of the world market actually strengthened the nation-state, since it developed as the expression of separate but interwoven national economies, each of them pursuing industrialization as a conscious policy under the aegis of states immensely more powerful than their pre-nineteenth-century predecessors. The individual economies were indeed not isolated, but interdependent. Nevertheless, the world market developed not on the basis of direct, unmediated market relationships between economic actors (firms, households, etc.), but on the basis of market relations mediated by the state. This necessarily produced a quite different pace, geographical diffusion, and sectoral structure of industry and economic activity than would otherwise have been the case.[3] In particular, although the expansion of integrated national economies did not necessarily conflict with the development of the world market in the long run (in a sense providing its building bricks), the mediation of international economic relationships by state policy inevitably tended to transform the competitive struggle of capitalist corporations into a battle of nation-states. Competition between nation-states intensified as competition between firms increasingly reached beyond national boundaries.[4] By the latter part of the century, with the acceleration of European industrialization, the formation of the world market simultaneously involved the strengthening of the nation-state. The ideology of nationalism grew correspondingly stronger and proved capable of supporting rightist as well as leftist policies.

Nationalism itself, however, remained a vaguely respectable notion in the socialist movement. Its sins were

3. Weber notes the case of nineteenth-century Germany, where, he argues, the location of industry represented an adaptation to the politically determined frontiers of the unified state. H.H. Gerth and C. Wright Mills (eds.), *From Max Weber*, p. 162.
4. This tendency was aggravated by concentration and cartellization of industry, which promoted closer and more institutionalized relationships between the state and the dominant firms in the economy. Cf. Heinz Gollwitzer, *Europe in the Age of Imperialism 1880-1919*.

generally ascribed to imperialism through an illogical, though understandable, Rousseau-like extension of the rights of the individual to the nation ('a nation which oppresses others cannot itself be free'), as exemplified in the stream of denunciations of the evils of colonialism that poured from the congresses of the Second International. The failure of nationalism to measure up to its democratic reputation was either ignored or imputed to imperialism, all the more readily inasmuch as the mounting attachment of the working class to the nation, associated with what Carr has called the 'socialization of the nation' in the late nineteenth century,[5] was becoming increasingly evident. The *political* evils of nationalism *in Europe* — which led ultimately to fascism — were transformed by a sleight of hand into the *economic* evils of imperialism in *Africa and Asia*.

2. Lenin's Position Before 1917

The extensive Marxist discussion of imperialism during the late nineteenth and early twentieth centuries, before the appearance of Lenin's *Imperialism: The Highest Stage of Capitalism*, had firmly linked the phenomenon to protectionism and monopoly (this was especially clear in the works of Hilferding). The advance from this notion to the theory of an over-ripe or moribund monopoly capitalism seemed easy, although many difficult (indeed, sometimes impossible) links had to be forged in the argument. What was really

5. E.H. Carr, *Nationalism and After*, p. 19. By this term Carr conveys the fact and process whereby national policies reflect the increasing integration of the working classes into the life of the nation and the consequent transformation of national policy such that dealing with the economic and social claims of the working classes becomes a central concern. 'The defence of wages and employment becomes a concern of national policy and must be asserted, if necessary against the national policies of other countries; and this in turn gives the worker an intimate practical interest in the policy and power of his nation. The socialization of the nation has as its natural corollary the nationalization of socialism.'

new in Lenin's *Imperialism*, at least in its emphasis, was the vision of a handful of parasitic monopoly capitalist states feeding off more than half of humanity in the colonies and semi-colonies. The combination of the pre-Leninist emphasis on restriction and monopoly with Lenin's own emphasis on exploitative parasitism produced the notion of monopoly capitalism (=imperialism). If followed that imperialism and capitalism (which, through monopoly capitalism, had now become synonymous) could then be regarded as *generally* reactionary, despite Marx and Engels's, not to mention Lenin's own, references to the industrialization of the colonies by imperialism. The intrinsic attractiveness of Lenin's doctrine, together with the position he acquired as leader of the October Revolution and head of the Soviet state, transformed his views into central tenets of the world revolutionary movement.

Lenin has been described as the mediator between Marxism and the East.[6] As a citizen of the Tsarist multinational state, rapidly developing industrial capitalism but none the less still characterized by Asiatic backwardness, heavily dependent on the West economically yet oppressor of the East, he was ideally placed for this role.

From early in the twentieth century, Lenin became increasingly aware of the revolutionary potential of the East. This awareness was in particular the product of the effects of the 1905 revolution, which ignited national-democratic movements in the periphery of the Russian empire. These movements highlighted the tendency of social and national demands to merge and reinforce each other in explosive fashion. Even more powerful examples were provided by the nationalist revolutions in Persia (1906), Turkey (1908), and China (1911).

These revolutionary upheavals were fitted into the concept of bourgeois-democratic revolution elaborated by Lenin in his 1914 pamphlet *On the Right of Nations to Self-Determination*, which portrayed the establishment of a nation-state as the essential framework for the development

6. Schram and Carrère d'Encausse, pp. 4 and 6.

of modern capitalist societies, and nationalism itself as integral to the process of establishing a nation-state. Lenin held that it was not crucial that the bourgeoisie was little developed in some of the societies concerned, since the heart of the bourgeois-democratic revolution was the agrarian question, i.e. the dispossession of the feudal landowners. In other words, the class central to the bourgeois-democratic revolution was the peasantry, whose emancipation created the social basis for the development of the bourgeoisie.[7]

There was, however, an ambiguity in Lenin's view of the nature of the national and colonial revolution. He never finally decided whether he was dealing with an anti-imperialist or anti-capitalist revolution in the East.[8] Although in theory it was undoubtedly the former (and therefore a bourgeois revolution in essence), in practice the national movements of the East targeted the principal centres of advanced capitalist power in nearly every case. However bourgeois they may have been in essence, it seemed sheer folly to ignore them in the context of the strategy of 'world revolution'.[9]

We have already touched upon the intellectual ambiguities and potential for political confusion of the concept of 'world revolution', as the conflation of two different social movements with inherently contradictory aims, the fusion of which (or alliances derived therefrom) has generally

7. Fernando Claudín, *The Communist Movement: From Comintern to Cominform*, p. 262. It might be added that a negligible bourgeoisie implied a small working class, apart from employees of foreign firms and the colonial administration. In turn, a small working class would likely imply greater revolutionary bravado on the part of whichever sections of the exploiting class were leading the national movements. But this is to refer to the actual situation in the East, rather than to Lenin's view of it.
8. An example of this ambiguity appears in his article of 1908 'Inflammable Materials in World Politics', in which he salutes the appearance in Asia of tens of millions of proletarians (cited in Schram and Carrère d'Encausse, p. 23).
9. A recent study reaches the same conclusion (on the basis of a very different analysis): '. . . one of the fundamental characteristics of Lenin's paradigm . . . (is) . . . a subordination of scientific exigencies to those of political activity.' G. Arrighi, *The Geometry of Imperialism: The Limits of Hobson's Paradigm.*

been transitory, uneasy, and often disastrous for the socialist side. But it was nevertheless a key concept in Lenin's outlook, oriented to revolutionary tactics of a voluntarist character.

The potential contribution of the East to (basically anti-capitalist) world revolution was further enhanced by a shift in Marxist doctrine initiated by Trotsky in 1905 and eventually accepted in a modified and more cautious form by Lenin to the effect that the historic tasks of a particular ruling class might, as a result of subsequent historical developments, come to be performed by some other class entirely. Specifically, it might, and probably would in a number of cases, fall to the proletariat to accomplish the tasks of the bourgeois-democratic revolution, which would be effected under working-class hegemony. In practice, this could mean that the dynamic, pent-up forces of peasant insurrection (Lenin's version of the bourgeois-democratic revolution) might be released, but their bourgeois potential controlled by the proletariat, relatively small though its numbers might be. (The concept of the vanguard party, developed in 1902, had already partly provided for this problem, relying on organization, discipline, and hierarchy in the working-class party to compensate for lack of both numbers and a democratic environment.)

Thus, one side of the coin was Lenin's recognition of the revolutionary potential of the East. The other was his growing disenchantment with what he saw as the increasing reformism and opportunism of working-class politics in the West. He was himself witness to this at the 1907 Stuttgart Conference of the Second International, with specific reference to the colonial question. But the matter went deeper. Lenin never fully understood Western political democracy: he appreciated neither the dilemmas it presented to Western Marxists nor the attempts to resolve them, even those made in a non-opportunistic spirit. He thus perceived a world in which the Western proletariat was becoming more reformist and less revolutionary, while the Eastern masses were increasingly becoming the 'inflammable material' that would set the edifice of Western capitalism ablaze.

As early as 1907, commenting on the Stuttgart Congress, Lenin had delineated the prospect of the Western working class living parasitically off the fruits of colonialism.[10] With the outbreak of the World War and the capitulation of the majority of the Second International, this prospect seemed even more plausible.

The evolution of Lenin's integration of the Eastern liberation movements into his perspective of world revolution may be traced through his changing conceptualization of the national question. Before the First World War he held the classical Marxist view of the *conditional* recognition of the right of national self-determination in accordance with the progressive character of the creation of nation-states in the first stage of the national revolution.[11] The second stage of the national revolution corresponded to 'the development and growing frequency of all sorts of relations between nations, the breaking down of national barriers, the creation of the international unity of capital, and of economic life in general, of politics, of science, and so forth'.

But in his April 1916 theses on *The Socialist Revolution and the Right of Nations to Self-Determination*, Lenin introduced two crucial innovations. In practice the second stage of the national revolution had been relegated to a socialist future, so that the national question was regarded as fundamentally still a bourgeois-democratic question. With the outbreak of the First World War Lenin concluded that the weight of capitalism's contradictions had proved intolerably onerous and that because of the uneven development of capitalism, although individual countries would advance towards socialism through sequential stages

10. 'The International Socialist Congress in Stuttgart' (1907), published in *Proletary*, No. 17, excerpts in V.I. Lenin, *The National Liberation Movement in the East*, Moscow, 1962, pp. 10-11, and in Schram and Carrère d'Encausse, p. 134 et seq.

11. As spelled out in the discussion on the Poronin Resolution in 1913. Cf. E.H. Carr, *The Bolshevik Revolution 1917-1923*, Volume 1, p. 431.

(unless some external force disrupted this process), it was possible that different stages might co-exist simultaneously on a world scale. Lenin concluded that in the imperialist countries 'all the objective prerequisites of the realization of socialism had now been created'.[12] This changed the whole complexion of the national question.

In addition, Lenin divided the world into three principal types of countries: (i) 'the leading capitalist countries of Western Europe and the United States', where 'bourgeois-progressive national movements are long ago finished'; (ii) Eastern Europe 'and especially Russia', where 'the twentieth century has especially developed bourgeois-democratic national movements and sharpened the national struggle'; (iii) the 'semi-colonial countries like China, Persia, and Turkey and all colonies', where 'bourgeois-democratic movements are either only just beginning or far from finished'.[13]

The effect of these innovations was that in the transition period between the bourgeois and socialist revolution in Russia, 'the line between the bourgeois and socialist stages of development in the national struggle had also become blurred'.[14]

In the light of the political assumptions outlined here — the revolutionary role of the bourgeois-democratic revolution in the East; the potentially hegemonic role of the proletariat in the bourgeois-democratic revolution; the concept of the 'world revolution' — and of Lenin's shift of the national question from the bourgeois to the socialist stage,

12. Cited in Carr, p. 433.
13. Ibid., p. 433.
14. Ibid., p. 434. These innovations, as Carr points out, represented not only a theoretical movement towards grasping the transition from the bourgeois to the socialist stage of the national revolution, but a refinement of the analysis of the bourgeois stage, insofar as the bourgeois national struggle could now become not only anti-feudal, but also, and sometimes simultaneously, anti-imperialist. This was a direct consequence of the analysis contained in *Imperialism*, which saw reactionary twentieth-century monopoly capitalism as parasitic upon its colonies and semi-colonies, replacing the progressive, competitive capitalism of the nineteenth century.

combined with a certain blurring of the distinction between the two stages, *Imperialism* (published in 1916 after the April theses) appears as the logical culmination of more than a decade of consideration of the tactics of world revolution, especially as applied to Russia. It was simultaneously an important link in the tactical chain carrying that consideration onwards.

The place of *Imperialism* in Lenin's revolutionary strategy has nowhere been more succinctly summarized than in Schram and Carrère d'Encausse's *Marxism in Asia:*

'In ... *Imperialism, The Highest Stage of Capitalism,* Lenin ... developed the idea according to which it was colonial exploitation which lay at the root of the corruption of the proletariat, for the profits from the colonies had made it possible for the bourgeoisie to encourage "opportunist" (i.e. moderate and reformist) tendencies in the working class. But imperialism, which eats away at the dynamism of the proletariat of the advanced countries, has, in the dependent countries, exactly the contrary effect, since there it serves to develop nationalist tendencies. Given this link between the national problem and imperialism, Lenin considered that no revolutionary could henceforth deny the importance of national movements. For his part, he regarded the national struggle against imperialism as an integral part of the overall struggle of the proletariat for its liberation, since the national struggle could not achieve its objectives without the destruction of the colonial system. Furthermore, seen in the context of imperialism, the national problem is the factor which connects the non-European world to the problem of the world revolution and constitutes a link between the developed West and the backward East.'[15]

3. The Evolution of Comintern Policy

With the establishment of the Soviet state in 1917 and of the
15. Schram and Carrère d'Encausse, p. 24.

Communist (Third) International in 1919, and with the concurrent foundation of Communist parties throughout Asia, Africa, and Latin America, the revolutionary movement's view of imperialism ceased to be of primarily theoretical concern and became a matter of practical politics as well. The Comintern was the formal link between the Soviet state and the national parties and provided the theoretical rationale for the policies adopted by both the new state and the national parties. Moreover, Comintern Congresses, at least up to 1924, were not mere formalities, but undoubtedly had important effects on the formulation of policy. The debates of the first five or six Comintern Congresses must have had significant effects on many of the future leaders of the world's Communist parties. In tracing the evolution of the Marxist view of imperialism, it is therefore appropriate to examine treatment of this question in the Comintern Congresses.

The two principal themes around which controversy crystallized were the overall role of colonial and semi-colonial struggle in the world revolution (which has been called the 'strategic question') and the 'tactical question' of class alliances, i.e. with which other classes, if any, the proletariat or its party should be prepared to ally and under what conditions.[16]

The strategic problem, of course, threatened to become metaphysical (as indeed it did in the 1960s), since it could all too easily be posed at too general a level to yield useful guidance. But this danger was less pressing in the 1920s, when aspiring leaders of vigorous, newly-born or incipient social movements in the East were thirsting for guidance, experience, and discussion, and when the fate of the 'world revolution' (and with it the young Soviet state) might well depend not only on the particular tactics of the more experienced Western leaders, but also on the material help

16. Schram and Carrère d'Encausse have drawn attention to the cultural aspect as a separate issue, i.e. the problem of how, in the context of what was essentially a modernizing movement, the peoples of the 'East' were to retain their 'identities'. From one angle this can be regarded as an element of the tactical debate, via nationalism.

(Comintern agents, financial assistance, military advisers, mobilization of metropolitan support, etc.) the Comintern could choose to allocate depending on its strategic criteria.

These considerations were grounded not only in the material resources commanded by the Soviet state, but also in the fact that the Communists of the imperial countries — especially Britain, France, and Holland — could themselves play an important role in aiding the exploited masses in their empires to organize against the common foe. This was not merely a matter of resource allocation; the political repercussions within the imperialist countries of aiding working-class, communist, or national liberation movements in the colonies had to be measured, and they could not always be assumed to be positive, at least in the short run.[17]

Perhaps equally important was the *indirect* effect of the strategic debate on the tactical problem, for the discussion on the strategic role of the colonial and semi-colonial masses in the world revolution added new nationalist dimensions to the problem of class alliances. The problems of 'world revolution' and 'class alliance' were in turn related to the diagnosis, and more especially the prognosis, of imperialism.

The First Congress of the International in 1919 paid little attention to national and colonial problems. All eyes were focused on the West, whence the greatest danger of bourgeois counter-revolutionary intervention loomed, and particularly on Germany, where the high hopes for world revolution were concentrated. Despite Lenin's Eastern emphasis, the first Comintern Congress reiterated in no uncertain terms the traditional Marxist view of the relative importance of the roles of East and West in the eradication of colonialism: 'The emancipation of the colonies is possible only in conjunction with the emancipation of the metropolitan working class. The workers and peasants not only of Annam, Algiers, and Bengal, but also of Persia and Armenia, will gain the opportunity of independent existence

17. Both the French and British parties were variously found to be laggards, for opportunist reasons, in their anti-imperialist solidarity.

only when the workers of England and France have overthrown Lloyd George and Clemenceau and taken state power into their own hands.'[18]

By the Second Congress in 1920, however, the situation had changed, and this became one of the historic Congresses on the national and colonial problem, its debates and theses being frequently cited subsequently. The shift in emphasis was in part due to the beginning of the ebb of the revolutionary tide in the West and its flow in the East. Also, however, delegates from the East, in particular the theoretically sophisticated M.N. Roy of India, were attending the Congress for the first time.[19] The German and Hungarian revolutions of 1919 had been defeated, and the Red Army halted at the gates of Warsaw. Moreover, with the collapse of Germany and Turkey, Western intervention was concentrated precisely where the legacy of Tsarism had left the greatest divisive potential: in the East. It was there that the rising nationalism of the non-Russian peoples of the former Tsarist empire offered British imperialism a particularly tempting target. The armistice permitted a shift of Allied resources from Europe to Asia for the campaign against Bolshevism. This involved not only supplies to white Russian armies but also moves against Soviet forces by British military contingents in the Caucasus and Central Asia. 'Through this British action, the Middle East became in 1919 the theatre of an all but declared war between Great Britain and the RSFSR.'[20]

18. Cited in Claudín, p. 246.

19. Claudín attributes the change also to the appearance of the national and colonial question in Russia itself. However, this appears to have been reflected not in the Second Congress debates (July 1920), but in those of the Baku First Congress of Peoples of the East, held in September of the same year, where the problems of revolution in the East were again discussed. The general point may be made here that it is by no means clear that Comintern theory at any time became *purely* the rationalization of the requirements of Soviet *realpolitik*. At least up to 1928, particular doctrines had to be debated, argued for, and won in ideological terms. For examples of the continuing importance of theory, see S.F. Cohen, *Bukharin and the Bolshevik Revolution*, pp. 252 ff.

20. Carr, p. 237.

Thus, because of the search for new sources of revolutionary energy to renew the faltering offensive against the Western capitalist powers and because of the urgent needs of Soviet survival, the strategic and tactical aspects of the Eastern question were treated most seriously at the Second Congress. Moreover, delegates from the colonial and semi-colonial countries were generally unwilling to accept a perspective that delayed their liberation until the conquest of power by the Western proletariat. The Eurocentric emphasis of the First Congress was therefore abandoned; never again did the Comintern describe colonial liberation in any country as dependent on metropolitan revolution. At the same time, the Comintern did not abandon its view that the Western proletariat would play the key role in the world revolution, although realization of that role was made contingent on circumstances relating to the end of colonial exploitation. Meanwhile, the colonial revolution moved to a much more central position on the world revolutionary stage.

The two principal contending perspectives in the debates were counterposed in the draft theses presented in Commission by Lenin and M.N. Roy. Roy's position on the strategic issue was that priority should be accorded the anti-imperialist struggles of the peoples of the East over the socialist movement of the proletariat of the West, on the grounds that the latter would never wage a vigorous revolutionary struggle so long as colonial profits maintained its high living standards and sapped its militancy. This was an ultimate extension of the line of reasoning with which Lenin himself had been concerned, as we have seen, for some years. But Lenin was too deeply imbued with the classical Marxist tradition to go so far in this direction, especially since he regarded both the nationalist (anti-imperialist) movement and the colonially based corruption of the Western working class as temporary. Above all, he, like Marx, saw socialism as the product of Western civilization and therefore envisaged its decisive inauguration as coming from the West.

The tactical question at issue was this: 'which class should take the leadership in the revolutions of the East, and which allies, if any, should the working class be prepared to seek and with what guidelines in mind should it seek such allies, whether or not in the leadership of the revolutionary movement?' Roy held that the proletariat in the colonies and semi-colonies, and especially in India, should have no truck with bourgeois allies and should endeavour to take leadership of the national liberation movement forthwith, thereby assuring a more resolute struggle against imperialism and a fortification of the position of the working class vis-à-vis other classes. Moreover, he did not trust the bourgeoisie to lead any movement in which the working class was involved without using the opportunities thereby afforded to harass, crush, or otherwise retard the workers' movement.

Lenin, on the contrary, held that the social base of the Eastern national liberation movements was bourgeois or proto-bourgeois (peasant), and that their social function was to create nation-states, just like nineteenth-century nationalism in its struggle against feudal absolutism. The complication of imperialist control did not significantly alter this perspective, which contrasted somewhat with Roy's emphasis on social revolution. Lenin pointed out that the working class was proportionally minute in the population of the countries concerned and was extremely backward culturally (often simply illiterate). He noted that efforts to establish a Communist party in India had so far failed completely. There was, he held, no practical alternative to temporary bourgeois leadership of the liberation movements, which was in any case appropriate since the tasks of the bourgeois-democratic revolution had not yet been accomplished in these countries.

Nevertheless, there *was* a proletariat, however small, in the mines, plantations, and docks, on the railways and in the government offices and public works and other government departments, and in a small but nevertheless growing factory industry. M.N. Roy was himself testimony to its existence. Lenin took the point and modified his theses accordingly; he argued that although bourgeois-democratic objectives and bourgeois leadership were the order of the day at the present stage, the working-class movement should ally only with revolutionary nationalist elements. This was a change from his initial formulation, which stipulated an alliance with 'bourgeois-democratic' elements. Lenin did not regard this as a change of substance. He believed that since the heart of the bourgeois-democratic revolution was the land question (breaking the power of the feudal land-owners),[21] the peasantry was the crucial class and any real bourgeois-democratic revolution would have to involve the peasantry on a broad scale. The question of separating the revolutionary sheep from the goats among the bourgeoisie was therefore relatively unimportant. Roy, in turn, allowed the desirability of occasional cooperation with bourgeois nationalists, but insisted that Communists should strive to seize leadership of the national liberation movements from the outset. Both Lenin and Roy agreed that the independence of the working-class movement and its party had to be maintained.

The Congress approved both sets of theses, effectively informing the bourgeoisie that the working class (and the Communists) intended both to cooperate with it against the imperialists and to overthrow it at the earliest possible opportunity once the imperialists had been evicted. In the meantime, 'bourgeoisies' had to be discovered that would cooperate with the Communists against the imperialists but not restrict the Communists' right to organize the workers and peasants against the bourgeoisie and landlords.[22] In practice, Lenin's emphasis on bourgeois hegemony was to prevail in the years to come, while Roy's on independent proletarian action and leadership of the national movement was allowed to fade from sight. On the other hand, Lenin's

21. It is worth noting that Lenin's conception of the bourgeois-democratic revolution divested it of all political criteria relating to democracy. This was particularly damaging, compounding as it did his general tendency to underestimate the genuiness of Western bourgeois democracy.
22. Claudín describes this as a search for a 'white blackbird'.

stress on the (impossible) conditions for Communist cooperation with bourgeois nationalists was also forgotten, indeed rather quickly, first of all by Lenin himself (in the case of Turkey). In practice, the emphasis on bourgeois leadership of the national movements, combined with the tacit waiving by most Communist parties of the conditions for cooperation with bourgeois nationalists, later led to the ready manipulation of these parties by the bourgeoisie. The Communists and their supporters were often subjected to bloody massacres once they had served their purpose.[23]

Asiocentrism as a distinct nationalist cultural trend tended to lend added force to Lenin's as opposed to Roy's approach to class alliances. Although in his world revolutionary ('strategic') outlook Roy undoubtedly cast himself as the most extreme Asiocentric, his approach to class struggle and alliances in Asia itself implied a sharp demarcation of workers and peasants against capitalists and landlords, rather than the nation as a whole against imperialism. In effect, then, he combined intense Asiocentrism with practical anti-nationalism. But insofar as Asiocentrism was a *general* phenomenon at Comintern Congresses, its principal effect was to strengthen nationalist tendencies within the Communist movement and to add greater relative weight to Lenin's thesis stressing the importance of bourgeois leadership.[24] Although the view that located the source of the downfall of world capitalism in the East could also be held by those who advocated working-class hegemony in the anti-imperialist struggle, clearly it was more likely to lend additional weight to Lenin's characterization of the national liberation struggle.

23. At least part of the responsibility for this disastrous outcome must be laid to the sheer political naiveté of supposing that the bourgeoisie would pay no attention to the freely proclaimed intentions of the Communists to eliminate them after the victory of the anti-imperialist struggle.

24. In general, the more powerful the nationalist influence culturally, the greater was likely to be the emphasis on alliance with or acceptance of leadership by the 'national bourgeoisie'. This was notable for example, in the case of Muslim Communists of the USSR at the 1920 Baku Congress. See Schram and Carrère d'Encausse, p. 34.

Another issue on which Lenin and Roy agreed, the long-term implications of which were fateful, was the role Soviet power could play in permitting the Eastern countries to attain socialism without passing through capitalism. In this connection Lenin even developed a conception of 'peasant soviets' and suggested modifying the structure of the party to take account of its peasant composition in some countries. Roy did not go so far, but he did envisage the possibility of combined peasants' and workers' soviets. For Roy, the possibility of the non-capitalist path for Asia depended on support from the victorious proletariat in 'the Soviet Republics of the advanced capitalist countries'; for Lenin, simply in 'the Soviet Republics'. Schram speculates: 'Did Lenin mean the same thing? Or was he thinking of the various "Soviet republics" scattered over the territory of the former Russian empire, which were soon to unite to establish the Soviet Union? It seems likely that if he had not yet, in July 1920, abandoned all hope of a revolution in Germany or elsewhere in Europe, he was already moving towards a prevision of a situation in which for a relatively long time, the Soviet Union alone would extend a helping hand to the peoples of Asia and thus permit them to avoid the capitalist stage of development. Thus the schema of Marx and Engels according to which Russia could avoid the capitalist stage if the victorious proletariat of the advanced capitalist countries of Western Europe supported the Russian revolution was transposed towards the East.'

The Third Congress of the Comintern in 1921 scarcely touched upon the national and colonial question — to the indignation of many of the delegates from the East, who appear to have attributed this to the Eurocentrism they felt they had detected at the Second Congress. The relative silence contrasted sharply with the continued upsurge of revolutionary upheaval in the East — in Turkey, Persia, and India, where an anti-British movement was sweeping the country in 1921. In China, too, Sun Yat-Sen had established a government in Canton and made contact with the Soviet regime.

There were, however, almost certainly profound reasons for the short shrift national and colonial matters received at the Third Congress. Just as Soviet security requirements had, at least indirectly, been instrumental in raising the issue at the Second Congress, so the same requirements were relevant in muffling it at the Third. A number of events occurred between the two Congresses that were bound to make the Soviet authorities hesitant to discuss these issues publicly. Two problems arose in particular, both highly embarrassing for the Soviet government, which to some extent might be regarded as a victim of circumstances. First, the right of self-determination had given way to de facto centralization in a number of cases concerning Asiatic Russia. The forces of reaction, both domestic and foreign (especially British and French), were using national aspirations,[25] first decisively awakened by the 1905 revolution, to attempt to bring about the disintegration of the USSR, which in the circumstances would have meant the wreck of the Soviet state. The workers' state felt it could survive only by forcibly remaining the possessor of the Tsarist empire. Accordingly, after the Baku Congress, Stalin, as Commissar of Nationalities, curtailed the power of the national Communist governments and instituted widespread purges to remove nationalist elements, which in many cases included Communists[26] (the most famous being Sultan Gabier).

25. The Muslim Communists at the Baku Congress of Toilers of the East in September 1920 opted clearly for an emphasis and heavy reliance on long-term alliances with bourgeois nationalists — a corollary of the extreme importance of nationalism in their outlook, the weakness of the Muslim working class, and the chauvinistic elements in the Russian working class in the Muslim lands.

26. Claudín argues that the failure to establish a genuinely autonomous Muslim state, i.e. with the right of secession and all the other rights formally guaranteed in the Soviet constitution, was a major factor in the Communists' failure in the Middle East and North Africa in this period. This seems unlikely, since attachment to the nation-state was not a strong sentiment for any section of the Islamic population then. The Comintern's opposition to pan-Islamism and its atheistic reputation, together with the naive policy of announcing in advance its intentions eventually to eliminate its proposed partners, seem adequate to account for the Communist failures.

As if this were not enough, the conflicting resolutions to which the Second Congress had committed the Comintern came home to roost. In a number of cases, most notably Turkey, but also Afghanistan, the Soviet government had provided material and diplomatic aid to facilitate the achievement of full independence from imperialism. Despite this, local Communists had been harassed and imprisoned, sometimes tortured and murdered, especially in Turkey. Moreover, Moscow's agreement with the Turkish government in 1921 had been signed *after* the murder of the leaders of the Turkish Communist party. Claudín calls these bloody episodes examples of failure of the Comintern due to its subordination to Soviet state interests, but clearly this is accurate only in a superficial sense, since the Soviet government was faithfully implementing the spirit and letter of the 'bourgeois hegemony' tactics voted at the Second Congress. Moreover, there is reason to believe that the policy practised by the Soviet regime was the one that would have received the support of the majority of the delegates had there been a vote on the issue. Certainly, the terms of the debate reflected little of Roy's concerns, though a little thought would have suggested that however weak the working class was at the time, Roy's points were bound to be of mounting importance in the future. Finally, the Comintern resolutions had to take the form of general guidelines to be interpreted according to local circumstances by individual Communist parties. This may be a somewhat ingenuous characterization of the Soviet government's relationship to Comintern directives and resolutions, but it does serve to point out that the Soviet party, no less than any other, had specific, practical responsibilities to which the resolutions had to be applied. The year 1921 was perhaps even more critical than 1920 in this respect. It was the beginning of the New Economic Policy, and there was hope of attracting foreign investment. The revolutionary tide had clearly receded in the West, and it was all the more imperative to ease the pressure in the East. This was the aim of the Turkish agreement of 1921, which, while strengthening the Turkish government against the Anglo-French alliance and leaving it free to deal with Armenia, in turn left Moscow free to tackle its own dissident Muslim nationalists, while safeguarding its oil. Finally, just three months before the Third Congress, a trade pact had been signed with Britain, one of the clauses of which was that neither side should engage in propaganda hostile to the other; the Soviet Union in particular promised to refrain from any propaganda that might incite the peoples of Asia to act against British interests.

At the time of the Third Congress Comintern policy as the rationalization of the state interests of the USSR and as the impulsion of world revolution became indistinguishable. This point is worth stressing, since it has escaped the attention of so many otherwise perceptive observers. We shall see that there did come a time when the Communist International became nothing more than an instrument of Soviet state policy, but this will be seen to have been the result of the institutionalization of a great change in the social location and ideological function of Marxism. As important as this institutionalization of manipulation by Moscow was to become, it was fundamentally a secondary phenomenon. All the mistakes allegedly resulting from the over-centralized conception of the Comintern had much deeper roots in a combination of mistaken political analysis and the unforeseen (and largely unforeseeable) changed role of Marxism from a movement for democratic working-class socialism to a movement for the modernization of backward societies.

The Fourth Congress of the Comintern, in December 1922, marked a return to a more militant attitude towards bourgeois nationalists. The theses did acknowledge that the bourgeoisie and intelligentsia would play a major role in the early phases of the colonial revolutionary movements: 'In all these countries, at first, the indigenous bourgeoisie and intelligentsia are the champions of the colonial revolution-ary movements.' Moreover, 'as the bourgeois-nationalist intelligentsia draws the revolutionary working-class movement into the struggle against imperialism, its representatives at first also take the lead in the newly-formed trade-union organizations and their activities.'[27] The theses went on to note that bourgeois nationalists saw in the Soviet Union a practical ally against imperialism, but then warned that 'the representatives of bourgeois nationalism, taking advantage of the political authority of Soviet Russia and adapting themselves to the class interests of the workers, clothe their bourgeois-democratic aspirations in a "socialist" or "communist" garb in order – although they themselves may not always be conscious of this – to divert the embryonic proletarian associations from the direct tasks of class organization'.[28] Further, noting that the national bourgeoisie in some Asian countries had strived for conciliation with imperialism during the two and a half years since the Second Congress, the theses of the Fourth Congress attributed this shift to bourgeois fear of the peasantry: 'The bourgeois nationalists (in India, Persia, Egypt) fear the agrarian watchwords, and their anxiety to prune them down bears witness to the close connection between the native bourgeoisie and the feudal-bourgeois landlords, and to the intellectual and political dependence of the former on the latter.'[29]

The theses held that the class character of the anti-imperialist movement and the fact that its decisive victory would be incompatible with the maintenance of the domination of world imperialism meant that the objective tasks of the colonial revolution exceeded the bounds of bourgeois democracy. The ruling classes in the colonial world are thus 'unable to lead the struggle against imperialism insofar as that struggle assumes the form of a revolutionary mass movement.' The conclusion — stated more forthrightly than at the Second Congress — was that the 'young proletariat of the colonies must fight for an

27. Claudín, p. 260.
28. Ibid. A similar warning was issued at the Second Congress.
29. Cited in Claudín, p. 226.

independent position in the national liberation movement and become its leading force.'[30]

The Fifth Congress in 1924 again paid little attention to the anti-imperialist struggle, focusing mainly on Europe. It did, however, adopt a more conciliatory attitude to the national bourgeoisie than the Fourth Congress had (although the latter had rejected Roy's theses). In part this attitude was attributable to the commencement of a period of Soviet policy during which Anglo-French imperialism was regarded as the principal enemy; the bourgeois national movements and bourgeois governments in semi-colonial countries were considered the only potential allies of any substance in undermining the enemy's rear lines.

The Sixth Congress (1928) was concerned to explain the Chinese disaster of 1927, itself the logical outcome of the whole Leninist approach to bourgeois hegemony over the anti-imperialist movements (an approach that was followed, it should be noted, by both the Soviet and Chinese Communist parties). This Congress also conducted a more general discussion of the national and colonial question, with a report presented by Kuusinen. Despite the opposition of the two parties most directly concerned with empire — the British and the Indian, functioning in the biggest imperial power and the biggest colony — the theses adopted at this congress finally proclaimed outright that imperialism was economically retrogressive in the colonies. The Comintern thereby jettisoned Lenin's formal obeisance to the classical Marxist position on the matter in his *Imperialism* and asserted instead that imperialism retarded both industrialization in particular and capitalism and the development of the productive forces in general. The resolutions of this congress formalized the surrender of the Marxist analysis of imperialism to the requirements of bourgeois anti-imperialist propaganda.

30. Claudín states that the main weakness of the Fourth Congress was its excessive abstractness and neglect of the fact that the working class in most colonial and semi-colonial countries was too weak numerically to assume the leading role assigned it.

4. The Comintern's Conclusion

From the very inception of the Comintern the requirements of the world revolution and those of the defence of the Soviet state were inextricably interlaced. This had special significance with regard to the colonies and semi-colonies, for the principal enemy of the young Soviet state, Britain, also happened to be the principal colonial power; moreover, British colonies or spheres of influence were contiguous with Russian territory. Distinctions between the exigencies of world revolution and of the defence of the Soviet revolution were especially difficult to sustain under such circumstances.

The theory of imperialism as elaborated by Lenin in 1916 had stressed that the entire system of exploitation on which modern (i.e. monopoly) capitalism was based rested on colonial exploitation. This suggested a more profound motive for emphasis on the anti-imperialist struggle than would have been generated by defence of the Soviet Union alone, since anti-imperialist struggle weakened capitalism not only indirectly by aiding the first socialist state, but also directly by striking at the socio-economic roots of the modern system itself.

This fusion of world revolution and Soviet international security requirements affected the Communist view of imperialism, lending nationalism greater scope to influence Marxism, both conjuncturally and durably. Two principal, mutually reinforcing, imperatives were at work here: the ideological and political requirements of the tasks of Soviet industrialization; the associated requirements of enhancing the security of the Soviet Union by supporting national revolts in the Third World.

This naturally strengthened the already existing tendencies to minimize or deny the economically progressive role of imperialism in the colonies and to exaggerate the differences between the indigenous bourgeoisie (and other ruling groups) and imperialism, an emphasis that already underlay Lenin's theses adopted at the Second Congress. In this context, it was entirely logical that the Sixth Congress in 1928 should have sealed the debate, definitively characterizing imperialism as economically reactionary in the colonies and semi-colonies. This is not to say that the Comintern's view of imperialism was no more than a rationalization of political practice. The 1928 Congress itself temporarily de-emphasized collaboration with the 'national bourgeoisie', which could have been accomplished more coherently had the economic character of imperialism been deemed progressive.[31]

If the 1928 'shift' in the theory of imperialism merely ratified what had come to be the dominant view since Lenin's *Imperialism*, changes in other aspects of theory were of more significance. Among these, critical for the period after the Second World War and for the future of Marxism more generally were, in particular: the blurring of the distinction between bourgeois-democratic and socialist revolution in Third World countries (indeed, the virtual disappearance of any clear criteria for distinguishing socialist revolutions or paths of development); the loss of any distinction whatever between anti-imperialist and anti-capitalist or socialist struggle; and the genesis of the concept of the non-capitalist road of development.

31. The British and Indian parties argued that imperialism was advancing the industrialization of India.

5
Post-War Marxist Analysis of Imperialism

After the Second World War, especially in the late 1960s, various independent Marxist analyses of imperialism were advanced parallel to the official Communist view. Both trends agreed that imperialism was not only a factor retarding modernization, but also constituted the principal impediment both to the rapid achievement of an advanced society and to the eradication of poverty. The fusion of 'imperialism' with 'capitalism', which Lenin had already achieved by defining imperialism as monopoly capitalism and monopoly capitalism as the present stage of capitalism, was further strengthened by the notion of neo-colonialism and by the elaboration of a conspiratorial interpretation of the concept of the 'world market'. The Leninist assessment of imperialism as unable to modernize backward societies was thus extended to apply to capitalism in general.

That imperialism has had and still has disastrous effects on the economies of Third World countries is a tenet of the Marxist outlook probably accepted by a majority of those in the West who have any view of the matter at all. The outstanding success of Lenin's *Imperialism* is rather remarkable in view of the unprecedented progress in modernization achieved in the Third World under the aegis of imperialism/capitalism after the Second World War. How can we account for the continued success with which the theory has resisted the facts that belie it?

1. The Fiction of Underdevelopment

The problems of underdevelopment and world poverty, which had previously been the concern mainly of specialists, became common coin in the West after the Second World War. They were aspects of a world that was much more interconnected, with the growth in power of the Soviet Union, the rise of the United States to leadership in the West, and the achievement of independence by most formerly dependent territories. This drawing together of humanity advanced by leaps and bounds after 1945 and contributed to impelling acceptance of the Leninist world-view of imperialism, which has since become the most generalized ideology concerning the process of unification of mankind.

The Second World War had brought the peoples of Latin America, Asia, and Africa onto the world stage much more prominently than before, stimulating movements for national independence that fused with demands for a better life. These movements and demands grew vigorously in the climate of political competition between the USSR and the West in the Third World. Purely economic factors also made the Third World more important. No matter how apparently nominal newly won independence may have been, it clearly offered greater possibilities for a switch of masters, since it afforded greater scope for the exercise of relative *economic* power to shift alignments. But political independence was in fact more than nominal, and was generally associated with expanding economic activity. The importance of Third World markets thus increased at the same time as Western expansion stimulated the demand for raw materials from the Third World.[1]

Alongside these developments and connected with them there was a burgeoning of Third World nationalism, which

1. The trade stimulus to postwar industrialization in the Third World was probably at least as strong as it was for industrialization in nineteenth-century Europe. The dramatic rate of postwar industrialization and the unprecedented progress in modernization achieved in the Third World is documented in chapter 8, below.

intensified after independence and gained added momentum from the large number of new nations and the aspirations for social and economic improvement associated with nationalism. These movements, although not inherently pointing in a democratic or socialist direction, often employed a radical-leftist ideology. In so doing they touched a sympathetic chord in the West, where there has been a steady (left) radicalization of the intelligentsia, accelerating somewhat after the late 1960s.[2]

It is against this background that the rise of the fiction of underdevelopment must be situated. This fiction is but the other side of the coin of the ideology of neo-colonialism (the postwar version of Lenin's *Imperialism*), and the two have mutually sustained each other, for although either taken singly is implausible, together they look quite credible.

In general, the underdevelopment fiction maintains that the peoples of the Third World have been getting steadily worse off ever since the industrial revolution in the West. They have become gradually worse fed, worse housed, more disease-ridden; increasingly forced into malodorous slums; unable to find worthwhile (or any) employment; and subjected to inhuman conditions and rising inequality of wealth and income.

This conception depends for its ideological dominance on Third World nationalism, and on the populist leftism that has increasingly marked the Western intelligentsia and the left in general since the Second World War. Its specific doctrines have been extrapolated from the Leninist theory of imperialism with the assistance of that portion of the professional intelligentsia concerned with economic development, whose occupational location has placed them in the

2. Especially affecting the younger generation in the social science faculties of the universities, whose numbers have been increased by the demand for their services by the numerous non-university national and international bodies dealing with the social and economic problems of the Third World. This group forms the core of those who have been subject to Third World nationalist and vulgar-Marxist pressures on 'underdevelopment' and who have in turn done most to elaborate the underdevelopment fiction.

cross-fire of Western leftism and Third World nationalism. Before dissecting the underlying assumptions of this view, I will anticipate chapters 7 and 8 by pointing out that the term 'underdevelopment' actually corresponds to no objective process.[3]

There is no evidence that any *process* of underdevelopment has occurred in modern times, and particularly in the period since the West made its impact on other continents. The evidence rather supports a contrary thesis: that a process of *development* has been taking place at least since the English industrial revolution, much accelerated in comparison with any earlier period; and that this has been the direct result of the impact of the West, of imperialism.

The point is easily illustrated. Those definitions of underdevelopment that do not describe it simply as the condition of not having reached the level of living standards and productive forces that prevails in the advanced countries almost invariably emphasize such features as mass unemployment, chronic underemployment, shanty towns, gross overcrowding, pressure on the land, and so on.[4] All these evils, however, stem from population growth — fewer babies dying before the age of five, and more adults living longer than before — which is the most fundamental indicator of *improvement* in living standards, brought about precisely by the impact of the West through the imperialist introduction of modern transport, hygiene, medicine, and the general stimulus of the productive forces (permitting better nutrition).

The fact is that the West did *not* industrialize while the rest of the world stood still, *nor* did that industrialization retard the development of the rest of the world. Rather, the

3. It may be taken to correspond to the *fact* of different levels of living standards and of degrees of development of the productive forces — and to an *ideological* process.

4. See André Gunder Frank, *Latin America: Underdevelopment or Revolution*, p. 381; A.G. Frank, *Capitalism and Underdevelopment in Latin America, Historical Studies of Chile and Brazil*, p. 206; P. Bairoch, *Economic Development in the Third World Since 1900*, pp. 168, 200, 203; S. Amin, *Accumulation on a World Scale*, Volume 2, pp. 381-2.

industrialization of the West from the late eighteenth century onwards (especially from the mid nineteenth century for most countries other than Britain) tended to initiate and then accelerate modern development in the rest of the world, which otherwise would have remained comparatively stagnant. Western economic expansion aroused the non-Western world to a modernization process for which its own internal development had not yet prepared it. There were three main aspects of this impetus: destruction of pre-modern cultures and modes of production; stimulation of aspirations new in both degree and kind; implantation of elements of modern civilization, both culturally and economically. Indeed, nationalism fused these elements, combining the emotional forces released by the traumatic break with the past and the aspirations engendered by comparison with Western achievement.

But the picture was not one of simple progress. The nationalisms created largely by imperialism became the principal *political* instrument of modernization, but they were hot-house plants, exhibiting to an extreme degree elements of irrationalism and moral imbalance that partially counteracted the individualist culture introduced by Western capitalism. It will readily be seen that the Leninist theory of imperialism, with its emphasis on robbery, exploitation, and parasitism and its denunciation of Western pillage of the Third World, was perfectly suited to the psychological needs and political requirements of Third World nationalists. The theory of imperialism (and more recently of neo-colonialism) thus found sturdy support from major social movements in both the West and the Third World at precisely the point that the facts of reality were even more damaging to it than before.

2. Explaining the Non-Existent

The quality of postwar literature on imperialism has naturally suffered from ascribing rising significance to a phenomenon of declining importance. In principle, an alert Marxism could have initiated searching discussion on the shape of *the post-imperialist world*; but merely to make this point is to remind oneself how little modern Marxism, whether 'independent' or 'Stalinist', has been able to comprehend anything in the world other than the old familiar themes in slightly altered guises.[5]

Neo-colonialism is a case in point, on which we need not linger here except to state that the contention that political independence did not fundamentally alter the relationship of economic exploitation and/or control between metropolis and colony both provided a hinge by which to transmit the Leninist theory of imperialism into the period of independence and permitted the negative effects of imperialism to be divorced from formal political control, thus leaving the door open for the claim that the impersonal forces of the world (capitalist) market had equally negative effects. In one common version, these effects are attributed mainly to semi-conspiratorial manipulation by large firms and international organizations and to blackmail (often covert) by the imperialist states themselves. This approach not only facilitates transition to the notion that the world market is the source of inequality between the 'metropolis' and 'periphery' but also lends the concept of the world market a permanently sinister aura in the eyes of the petty-bourgeois left, in strange contradiction to Marx's basically optimistic analysis of the effects of its extension.

This contrast between the view of the world market as a progressive factor opening backward societies to disruptive and liberating influences and the view that it is the source of the extension into precapitalist societies only of the anarchy and irregularity of capitalism is related to two other features of the postwar anti-imperialist outlook. First, the idea that the world market is the root of international

5. Arrighi (p. 17) notes that by the end of the 1960s, 'even those scholars who were most alert to the changing pattern of international capitalist relations felt obliged to pay a tribute to Lenin where none was due, compounding the confusion'.

exploitation tends to dissolve any distinctive *imperialist* aspects of such exploitation and to equate it merely with the extension of specifically capitalist relationships across international boundaries. In turn, this blurs the demarcation between the negative effects of the growth of capitalism as an indigenous phenomenon and the negative effects of the impact of the advanced capitalist countries (imperialism).

Second, the existence of a group of underdeveloped socialist countries has fostered the presumption that an alternative superior to capitalist modernization already exists, and thus that any capitalist modernization of a backward country is practically second-best. The blurring of the distinction between imperialist and capitalist exploitation and the existence of modernizing socialist countries together militate against any view that exposure of Third World countries to the world market can be progressive.

It may be noted with regard to this last point that it does not follow from the existence of backward but modernizing socialist countries that socialism is functionally superior to capitalism in industrializing any given society simply because it is a historically superior mode of production. The apparent success of the Soviet Union in this respect may be due to specific factors that are not necessarily or easily repeatable. Moreover, there are many dimensions to modernization, and it may well be that what is second-best in one respect may be best in another, e.g. the flowering of individualism or political democracy. In addition, a more realistic approach to the whole question of modernization may conclude that it is impossible for some societies to progress effectively through capitalist development, whilst others may be unsuited to socialism. Different phases of the process may require different socio-economic orientations, as was true in Russia. Whatever the specific circumstances, however, to avoid utopianism — the assumption that the adoption of central planning, an egalitarian ideology, and a one-party system is the key to the most effective modernization policy — does not at all mean to rely on automatic capitalist progress.[6]

In sum, the combination of identification of imperialism with the growth of Third World capitalism and the stigmatization of capitalism as a second-best method of modernization strengthened anti-imperialist ideology immeasurably. This ideology was further fortified by the fact that the characterization of capitalist development as 'second-best' was associated with the presumption that the best, the socialist, path to modernization, was also the most 'natural' in some sense; failure to adopt it implied a measure of distortion, caused, of course, by outside forces. Thus, although imperialism and capitalism became inextricably intertwined in such a way as to condemn *all capitalist development*, the demonology and practical utility of denouncing *external* or *foreign* sources of exploitation was retained.

The interrelationship between anti-capitalist and anti-imperialist ideology thus became quite complex. On the one hand, anti-imperialist and anti-capitalist rhetoric and ideology in the Third World overlapped to a large extent, became closely interwoven, and supplemented and strengthened one another in practice. On the other hand, the fact that the two never fused completely always left the foreign devil to be called out, to fortify the position of those who wished to strengthen themselves against imperialism without opting for a socialist path.[7] Despite the frequent difficulty in distinguishing anti-imperialist from anti-capitalist propaganda, the external element in the alleged

6. Although capitalist development opens up new opportunities for human progress, this does *not* mean that human progress automatically results. Conscious political intervention of a correct sort is a *sine qua non* of human progress. Incorrect political intervention, or merely leaving the process of capitalist development to work itself out, may result in reactionary solutions to the contradictions raised by capitalist development, and may push humanity back morally, culturally, and in the end even materially.

7. In Brazil, for example. One curious result of the partial fusion of anti-capitalist and anti-imperialist propaganda has been that the development of Third World capitalism has been accomplished to a not inconsiderable extent under the aegis of anti-capitalist ideology and rhetoric.

failure or inadequacy of indigenous Third World capitalist development has remained a constant theme.[8]

The pursuance of this theme in the objective circumstances of *accelerating* Third World capitalist development and widened room for manoeuvre by independent Third World states necessarily produced ingenious theories designed to explain non-existent phenomena.[9]

The theoretical difficulty was to explain how international economic relationships could be exploitative only of the less developed countries in a world of independent nation-states. Why, for example, was direct US investment in Europe not imperialist, whereas in Guatemala it was? One answer was that the difference was merely one of degree. But the search continued for an explanation of how imperialist exploitation could endure in eras of juridical equality between nations, which apparently implies the elimination of institutional-political distortions of relative bargaining positions.[10]

Another sort of answer was to advance 'vicious circle' type explanations. The heart of these is the claim that once a large difference in the level of the productive forces in metropolitan and peripheral countries has been established, it tends to generate a self-reinforcing momentum, so that, for example, the existing division of labour at independence so impoverished the less developed countries that they were unable to accumulate sufficient capital to industrialize. This, of course, was pure dogma. It could as well be claimed

8. The recurrence of this theme in official Communist literature is not surprising in view of its link to Soviet diplomacy. Its recurrence in the literature of the independent Marxist left is due to the psychological difficulty of combining an objective appraisal of capitalism with consistent opposition to it.

9. A related phenomenon is the enormous proliferation of explanations of the non-existent secular deterioration of the terms of trade of the Third World. (A recent summary of the plethora of contributions on this theme is contained in J. Spraos, 'The Statistical Debate on the Net Barter Terms of Trade Between Primary Commodities and Manufactures', *The Economic Journal,* 90, March 1980.)

10. It never occurred to anyone (on the left) to study the development of *more equal* bargaining relationships with the establishment of formal sovereignty.

that the high level of development of the productive forces of the metropolitan countries would eventually generate retarding pressures, to which the peripheral countries would not be subject, a proposition that, at least superficially, would seem to have more in common with Marxism than the vicious-circle approach.[11] Moreover, the latter explanation was open to the objection that the vicious circle could be rendered virtuous through state intervention. Depictions of vicious circles were therefore generally accompanied by emphasis on the network of cultural, political, and economic relationships that limited the capacity of Third World states to break out of the circle in this manner. Investigation was thus shifted away from specific economic relationships like capital export or the terms of trade; instead there was discussion of the totality of relationships binding periphery to metropolis and subordinating the former to the latter. The most sophisticated of such approaches was the 'dependency' school, developed among Latin American social scientists in the 1960s;[12] this approach was flexible enough to allow for the reality of some development in Latin America, though limiting it conceptually within externally determined constraints.

The postulation of the mounting importance of a declining phenomenon leads to a historical outlook typically characterized by two interrelated assumptions: 1) that the 'dependent' (or, at an earlier age, colonial) international division of labour is in some sense unnatural; its existence therefore implies that an alternative, 'normal' development has been displaced artificially; 2) that if this 'normal' development has not occurred, it is because peripheral economies have been externally conditioned and not because of their internal contradictions.

To assert the latter proposition is to draw attention to the

11. The Myrdal cumulative causation approach (G. Myrdal, *Economic Theory and Under-Developed Regions*) has generally been adopted by the left in analyses of imperialism, despite its anti-Marxist conception of the nature of social change.

12. Amin's *Accumulation on a World Scale* might be considered a non-Latin-American dependency model.

fact that no Marxist has examined the contrary hypothesis, namely that the external factors have been secularly (if not steadily) *reducing* the relative backwardness of Latin American society rather than limiting or constraining its progress.[13] Indeed, more complex hypotheses may be advanced as to the interrelationship of external and internal forces in Latin American development without involving the concept of dependence at all (whether increasing or decreasing). In general, dependency theorists attribute to dependent development all the evils that they would prefer to see omitted and apparently imagine were absent during the 'non-dependent' development of Europe in the nineteenth century. This approach is not only ahistorical, but clearly utopian.

3. Theory of Imperialism and the National Bourgeoisie

The Communist movement meanwhile had little new to contribute to the theory of imperialism after the Second World War, except a stereotyped picture of Latin American and most other pre-industrial societies as feudal or semi-feudal, this structure allegedly supported by imperialism and opposed by the national bourgeoisie. This formula served to rationalize a political strategy that upheld that it was necessary to complete the bourgeois revolution before aiming for socialism; and this, of course, required cooperation with the national bourgeoisie. Analysis of the dynamic and structure of the societies concerned thus became largely a by-product of the theory of imperialism, which in this sense itself became a theory of Third World capitalist development in its internal as much as its external

13. Since the dependency approach virtually excludes this hypothesis by assumption, we must certainly reject Cardoso's plea in defence of dependency theory that 'the effect of dependency theory on the sociological imagination has been positive'. (F.H. Cardoso, *The Consumption of Dependency Theory in the United States*, p. 18.)

dimensions (exemplified by the diverse uses to which the term 'national bourgeoisie' was put).

Collaboration with the national bourgeoisie was a hallmark of the Communist movement from the later years of Stalin's life, and especially after the Twentieth Congress of the Soviet Communist Party. In the case of Latin America, dependency ideology in its crudest form readily lent itself to this sort of political strategy. In an attempt to strike at the political roots of revisionist Communism, Gunder Frank mounted a polemic against the underlying theory of imperialism, arguing that the problem of underdevelopment arose not from imperialism's preservation of pre-war non-capitalist social structures (like feudalism), but from its transformation of all peripheral countries into capitalist societies. It was their *capitalist* nature that retarded their progress. This being so, there was no point in looking to vigorous independent development sparked by a national bourgeoisie, since capitalism already existed. This amounted to an inglorious attempt to sidestep the difficulties for traditional Marxist theory arising from the existence in Latin America of bourgeoisies capable both of acting independently of imperialism (in their own interests) and of cooperating with it (also in their own interests). In effect, Gunder Frank did away with the problem by eliminating the bourgeoisie but retaining capitalism.

Part Two:
The Rise of Third World Capitalism and the Positive Role of Imperialism

To the crude conditions of capitalistic production and the crude class conditions corresponded crude theories. The solution of the social problems, which as yet lay hidden in undeveloped economic conditions, the Utopians attempted to evolve out of the human brain. Society presented nothing but wrongs; to remove these was the task of reason. It was necessary, then, to discover a new and more perfect system of social order and to impose this upon society from without by propaganda, and wherever it was possible, by the example of model experiments. These new social systems were foredoomed as Utopian; the more completely they were worked out in detail, the more they could not avoid drifting off into pure fantasies.

Friedrich Engels SOCIALISM: UTOPIAN AND SCIENTIFIC

6
Colonialism:
Dr Jekyll and Mr Hyde

1. Morality and Historical Analysis

Marxists have been wont to stress imperialism, as opposed to colonialism, as the key concept in understanding international exploitation and domination. This has sometimes led to minimization of the specific role of state-territorial control in the transformation of precapitalist societies and has blurred the important differences between colonial and semi-colonial or neo-colonial conditions. This tendency goes back at least to Lenin, who insisted in his *Imperialism* that Kautsky's limitation of imperialist exploitation to the colonies had to be condemned. Lenin held that imperialism was essentially an economic relationship governed by the necessity for capital export, which was in turn the characteristic feature of the new stage of capitalism. To restrict the phenomenon to the metropolitan-colonial relationship was to restrict the universality, and therefore the theoretical validity, of the new stage of capitalism, making it contingent on particular political circumstances. Moreover, as a theory of colonies, the idea of imperialism became much less compelling as an explanation of the origins of the First World War.

Colonialism, I would argue, must be analysed separately as a specific stage and aspect of imperialism. Moral standpoints and therefore analyses have been affected by the fact that colonialism, as opposed to non-colonial imperialism, involved the explicit use of non-democratic political and military force against the colonial population, together with the much stronger element of deliberate motivation implied by the assumption of governing responsibility. These aspects have strengthened the moral impact of condemnation of imperialism, but have also reinforced proclivities to analyse history in terms of utopian alternatives. The moral condemnation of imperialism in modern democratic terms acquires greater force from imperialism's imposition of regimes and policies without any formal democratic sanction by those directly affected. Even if colonial rule and policies met with genuine social acceptance, as was often the case, they lacked that democratic legitimation of rulers and their policies which, together with the national identity of rulers and ruled, had become touchstones of moral and political acceptability in the West and in that part of the Third World most strongly impregnated with Western values.

This is to be contrasted with the (largely hypothetical) situation in which the sins of imperialism are ascribed to mainly impersonal forces, such as the destructive effects of the world market or of exploitative foreign investment. In this case, much of the moral onus for flouting the ethics of democratic legitimacy in the context of the independent nation-state is removed, whatever may be the concealed, indirect, or irregular use of force to maintain the semi-colonial or neo-colonial status.[1]

Moreover, conditions under which economic relationships were controlled and mediated by the colonial state in accordance with more or less definite policy priorities naturally gave rise to visions of alternative, indigenously controlled state policies that would be equally potent but have different effects. Such visions have been used as tools of historical analysis, a procedure whose illegitimacy lies not in its speculative aspect (for how otherwise than by

1. In the event, the particularly 'blameworthy' aspects of colonialism have been ascribed in the post-colonial era — illogically — to 'imperialism' (neo-colonialism). But this has been possible only because of the illegitimate continued use of the term 'imperialism' during the post-imperialist epoch.

speculation could we make the judgement, for example, that the French revolution brought about more fundamental changes than would otherwise have occurred?[2]), but rather in the assumption that equally effective nation-states would or could have arisen, and would or could have formulated modernizing aims, without colonialism.[3]

It is natural that nationalist mythology should equate 'immoral' with 'inefficient for the nation' (since were it otherwise, if imperial and undemocratic rule were beneficial to the 'nation', this would imply that the 'nation' was unable to achieve what the foreign ruler could). But there is no need for Marxists to accept the implicit proposition that all societies develop at the same pace and can register approximately the same achievements at any given time. Of even less merit is the alternative proposition: that to judge other societies by 'our' standards is ethnocentric (or Eurocentric) and betrays deplorable arrogance and insularity. The first assumption is factually incorrect; the second logically implies the abandonment of any conception of human progress. Nor need Marxists cavil at the thought that progress sometimes requires the use of force. Marx himself, in opposing Proudhon's sentimental approach to historical analysis,[4] quite justifiably argued that the most progressive society in the world (the United States) rested upon slavery; and he and Engels, however reluctantly, opted for Bismarckian industrialization of Germany rather than none at all.

2. Speculation (historical or otherwise) is essential to social science. But it is important to distinguish clearly between the propositions that alternative solutions are theoretically conceivable, that they are practicable, and that they are actually likely to be adopted.
3. This assumption about the desirability and possibility of effective development in the absence of colonialism has been voiced with particular clarity by Thomas Hodgkin ('Where the Paths Began', chapter in Fyfe, ed., p. 11), who regards imperialism as 'essentially retrogressive, destructive of African Civilization (which did not require colonial conquest to develop in interesting and fruitful ways)'.
4. Lichtheim has argued that the gloomy certainty that progress was likely to be painful was precisely the factor that distinguished Marxists from the utopians. G. Lichtheim, *A Short History of Socialism*, p. 318.

Force, especially armed force, was among the most normal features of intercourse between different societies and nations in the nineteenth century, including the societies and nations of Asia and Africa in their relations with one another. Nationalist denunciation of forcible colonization and the subsequent policies of imperialism as particularly immoral must rest on the peculiarly malignant effects of such colonization rather than on the use of force itself. This is especially true since the colonial record, considering the immense numbers of people involved, was remarkably free of widespread brutality. The issue here is not a moral one; rather, it is a question of what historical perspective to adopt in evaluating the contribution, if any, of colonialism to the progress of human unity and the realization of human capacities. The retrospective, partial, and discriminatory application of the moral principles of late liberalism to historical periods antedating the flowering of such 'standpoints of guilt' serves to obscure both the 'subjective' character (quite different from most earlier colonialism) and objective effects of modern colonialism.

In sum, if Marxist analysis is to rid itself of the incubus of nationalist mythology and liberal guilt, it must start from the firm ground of effects rather than motivations.

2. The General Effects of Colonialism

It has been customary for Marxists to analyse the effects of colonialism primarily in terms of 'economic development' rather than, for example, material welfare or cultural transfer. The latter factors have not been completely neglected, but Marxism's concentration has been on the former, for obvious reasons. To divorce economic development, however, from the material welfare of the population or from the intellectual and cultural foundations of the advanced technology, organization, and characteristic psychological traits on which it rests is to register only surface phenomena. Marxists have tended to do just that, to

minimize improvements in material welfare on the one hand
and to ignore (or even denounce) cultural transfer on the
other, focusing on aspects of colonial economic development
considered negative on the basis of an unhistorical ideal
type.

Apart from the fact that in the last analysis the material
welfare of the population is the aim of economic growth,[5]
initiation of a self-sustaining development process is largely
dependent on prior or parallel achievements in material
welfare, especially as regards the health, education, and
strength of the labour force and the provision of a volume of
incentive goods adequate to draw workers into the labour
market. There is therefore no justification for neglect of
welfare improvements, even from the standpoint of
economic development.[6] If we consider three of the elements
of material welfare particularly favourable to long-term
expansion of the productive forces — health, education, and
provision of new types of consumer goods — it will be seen
that the colonial era, far from initiating a reinforcing
process of underdevelopment, launched almost from its
inception a process of development, understood here in
terms of improvements in material welfare that also
constituted conditions for the development of the productive
forces.

The most dramatic, significant, and conclusive proof of
the advantages of Western colonization — which on any
reasonable humanistic standard ought to put all counter-
considerations into the shade — is the improvement in
health brought about by the colonizers. In nearly all cases,
mortality rates were on the decline and population growth in
unprecedented expansion within a few decades of the onset

5. This is a point Marxists are wont to emphasize when stressing the need
for 'inward centred' or 'human-needs oriented' development, but to ignore
when stressing the importance of industrialization (or failure of
industrialization) when the overall structural dynamism of the economy is
at issue.

6. A great many references to research on the effects of malnutrition on
labour productivity are contained in A. Berg, *The Nutrition Factor*, pp. 250-
1, n. 22 and 23. On the role of education in agricultural development, see D.P.
Chaudhri, *Education, Innovations and Agricultural Development*.

of colonial rule. By the late 1950s and early 1960s, for example, when colonial rule ended in Africa, the population had increased several-fold, a major change from its precolonial stagnation. Involved here was not simply the prolongation of life, but also the reduction of untold suffering from cruel ailments previously considered unavoidable natural phenomena, such as smallpox, diphtheria, and tuberculosis.[7]

Moreover (a point not incorporated in conventional measures of welfare), longer life-spans mean greater total consumption, if consumption levels per capita remain unaltered. These changes could not have been brought about to anything like the same extent without the powerful spur of commercialism, colonialism, and the organizational framework that necessarily accompanied them.[8] Further, these rapid improvements themselves stimulated policies of an even more far-reaching character through the regular

7. Kiernan's characteristic ahistorical adoption of impossibly high criteria for assessing the imperial record is interesting: 'Strachey finds some good words to say of British Administration in Egypt also. Cromer, greatest of the pro consuls, made the country at least semi-modern, reduced taxes, abolished the corvée (pages 86-89). If in spite of this the fellah showed few signs of growing prosperity, Strachey blames the over-growth of populations, as in all such cases, an inadequate excuse by itself.' V.G. Kiernan, *Marxism and Imperialism*, London, 1974, p. 88. Kjekshus has recently attempted to argue that: a) East African population was slowly growing throughout the nineteenth century; and b) this growth in population was turned into a decline as a result of the impact of the outside world. But the empirical basis for the first proposition is weak, as is the chain of casuality underlying the second. Besides, the phenomenal rate of population growth from about 1920 onwards is not denied. H. Kjekshus, *Ecology Control and Economic Development in East African History, The Case of Tanganyika 1850-1950.*

8. A comparison of the health and mortality records of the African colonies with those of Ethopia and Liberia, or of the record of Thailand with that of the Asian colonies, at once shows the difference made by colonial rule. The direct link between population change, the frequency and severity of famines, and the colonial impact is well illustrated by the case of Tanganyika: there was an upswing in population growth in the 1920s after the disappearance of general famines 'due to improved communications, the government's growing capacity to intervene, the spread of drought resistant crops, and wider participation in the commercial economy, which provided a certain protection against bad years, even if it was only through labour migration'. J. Iliffe, *A Modern History of Tanganyika*, p. 315.

involvement of government in the economy prior to the Second World War.[9] Indeed, future historians will likely consider the population explosion one of the crucial causes of the unprecedented advance in human welfare achieved during the twentieth century, its effects in stimulating the reorganization of human society (especially backward societies) so as to produce an ever greater volume of output far outweighing any initial per capita stagnation or decline.[10]

Turning to the provision of incentive goods (consumer goods in a variety and at a price and quality unobtainable before colonial rule, the importation of which was made possible by the expansion of income from primary production), we may note that the bulk of imports into Africa during the colonial period was destined for Africans in the low-to-middle income categories. Imports from developed countries into West Africa did *not* displace simple techniques in West African textile production and other crafts. A substantial decline in the *proportion* of goods supplied by domestic industry from the mid nineteenth century to the 1960s was accompanied by an *absolute* rise in the volume of a number of items of traditional production, because the market underwent a massive expansion during this period.[11] Where declines in traditional crafts occurred, it was usually because of alternative employment opportunities, not because of competition from imported products.[12]

Hancock describes the situation in Ghana in 1946 as follows:

'We must remember that the opening up of Africa is a very recent occurrence, and we must admit that the traditional way of life in that continent imposes many hindrances to rapid economic transformation. And yet the transformation

9. Gann and Duignan, pp. 262-3.
10. As we shall see, such deleterious effects of population growth were comparatively rare — and certainly localized.
11. A.G. Hopkins, *An Economic History of West Africa*, pp. 250-1.
12. Marion Johnson, 'Technology, Competition, and African Crafts', in C. Dewy and A. Hopkins, eds., *The Imperial Impact: Studies in the Economic History of Africa and India*.

has in some parts been amazingly rapid. I know an agricultural statistician in the Gold Coast who made it his business during three or four successive years to tabulate the detailed economic facts of ordinary life in a typical village of the cocoa producing country. He examined the village through his statistician's microscope; he set down all the multitudinous facts of land ownership and productivity, purchase and sale, credit and debt, expenditure and charity, diet, clothing and educational attainment. He calculated that the average annual income of a village family, in cash and in kind (the larger half being in cash), amounted to £23 18s. 6d. This may seem a pretty small figure when measured by the money standards of Europe and America; but we have to remember that a family in the Gold Coast can buy all the food it wants for a few pennies a day. Even if we take the money measurement, the Gold Coast farmers are better off than the majority of peasants in Romania and other countries of South Eastern Europe. If we take the welfare measurement, they are immensely better off. We can translate their incomes into terms of plentiful food (although it contains too large a proportion of carbohydrate), adequate and often very beautiful cotton clothing, a fairly wide distribution of useful manufactures such as bicycles and sewing machines, and a sprinkling of luxuries, including tobacco for smokers and sweets for children. To these items we ought to add the public utilities and social services — communications, water supply, schools, hospitals and the like — which are still underdeveloped but nevertheless satisfy the elementary needs of a community advancing along the road of progress. Now let us cast our mind back a brief half century. We shall find it difficult to discover at that time even the faintest glimmer of progress. We shall see instead the dense tropical forest and a sparse population hacking at it in the feckless routine of shifting cultivation: we shall see a primitive economy yielding a primitive livelihood.'[13]

This graphic, impressionistic picture may be supplemen-

13. W.K. Hancock, *Argument of Empire*, pp. 79-80.

ted by noting that Nigerian producers quadrupled the purchasing power of their exported cash crops from the turn of the century to about 1950, so that a market for consumer goods was formed that provided the basis for import-substitution industrialization beginning in the late 1950s.[14] Although British West Africa was particularly well placed to benefit from expansion of colonial cash crops owing to the lack of white settler communities and the fact that production was carried out by independent farmers and not foreign-owned plantations, similar trends were evident throughout Africa, as the import statistics and subsequent growth of import-substitution manufacturing readily testify.[15]

The effects of colonial rule on the supply of consumer goods in India are less clear. Comparison with the time of Akhbar is necessarily even more dependent on the impressions of observers than in the case of Africa, which was colonized much more recently. Griffiths has carefully summarized the evidence concerning sixteenth-century Mughal India, reporting the unanimous verdict of all observers that the poverty of the common people was appalling, while noting that contemporary observers have remarked on the same feature of Indian society today. In his carefully balanced account Griffiths is yet able to note definite improvements in the provision of clothing (especially important for the cold winters of northern India, and all the more significant in illustrating the ultimately beneficial effects of the triumph of Manchester cotton over the hand-loom weavers), in housing in some areas, and certainly in the quantity and quality of household utensils.[16]

14. A.G. Hopkins, *An Economic History of West Africa*, pp. 126 ff.
15. For the case of Tanzania, see J.B. Sender, 'The Development of a Capitalist Agriculture in Tanzania: A Case Study with Detailed Reference to the West Usambaras', unpublished doctoral thesis, University of London, 1975.
16. P.K. Griffiths, *The British Impact on India*, (first published, 1952), London, 1965, pp. 447-478. The beneficial impact of colonial rule on the domestic textile industry in the later period has been hinted at by K.N. Chaudhuri, *India's Economy in the Nineteenth Century*, p. 36: 'The general expansion in India's economy in the 19th century brought about by the

Above all, with the creation of adequate road and rail communications and the establishment of an effective central administration, the virtual elimination of famines after the beginning of the twentieth century at last removed an ancient scourge.[17]

Progress in the establishment and expansion of modern education in the colonial countries has been almost as dramatic as progress in health. Some indication of the enormous progress made is given by Bairoch's comparison of Third World educational achievement with the results scored in the industrialized countries at an analogous stage of their development. According to his calculation, the elementary-school enrolment ratio in Third World countries was about 57 per cent in 1970 (up from 45 per cent in 1960). This figure is approximately the same as that in Europe (excluding Russia) in about 1860, when the percentage of the labour force employed in agriculture was 55-60, as compared with slightly below 70 for the underdeveloped countries today; the proportion of the working population employed in manufacturing industry was about 18-20 per cent, as compared with 10 per cent in the underdeveloped countries today.[18] With regard to secondary and higher education, Third World achievement is superior, at least quantitatively, to that of the industrialized countries at a similar stage of their development: 'in general, levels of attendance achieved by the Third World in 1970 are much higher than those in the industrialized countries at the time when they had attained a similar stage of development. Thus a secondary education

construction of railways and the extension of agriculture, together with the rapid development of the cotton mills in the 1870s and 1880s, might actually have increased the size of the textile industry proportionately from what it had been in pre-British days.'

17. Ibid., chapter XIX. More recently, it has been noted: 'British rule was accompanied by a large growth in population ... This evidence does not fit very easily with theories which postulate a decline from an already "subsistence" standard of living in 1858.' W.J. Macpherson, 'Economic Development in India Under the British Crown, 1858-1947' in A.J. Youngson, *Economic Development in the Long-run*, Unwin, 1972.

18. P. Bairoch, *The Economic Development of the Third World since 1900*, p. 138.

attendance rate of about 20% (the 1970 Third World figure) was only achieved by the developed countries in the decades between 1930 and 1950, i.e. at the moment when their per capita standard of living was about six to eight times as high as that of the currently less developed countries.'[19]

These advances are the more remarkable if it is recalled that before 1900 there was no formal education in Black Africa beyond a scattering of Koranic schools on the fringes of the forest belt,[20] and that Indian education was largely confined to Sanskrit, which bore no relation to the cultural or practical exigencies of overcoming poverty.

The significance of the introduction of Western education goes far beyond the acquisition of skills required to obtain jobs in the modern sector. It is true that the education introduced during the colonial period was marred by many features ill-adapted to the conditions and needs of the Third World: neglect of agricultural, engineering, and technical education in favour of the arts and pure sciences, and 'combination of Arnoldesque muscular Christianity with the feudal traditions of the old universities'.[21] Observing such absurdities, it is only too easy to overlook the more profound effects of Western education in dissolving traditional outlooks in a manner which, however traumatic, could only facilitate individualism, rationality, and a democratic outlook. In Africa, for example, missionary education, with its emphasis on the individual conscience, implicitly constituted an implacable foe of the rule of tribal custom. The link between education, achievement, and status was deeply subversive of the hierarchical features of most precapitalist societies. The association of modern education with societies that combined enormous economic,

19. Ibid., p. 140. The adjusted enrolment ratios for primary and secondary schools in Third World countries have increased substantially since 1970. See World Bank, *World Economic and Social Indicators* (April 1978), Report No. 700/78/02, pp. 40-43.

20. All black African universities, at least until the late 1960s, were products of Western initiative.

21. T. Balogh, 'Oxbridge Rampant', in *The Economics of Poverty*, Weidenfeld, 1955, pp. 98-101.

technological, and military power with parliamentary democracy and individual rights represented a major liberating force in custom-bound societies and an important cultural export, which in the end was used against the colonial power itself. Indeed, the more perspicacious British rulers of India deliberately promoted modern education with a view to strengthening the progressive forces in Indian societies against late British and Indian reaction.[22] It scarcely need be emphasized, moreover, that education was one of the crucial elements in economic progress, encouraging the development of the market and providing the elementary literacy and numeracy without which no modern economy could take root (quite apart from the range of specialized skills that would be required as the economy became more diversified).[23]

Imperialism was the means through which the techniques, culture, and institutions that had evolved in Western Europe over several centuries — the culture of the Renaissance, the Reformation, the Enlightenment, and the Industrial Revolution — sowed their revolutionary seeds in the rest of the world. This culture was in many respects unique, and contributed much of value to humanity. In no case (with the partial exception of Japan) can it be argued that without the impact of the West this cultural transfer, which was inseparable from the transfer of technique, could have been possible at any remotely similar pace. It is often maintained against this view that these results were achieved by great brutality and the traumatic shattering of traditional ways of life; that had Africa and Asia been left to their own devices they would have been able peacefully to acquire whatever the West had to offer, as Japan did; that in any case the actual achievement of the West, especially in terms of industrialization, has been woefully inadequate;

22. Griffiths, chapter XXV. See also Anthony Sampson, *The Seven Sisters, The Great Oil Companies and the World They Made*, pp. 175 and 300
23. In the case of pre-literate societies, the immense technological advance made possible by the ability to keep records should not be forgotten. This point alone should be sufficient to silence those who hold that African development was frustrated by European colonialism.

and that whatever the limited gains of economic modernism, they have been more than counterbalanced by subsequent freezing of the economy into a colonial division of labour and a dynamic of cumulative underdevelopment.

There is, however, no room for equivocation over this matter, over the results of imperialism's forceful incorporation of the bulk of humanity into the modern world. If we say, with Emerson, that, 'imperialism scattered the revolutionary seeds of Western civilization in haphazard fashion over the surface of the globe and started them on the first flowers of their growth,'[24] then as Marxists, products of that civilization who aspire to carry it to new heights, we must accept the view that the epochal imperialist sweep was indeed a titanic step towards human unity (on the basis of the greatest cultural and material achievements so far attained by humanity).

It would, however, be somewhat daunting if this judgement were advanced only by Westerners. If such allegedly world-shaking improvements have taken place, one would think that some positive recognition of the fact would be registered by the beneficiaries. But the imperialist achievement seems greeted only by showers of abuse from these beneficiaries. The appearance, however, is misleading. In the interval between the first constructive impact of imperialism on Africa and Asia and the growth of modern nationalist movements (its second constructive impact), with their necessarily irrational calculus of the effects of imperialism, a generation of educated Africans did enthusiastically welcome the imperialist conquest.[25] Nor was clear-sighted recognition of the positive effects of imperial rule lacking in the older civilization of India.[26]

24. R. Emerson, *From Empire to Nation*, p. 20.
25. Duignan and Gann, *Burden of Empire*, pp. 364-5.
26. A striking example was the protest of the Indian reformer Rammohan Roy against the foundation of a Sanskrit College in Calcutta in the early nineteenth century: 'When this seminary of learning was proposed, we understood that the Government in England had ordered a considerable sum of money to be devoted to the instruction of its Indian subjects. We were filled with sanguine hopes that this sum would be laid out

If the rise of modern nationalism has shifted attitudes, ideologies, and rhetoric in a very different direction, it has nevertheless failed to alter the fundamental effort to assimilate Western culture, values, and technical achievements.[27]

---

in employing European gentlemen of talents and education to instruct the natives of India in mathematics, natural philosophy, chemistry, anatomy and other useful sciences which the natives of Europe have carried to a degree of perfection that has raised them above the inhabitants of other parts of the world. We now find that the Government are establishing a Sanskrit school under Hindoo pundits to impart such knowledge as is already current in India. The pupils will here acquire what was known 2000 years ago, with the addition of vain and empty subtleties since produced by speculative men such as is commonly taught in all parts of India. The Sanskrit language, so difficult that almost a lifetime is necessary for its perfect acquisition, is well known to have been for ages a lamentable check on the diffusion of knowledge; and the learning concealed under this almost impervious veil is far from sufficient to reward the labour of acquiring it. If it had been intended to keep the British nation in ignorance of real knowledge, the Baconian philosophy would not have been allowed to displace the system of school-men which was best calculated to perpetuate ignorance. In the same manner, the Sanskrit system of education would be the best calculated to keep this country in darkness, if such had been the policy of the British legislator. But as the improvement of the native population is the object of the Government, it will consequently promote a more liberal and enlightened system of instruction embracing mathematics, natural philosophy, chemistry and anatomy with other useful sciences which may be accomplished by employing a few gentlemen of talents and learning educated in Europe, and providing a college furnished with the necessary books, instruments and other apparatus.' Cited in Griffiths, pp. 248-9. It is also worth recalling the polemics of Lenin and Plekhanov against Slavophile tendencies, and the fact that the first Marxist nuclei of what was later to become the Russian Social Democratic Labour Party did not hesitate to advocate the path of Westernization. See Lucio Colletti, 'The Question of Stalin', *New Left Review*, 61, 1970.

27. 'The case for identifying the modern West with progress can perhaps rest on this pragmatic ground, that the peoples most affected are themselves making such an identification, even though they often also want to hold onto as much as they can of their traditional culture.' Emerson, *From Empire to Nation*, p. 14. The vigorous protests against the attempts of colonial governments to introduce vocational elements (perceived as an inferior form of education) into school curricula were a clear example of positive, instrumental attitudes to Western culture. An example of such protest is discussed in W.A. Dodd, *Education for Self-Reliance in Tanzania, A Study of its Vocational Aspects,* Centre for Education in Africa, Institute of International Studies, p. 14. In India in the nineteenth century the intelligentsia hailed the new (British) system of education. (Poromesh Acharya, 'Indigenous Vernacular Education in the Pre-British Era: Traditions and Problems', *Economic and Political Weekly*, December 1978.

3. The Development of Underdevelopment

Widespread Marxist criticism of the theoretical basis of André Gunder Frank's thesis of undervelopment co-exists with equally widespread agreement that imperialism has induced a process of developing underdevelopment in the Third World. The limited elements of modern technology and modern capitalist society that have been introduced into the Third World are thus said to prevent the advance of the productive forces. The result is dramatically symbolized, for example, in the contrast between Australia and Canada on the one hand and India and Argentina on the other.[28] An essential element in the establishment of underdevelopment is colonialism (informal in the case of Latin America), which is seen as imposing essential elements of *control* that assure the determination of international economic relationships by the imperialist countries.

In this connection we must draw attention briefly to a problem to which we shall return at greater length: whether an element of conscious control is necessary in initiating the structures of imperial exploitation, especially that aspect centred on the allegedly exploitative international division of labour. One school of thought (e.g. Gunder Frank and many of the Latin American dependency theorists) sees underdevelopment as rooted in the penetration of capitalism as such from the mercantilist period onwards;[29] others see it rooted in the blockage of the initial penetration of

28. Cf. Michael Barrat Brown, *The Economics of Imperialism*, pp. 260-1. Africa is not referred to in this context since its late colonization invalidates comparison.

29. Cf. Immanuel Wallerstein, *The Modern World System: Capitalist Agriculture and the Origins of European World Economy in the 16th Century*. Hopkins notes: 'The political implications of this viewpoint hardly need stressing: if underdevelopment still had a pre-capitalist basis then the orthodox Marxist strategy would be to promote the next historical stage, namely capitalism, by supporting a national bourgeoisie, whereas if capitalism permeated traditional societies as a result of international trade, then history is, in a manner of speaking, one step ahead of itself, and the national bourgeoisie becomes a target rather than an ally.' A.G. Hopkins, 'Clio-Antics: A Horoscope for African Economic History', in C. Fyfe (ed.), *African Studies Since 1945*, p. 45.

capitalism, its failure to continue in the form of a cumulative and progressive development of the productive forces. This failure was at least partially due, this view holds, to specific features of the character of capitalistic expansion in the nineteenth and early twentieth centuries, such as the free trade policy, colonial control, the particular orientation of foreign investment, etc. More generally, it was a result of *policy* rather than impersonal economic forces as such.[30] Policy, of course, may be considered essential in both approaches, but in practice it must play a larger role in the contingent historical approach. Emphasis on the artificial creation of underdevelopment (or less broadly, of a specific polarized Third World-metropolitan international division of labour) is clearly more consistent with the identification of 'distortions' in the pattern of Third World development and provides clearer guidelines to identification of the postwar economic effects of imperialism than the alternative, which sees underdevelopment as the result of the undifferentiated spread of capitalism to precapitalist areas.

On examination of the voluminous literature, the inauguration of 'underdevelopment' proves to be the alleged result of three interwoven processes: 1) the drain of surplus from periphery to centre; 2) the creation of a self-reinforcing international division of labour whose effects are to generate further self-reinforcing structural imbalances in the colonial economy; 3) the conservation of precapitalist modes of production in such a way as to arrest the advance of the productive forces. Let us consider these processes one by one.

The Drain of Surplus

The drain of surplus can be touched upon only briefly at this point. It should be noted, however, that for such a drain to

30. Cf. Barrat Brown, p. 97: 'For this reason, says Marx, the British Industrialist set out to destroy the East India Company and to develop cotton and other primary products in India to exchange for their manufactures. The neo-colonial assumption is that the world division of labour is not artificial at all.'

retard economic development it must be an *absolute drain*,
not simply an unequal 'transaction' that nevertheless leaves
both sides better off than before, or better off than they
would otherwise have been. Anti-imperialist literature has
generally misunderstood this point, yet it is essential for the
thesis that the development of the productive forces has been
blocked, since otherwise there is no reason why an absolute
drain of surplus should result from exploitation and
therefore no reason why exploitation should be inconsistent
with the expansion of the productive forces in the
periphery.[31]

Two pivotal mechanisms of surplus drain are generally
identified: that arising from the flow of profits from foreign
investments in the periphery back to the metropolitan
country, and that originating from allegedly unequal
exchange.[32] The argumentation on foreign investment
generally compares the outflow of profit with the initial
inflow of capital, or the total of the two flows over a selected
period of time; if the outflow exceeds the inflow, an absolute

31. In Marxist theory, exploitation is consistent with, indeed is the
condition for, the advance of productive forces under developed capitalism.
Theorists of underdevelopment have cited the example of the repatriation of
private fortunes to Britain as a major element in the 'drain of wealth' from
Bengal and have stressed the damage caused by private British trade to
Indian merchants and to the population of Bengal in general. However,
Marshall's research has shown: 'When Englishmen sent their fortunes
home they certainly contributed to Bengal's surplus of exports over imports.
But in the present state of knowledge it is not self-evident that this
contribution was on a scale to inflict major damage on the province. British
fortunes were matched by Indian ones, as the opulence of part of the Indian
community in Calcutta clearly showed. Indeed, it seems likely that
opportunities for secure and systematic accumulation of wealth were
greater under the British than they had been under the Nawabs.' P.J.
Marshall, *East Indian Fortunes: The British in Bengal in the Eighteenth
Century*, p. 270.

32. Cf. E. Mandel, *Late Capitalism*, pp. 345 ff. Characteristically, Mandel
produces figures for the relative gain of the imperialist world from foreign
investment and unequal exchange with the Third World (extremely dubious
figures, especially as regards the so-called gain of unequal exchange). He
illogically assumes that there is an absolute deduction from the total
resources of the Third World available before trade and investment
commenced. This is quite apart from the logical weakness in the unequal
exchange thesis even as regards relative gains.

drain is postulated. But since investment is generally value-creating, or profitable, it does not follow that an excess of repatriated profits over the original investment necessarily represents an absolute drain: the value-added will have also increased wages, salaries, and government revenues — a net gain compared to the situation if there had been no foreign investment. Before surplus can be drained it must first be created.[33] In terms of foreign exchange, the value-added retained in the host economy and not reflected in the simplistic calculation of outflows and inflows that so often underpins the evidence for surplus drainage may take the physical form of exports or of goods that compete with imports. Hence, the 'drain' does not even accurately represent the net foreign-exchange position, which may well be positive.

All that need be said about unequal exchange at this point is that there is a logical distinction between absolute and relative gains and losses; it is possible for both partners to gain, although one more than the other.[34] Unless trade is viewed as a zero-sum game in which the gain of one must be at the expense of the other, trade must be assumed to bring absolute gains even to the bargainer who loses relatively. In this case, the drain cannot retard economic development by reducing the reinvestible surplus. It is thus highly unlikely at first glance that either foreign investment or unequal exchange (supposing it to exist) causes any absolute drain of surplus compared to the situation that would pertain in the absence of the investment or trade, although it is possible to maintain that a greater absolute gain for the less developed country would result if the investment and trade were of a different character (for example, domestically financed or differently organized). On the contrary, imperialist trade

33. It may be argued that the alternative of domestic investment would have been superior and that the foreign investment has pre-empted this superior alternative. This is possible, but appears not to have been true in general. It raises the question as to why the domestic investment was not made.

34. Hopkins, p. 40, describes this as a product of conventional theory. It is, however, simply an elementary logical point compatible with any theory.

and investment almost certainly increase the capacity for further development through their augmentation of welfare and the productive forces.

The International Division of Labour

The poorest countries in the world have been those that, until recently, were almost exclusively suppliers of tropical food, minerals, and agricultural raw materials and that had little or no domestic manufacturing industry. This has lent much plausibility to the notion that the international division of labour was and is a significant cause of the relative poverty of the countries producing primary products. This international division of labour and the resultant poverty, it is argued, are consequences of imperialism, in both its impersonal economic effects and its conscious policies. These are, it is further maintained, the crucial characteristics of a primary-producing economy that tend to freeze the sectoral structure of the economy and accentuate the distortion to which this unbalanced structure gives rise, in such a way as to intensify the instances of underdevelopment in the economies concerned. (They are said to be unbalanced in that major sectors exist only to supply external markets, in contrast, supposedly, to the situation of the industrialized economies during their early stages of modern development.)

The validity of this line of argument depends on two questions: whether or not an alternative line of development to primary-product, export-led growth was possible or desirable for the polities concerned;[35] whether or not the export of primary products actually erected serious impediments to diversification, especially along the lines of industrialization. If an alternative line of development were

35. This is itself an ambiguous formulation, since without colonialism 'the polities concerned' would not have existed in most cases. However, the ambiguity is detrimental to the anti-imperialist case, since in general the polities created by imperialism were more conducive to economic development than their predecessors. 'Unite and rule' was a more frequent motto than 'divide and rule'.

impossible or undesirable, then the forcible and rapid integration of the colonial countries into the world market by the imperial countries could not be regarded as economically retrogressive. Even less so if the primary-product export sector ultimately proves capable of creating conditions for diversification.

The evolution of the international division of labour in its twentieth-century version was the product of the eighteenth- and nineteenth-century industrialization of Europe. The process occurred mainly during the second half of the nineteenth century, and the main outlines of the pattern were complete by the beginning of the First World War. In responding to the demand of the industrial economies for ever greater quantities of food, minerals, and agricultural raw materials, the colonies were not deviating artificially from some characteristic natural path of development represented, for example, by Britain during its industrialization. One need not accept neo-classical trade theory to realize that if modern development required foreign exchange — and it did [36] — the easiest and swiftest way for the colonies to obtain it was to cater to the booming European demand for primary products, just as at an earlier period the natural development for Britain was to sell cloth and textiles to a world market hungry for them. World-market conditions, especially towards the end of the nineteenth century, thus made exports of primary commodities the natural growth pole for less developed countries, since for most of them demand exceeded supply, whereas it was just at this period that rising tariff barriers and the earlier industrialization of much of Europe and North America made penetration of the world market for manufactures more difficult.

The economic orientation of the colonies from 1870 to 1914, however natural from the standpoint of the development of

36. A. Maddison, *Economic Growth in Japan and the USSR*, pp. 29-30. For the relationship between imports and economic growth in the postwar period, see H. Chenery and M. Syrquin, *Patterns of Development 1950-1970*, pp. 37 and 89. See also Kuznets, pp. 202-3, and M.R. Agosin, *On the Third World's Narrowing Trade Gap: A Comment*.

the world market, was by no means spontaneous, although it did incorporate important spontaneous elements.[37] The colonial state played a major role in initiating and encouraging cultivation of the crops and minerals required by the home economy, where necessary by coercion. Moreover, since the colonies had to pay their way, *any* exports that could be sold on international markets were supported, not only those considered particularly necessary for the colonial power. Does this imply that the colonies were deliberately ascribed a position in the evolving international division of labour different from and more detrimental than the one they would otherwise have assumed?

The development of the Latin American republics on the one hand and of Japan on the other suggests this answer: if the colonies had been capable of producing for the world market on any considerable scale left to themselves, their natural starting-point would have been the export of primary products. Latin America demonstrates this by example (since there was a choice[38]), Japan by exception. No non-European state evinced such extensively developed commercialism before the Western impact than Japan; none had such a thriving bourgeoisie, such well developed towns, such sophisticated trading and financial institutions, such an efficient and complex state machine. The thesis that Japan shows what could have been done had colonialism not stepped in and aborted indigenous development cannot sustain scrutiny.[39] The case of Japan rather demonstrates

37. For example, the development of exports of groundnut in northern Nigeria and of cocoa in western Nigeria near the beginning of the century. Neither, it should be noted, was the development of the European nations as modern industrial producers a spontaneous process. In fact, the coercive or 'extra-economic' methods used to encourage commodity production in Africa were rather similar to the mechanisms used in the attempt to undermine peasant property in, for instance, early modern France. See R. Brenner, 'The Origins of Capitalist Development: A Critique of Neo-Smithian Marxism', *New Left Review*, July-Aug. 1977, p. 74.

38. We shall see below the extent to which elements of external political control did permit choices as to the pattern of development followed by Latin American states.

39. The view that Japan experienced a particularly rapid or miraculous

that imperialism had to step in if an adequate flow of primary commodities were to be maintained, for the societies concerned were incapable of responding adequately to the demands of Europe without colonial rule.[40]

Nor is it clear why development *initiated* by primary commodity exports should necessarily remain so based. It has not in Australia, Canada, New Zealand, or the United States. Arguments to the effect that primary commodity exports suffer inherent disadvantages as potential 'engines of growth' are generally based on the wide fluctuations of earnings from these products,[41] the allegedly intrinsic lower productivity of agriculture than manufacturing,[42] the more limited backward and forward linkages of agriculture than manufacturing, and the alleged tendency for the terms of trade relative to manufactured goods to decline over time.

These arguments do not hold. There is no inherent tendency for agricultural productivity to be lower than productivity in manufacturing,[43] nor is there any secular tendency for the terms of trade of primary commodities to decline as against manufactures.[44] The relatively greater

transition to industrialization is also very suspect. See Radha Sinha, 'Agricultural Productivity in Meiji Japan', paper presented at International Economic History Congress, Edinburgh, 1978, mimeo.

40. Establishment of internal security and modern transport systems, especially railways, were the *sine qua non* of an adequate flow of exports.

41. Professor Clive Y. Thomas, *Dependence and Transformation, The Economics of the Transition to Socialism*, Monthly Review Press, 1974, p. 54. In fact, the instability of earnings from exports for developing countries has *declined* in the postwar period. Also, recent research stresses that fluctuating demand is not the source of export earnings instability; fluctuations in export earnings tend to originate at home, on the supply side. D. Murray, 'Export Earnings Instability: Price, Quantity, Supply, Demand?', *Economic Development and Cultural Change* (Dec. 1978). In addition, a significant and positive correlation between instability and growth is reported in O. Knudsen and A. Barnes, *Trade Instability and Economic Development: An Empirical Study*, 1976.

42. Barratt Brown, *Essays on Imperialism*, p. 72.

43. T. Balogh, 'Agricultural and Industrial Development', in *The Economics of Poverty*.

44. G.F. Ray, 'The "Real" Price of Primary Products', *National Institute Economic Review*, National Institute of Economic and Social Research, 1977.

linkages of manufacturing to other economic activities must be weighed against the initial historical problem of *which* kind of activity, in the specific historical context of initiating modern economic growth, will actually establish the greater linkages. If a manufacturing industry is initially heavily reliant on imported machinery, spare parts, and even raw materials and fuel, then the overall linkage coefficients will give a misleading index of the industry's stimulating effect on the rest of the economy as compared with expansion of new cash crops. Moreover, the absolute volume of income generated by the new industry may be more important than the linkage ratios, so that the overall effect on the economy of large-scale expansion of cash crops may be much greater than the establishment of some relatively small manufacturing industry, even if all the linkage effects of both industries remain within the domestic economy. This consideration is likely to have been relevant for most underdeveloped economies. The savings in earnings from primary commodities are not unambiguously detrimental to diversification. Indeed, they may be regarded as a potential stimulus to it. This argument has been applied primarily to planning in Third World countries after independence, and it is precisely in the post-independence period that vigorous progress in diversification, especially through industrialization, has shown that whatever obstacles to diversification primary production may have offered, they have not been decisive.[45]

Quite apart from all these considerations, since the technical conditions of production of different primary export commodities vary widely and since any given commodity can be produced by varying processes, it is

45. The specialization of part of the agricultural labour force in the production of a particular primary commodity for the market can itself generate demand for items of consumption to be satisfied by additional production by other sections of the agricultural labour force and by the growth of a domestic manufacturing sector. For evidence on rural-rural linkages and the degree to which increased rural incomes are spent on commodities produced in rural areas, see R.P. King and D. Byerlee, 'Factor Intensities and Locational Linkages of Rural Consumption Patterns in Sierra Leone', *American Journal of Agricultural Economics,* May 1978.

irrelevant to talk about primary commodities and their linkages in aggregate.[46]

The critique of development through primary production, however, may rest not upon the inherent characteristics of primary production as such, but rather on the specific historical circumstances under which it has been attempted. In particular, it has been argued that since primary production was initiated at a stage of the development of Third World countries at which there was little domestic demand for the products (especially minerals and raw materials for industry), a trade dependency on the developed countries resulted that would have been avoided had the economy's domestic resources been orientated primarily towards internal needs.[47] In itself, this would not represent a fatal impediment to diversification, but the very circumstances that caused this 'imbalance'[48] also result in the preponderance of foreign capital, skills, and other inputs that reduce the 'spread' effects which would otherwise have occurred — especially by draining away the surplus for reinvestment. Moreover, the demand of the European countries for Third World primary products, this argument runs, was a major factor in the scramble for formal empire, with all that colonial control implies in further restricting

46. For a detailed analysis of the 'substantial' differences existing between the characteristics and linkages of different staples' see: A.O. Hirschman, *A Generalized Linkage Approach to Development, with Special Reference to Staples, Economic Development and Cultural Change*, 25, 1977, p. 94. At the same time, note that it is not helpful to discuss *industries* and their linkages in aggregate. 'It is certainly illusory to suppose that all industries in the industrial sector have greater forward and backward linkages.' R.B. Sutcliffe, *Industry and Underdevelopment*, p. 84.

47. This point is especially emphasized by Thomas, p. 302.

48. It is an 'imbalance' only if autarky is the criterion of balance. From another perspective, the development of the world market, and specifically the advanced needs of the developed European countries in the late nineteenth century, to a point where Third World countries' primary commodities would find uses never dreamed of domestically and would be required in vaster quantities than their domestic demands — thus creating Thomas's 'imbalance'— ought to be regarded as a major historical bonus, giving the less developed countries advantages not enjoyed by Britain during the first Industrial Revolution.

spill-over effects. Since primary products in Africa and Asia were produced mainly under colonial control, the methods of extraction were quite different from what they would have been under independent regimes, and were in fact harmful to further diversified development. The cheap-labour policies of the foreign mine-owners severely limited the expansion of the market and thus the development of agriculture and secondary industry; and the associated internal training policies limited the extension of new skills. More generally, wherever wage-labour was needed in the colonial economy, a wide range of deliberate policy measures were adopted to ensure an elastic supply at comparatively low wages (labour and poll taxes, forced labour, seizure of land, etc.), all with the effect of restricting market expansion on the broad basis required for growth of manufactures. The element of foreign control was also decisive inasmuch as the market depended on rural producers selling cash crops, for they faced monopsonists in selling their produce and monopolists in purchasing imported goods, which further limited the expansion of the domestic market. In the case of settler colonies, deliberate restrictions on the productive activities of indigenous farmers again limited market expansion. Finally, the colonial state took deliberate measures to confine colonial resources to the production of primary commodities. Infrastructural development was so oriented, and industrialization, whether under the impetus of domestic or foreign capital, was blocked administratively or rendered impossible by free trade in manufactures with the metropolitan country, despite the fact that tariff barriers had been indispensable to every industrial nation (except Britain) in overcoming the handicap of Britain's critical lead and the consequent competition from cheap British manufactures. Such is the indictment.[49]

It can be compounded if Third World societies are treated

49. The colonial economy also often contained a legal framework for monetary policy, central banking, and the holding of foreign exchange reserves that constituted barriers to economic development in a number of countries.

as totalities and account is taken of the social structure that develops around the particular economic pattern based on primary production — one dominated by a small but wealthy elite to whom the major internal gains of commodity trade accrue, and whose consumption patterns are affected by their ties with Western capitalism. This imparts a bias towards imports, and therefore trade deficits, while it simultaneously restricts the growth of the mass consumption market.[50]

Three points may be made about this indictment of an orientation towards primary production *in the context of colonial control* (not as such):

1. It depends on the selective summation of negative aspects of primary-commodity development out of the experience of a wide range of countries over different periods of time; an equally selective summary of positive aspects could be made.

2. The lack of an independent state is critical to the maintenance of many (although not all) of the obstacles to diversification from a basis of primary products.[51]

3. Most of the 'backwash effects' described above do not actually *cause* underdevelopment — or in Myrdal's words, 'the initiation of a cumulative process towards the *impoverishment* of underdeveloped countries'[52] — but merely *limit* the spread effects of development. But these would in any case not have been present to anything like the same extent had there been no colonial control in the first place.

The second and third points taken together imply the

50. This is an amalgam of the view of Samir Amin, *Accumulation on a World Scale*, and Stephen H. Hymer and Steven A. Resnick, 'International Trade and Uneven Development', in *Trade, Balance of Payments and Growth*, J.R. Bhagwati, et al., eds.

51. We shall discuss this point in the context of Latin American informal colonialism.

52. G. Myrdal, *An International Economy*, New York, 1956, p. 95.

possibility that the post-colonial period will experience markedly accelerated advances in diversification as compared with the pre-colonial period, because of: a) the importance of an independent state in facilitating the transformation of a primary-commodity export sector into an engine of growth, and b) the existence of a latent 'spread potential'. This possibility is incompatible with the development of underdevelopment thesis — but the possibility has become an actuality.[53]

Defenders of the distorted structure view, of course, may argue that the new structure is also distorted. But since the new structure is becoming remarkably like that of the developed economies, it is not at all clear in what sense the economies of the less developed countries are becoming ever more underdeveloped. Nor can it be seriously maintained that the development of underdevelopment is confined to the colonial period, since the elements of modernization implanted then have served as the basis of post-independence diversification, even though the transition has not always been continuous.

In sum, the view that the integration of the Third World economies into the world market as suppliers of primary products for the advanced capitalist countries has frozen these countries in a distorted economic and social structure that creates a constant worsening of economic conditions as a result of the cumulative processes thereby initiated cannot

53. In 1960 primary commodities accounted for more than 86 per cent of the value of total exports of the developing countries; exports of manufactures for only about 13 per cent. By 1976 there had been dramatic changes — the share of primary commodities dropped to about 56 per cent, while the share of manufactures rose to about 43 per cent. World Bank, *Commodity Trade and Price Trends,* August 1978, p. 3. Manufactured exports from developing countries have grown with spectacular rapidity since 1960 — at rates of about 15 per cent per annum in real terms up to 1976. World Bank, *Annual Report 1978,* p. 15. In addition, decolonization commonly resulted in a marked diversification of sources of imports and destinations of exports. For a not untypical example of successful geographical diversification of export markets, see the data in M.A. Bienefeld, 'Special Gains from Trade with Socialist Countries: The Case of Tanzania', *World Development,* Vol. 3, No. 5, May 1975, p. 258.

be sustained. The position occupied by the less developed countries in the international division of labour was neither artificial nor less beneficial than the alternatives, given the state of development of the world market, as is shown by the evidence of non-colonial countries like Japan and those of Latin America. Moreover, there is nothing inherent in the economics or technology of primary production that prevents it from acting as a growth stimulus to a more diversified economy. Nor do the characteristics of primary production, in a *colonial context*, create irremovable barriers to diversification. The colonial situation merely restrains or limits factors of diversification that it has itself set in motion.

Preservation of Archaic Modes of Production

The preservation by imperialism of archaic or precapitalist modes of production may be considered a factor tending to rigidify an economy into a primary-commodity structure; or it may be regarded as a tendency that operates even when this structure is crumbling or has already broken down. In either case, this argument holds, it tends to hinder modernization of the economy concerned.[54] Preservation of precapitalist modes of production has most often been conceived as a socio-political process that embraces the entire society, frustrating and stultifying those progressive social forces which, without the intervention of imperialism, would have acted to modernize society. This analytical approach is generally applied to societies considered feudal, where it is supposed that imperialism, consciously allying itself politically and impersonally reinforcing economically the socio-economic structures of feudalism, prevents, or

54. The theoretical literature on 'preservation' is now fairly extensive. The most influential contributions have been those of E. Laclau, 'Feudalism and Capitalism in Latin America', *New Left Review*, No. 67, May-June 1971; C. Meillasoux, 'From Reproduction to Production', *Economy and Society*, Vol. I, No. 1, (Feb. 1972); N. Poulantzas, 'Internationalization of Capitalist Relations and the Nation State', *Economy and Society*, Vol. III, No. 2 (May 1974); Pierre-Philippe Rey, *Les Alliances de Classes*, Paris, 1973.

tends to prevent, the emergence of progressive bourgeois forces.[55]

A narrower sort of conservation may be said to operate with respect to specific modes of production within the overall society. Thus, peasant production may be 'conserved' in one geographical area by strengthening a landlord class, whilst capitalist agriculture is allowed to develop in other regions.[56] Sometimes the conserving forces may be analysed as more or less entirely impersonal, or as an unintended by-product of other policies. This is believed to be the case in Nigeria, where, it is argued, the taxation of the 'peasantry' for the benefit of the 'urban elite' and the multinationals effectively preserved the peasant mode of production and still prevents the generation of a surplus that would permit the development of capitalist agriculture.[57]

These views are anti-Marxist in the literal sense. Marx himself had no doubt that the destructive force of capitalism would far outweigh any conserving tendencies. In itself this is unimportant, but it is a useful intellectual corrective to the underlying leftist assumption that an anti-capitalist approach is necessarily Marxist — especially if we bear in mind that Marx was well aware that colonial powers would sometimes erect barriers (deliberately or otherwise) to the advance of the productive forces.[58] The Marxist position

55. This type of analysis has been widely applied to Latin America; also to China: Harold R. Isaacs, *Tragedy of the Chinese Revolution*, revised edition.

56. The similarity of this formulation (if stripped of its Marxist terminology) to the old concept of a 'dual economy' has been noted by Banaji, who in this context refers to the work of Laclau, Rey, Williams, et al. as exemplifying the neo-populist narodnik currents of 'third world political economy'. J. Banaji, 'Modes of Production in a Materialist Conception of History', mimeo, (n.d.), p. 26.

57. Gavin Williams, 'Colonialism and Capitalism: the Nigerian Base.' A Review Paper presented to the ASAUK Conference, Liverpool, 18 September 1974, p. 15 (mimeo).

58. Cf. Marx's comments on the stupidity of Britain's policies in India even in the general context of its progressive role there. An extremely unconvincing attempt has recently been made to suggest that Marx dramatically altered his views after the 1850s and that towards the end of his life there was little difference between his assessment of the impact of capitalism on precapitalist societies and that of, for instance, Samir Amin.

then, does not deny the possibility of preservation of pre-capitalist modes of production in specific cases; but it regards such cases as transitory, exceptional, or secondary, since the economy and society as a whole will be unable to resist the erosive and disruptive pressures of the capitalist market indefinitely. The process may be compared to a river whose currents and eddies build up barriers of accumulated rubbish to its own progress which are eventually dispersed as the dam itself creates pressures it is unable to contain. Nevertheless, much depends on what is meant by 'transitory'. Analytically, imperialism may set the forces of change in motion and may also, subsequently, erect barriers to these forces. If the barriers are not absolute, imperialism must be accorded the plaudits of the innovator. If the transitory blockage turns out to be of long duration, it must be an open question whether colonial force accelerated modernization.

I have already pointed out that the mere failure to encourage the spread effects of the initial introduction of elements of modern economic life does not in itself sustain the thesis of the development of underdevelopment, which must depend upon definite negative trends as compared with the pre-colonial situation, although examples of such failure generally constitute the bulk of the evidence in support of that thesis. It must be added that often what is seen as a failure of spread effects actually represents the uneven development of capitalism, in which the temporary stagnation of one sector may be the condition for the rapid advance of another.[59] Capitalism penetrates Third World

---

K. Mori, 'Marx and "Undervelopment": His thesis on the "Historical Roles of British Free Trade" Revisited', *Annals of the Institute of Social Science*, No. 19, University of Tokyo, 1978.

59. Uneven development does not mean *unchanging* imbalances. Thus, the stagnating sector will eventually benefit from the advance of the progressive sectors. This was the pattern of Japanese agricultural and industrial development, with heavy agricultural taxation supporting industry but delaying agricultural progress until the advance of industry reached a stage where it was able to provide agriculture with inputs adequate to permit massive gains in labour productivity. Cf. K. Okhawa

societies through a process that combines policy and unplanned expansion. Extraction of resources by nascent capitalist from precapitalist sectors (for example, from petty cash-crop producers in West Africa, where social differentiation has not proceeded very far) may temporarily delay the emergence of capitalist farming; but this in turn may simply serve to ripen the conditions for the growing manufacturing sector to invigorate the capitalist development of agriculture.[60]

We may therefore state two propositions. First, the misapprehension that precapitalist modes of production are being preserved arises from the logical error of assuming that the failure to encourage spread effects is equivalent to the initiation or enforcement of backwash effects. Second, the phases of conservation of backward modes of production in certain sectors are merely necessary conditions for the capitalist development of other sectors, which will in turn react upon the initially retarded sectors. These two propositions will be sufficient to explain most of the apparent cases of reactionary conservation.

The view that imperialism has helped to maintain feudal or semi-feudal systems against the thrust of a rising (and potentially industrializing) bourgeoisie is largely undercut by the almost universal willingness of feudal classes to transform themselves, at least partly, into capitalist industrializers once conditions are ripe.[61] This has been the

---

and H. Rosovsky, 'The Role of Agriculture in Modern Japanese Economic Development', *Economic Development and Cultural Change*, Volume 9, 1960.

60. In East Africa, regions that could have been regarded as classically 'underdeveloped' twenty years ago, merely serving as labour reservoirs for capitalist production units in other areas of the economy, have recently been the focus of a spectacularly rapid expansion of commodity production.

61. It may be judged that the non-ripeness of the conditions for industrialization is itself a function of feudally-based market restrictions, so that we are merely stating a tautology that sidesteps the crucial question of the *initiation* of industrialization. This objection is valid, especially as it concerns conflicts over government economic policy, but only as a short-term conjunctural phenomenon. The secular expansion of the market in Latin American countries ensured that there would be a longer run

case particularly in Latin America.[62] It should further be recalled that in most of Latin America and in the Philippines, Britain and the United States played an important role in overturning Spanish rule. Whatever restrictions may have been imposed on these countries subsequently were considerably less harmful to capitalist development than continued Spanish rule would have been.

Finally, in cases in which a modernizing nascent middle class (whether bourgeois or simply a vanguard of intellectuals) did challenge feudalism (or rurally-based modes of production whose exploiting classes would have had something to lose from the development of industry), this challenge was often a direct response to imperialism, which far from frustrating such a movement already in existence, created one that would otherwise have been very much slower to emerge.[63]

The preservation of peasant or petty-commodity modes of production is generally analysed as the result of deprivation of resources in order to sustain foreign or precapitalist modes of production (foreign firms or feudal landlordism), or even simply to fuel unproductive consumption. I have argued that this is more often an instance of uneven development, but further analysis of this matter must await discussion of the role of foreign enterprise.

convergence of the interests of haciendistas and urban businessmen, as the former invested in urban industry. This explains the non-appearance of the 'progressive middle class' so much anticipated in the 1960s by the liberal and radical intelligentsia. See, for example, the 'Introduction' by Claudio Veliz, in Claudio Veliz, ed., *The Politics of Conformity in Latin America*.

62. Indeed, in Latin America it seems that the classes called feudal would be more appropriately termed *landlord capitalist*. See K. Duncan, I. Rutledge, C. Harding ed., *Land and Labour in Latin America & Essays on the Development of Agrarian Capitalism in the 19th and 20th Centuries*, pp. 12 and 118.

63. China is a good example. See Andrew J. Nathan, 'Imperialism's Effects on China', *Bulletin of Concerned Asian Scholars,* Volume 4, No. 4, December 1972.

7

Dependency Theory as Nationalist Mythology

1. Origins and Aims of Dependency Theory

Dependency theory arose in Latin America in the 1960s in response to the alleged failure both of continental development and of theories attempting to explain it. More specifically, it was a reaction to what was considered the failure of import-substitution industrialization during the immediately preceding period.[1] But the inadequacy of existing theory and the propriety of formulating a new approach were grounded above all in the desire to elaborate adequate policies for national development. Analysis was secondary. In itself this need not have adversely affected analysis, had the theorists either controlled policy or

1. It has sometimes been described as a reaction to the ECLA Model, or the failures of that model. Though this characterization may be correct, it tends to obscure the fact that the ECLA and Dependentista approaches have much in common. Indeed, the latter may be described as the direct descendent of the former. Both allotted responsibility for Latin America's underdevelopment to extreme exposure to the world market (i.e. imperialism), and both accordingly called for inward-centred development. The partial failures of the ECLA approach produced the more nationalistic approach of the Dependentistas, a call for more of the same. Of course, the Dependentistas grossly exaggerated the failures of the import-substitution (ECLA) industrialization model. In particular, quite apart from factual inaccuracies and sheer guesses (in the form of assertions) borne of a wishful desire to see the 'wrong' kind of regime produce the wrong kind of results, much dependency theory attributes to particular conjunctural situations (e.g. reduced consumption, specific balance of payments crises) a structural character allegedly inherent in dependency itself.

represented a class or group realistically capable of doing so;[2] or, for that matter, had they been able to probe the politics of economic policy.[3] But since none of these conditions pertained, the policy orientation rendered analysis prey to nationalist utopias; actuality, potentiality, and desirability became hopelessly confused. The dynamics of Latin American capitalist development were approached on the basis of subjective-moralistic criteria, which not only produced conclusions widely at variance with reality, but even prevented the posing of the relevant questions, whether analytical or practical.

The failure of dependency theory even to pose the most crucial questions about the dynamics of Latin American society is the subject of section 3 of this chapter; in section 2, I shall offer a synthesis of the approach of the Dependentistas as a basis for the critique that follows.

2. Dependency as a General Approach

Dependency may be viewed as the complex of politico-economic relationships that bind the advanced capitalist countries of the 'centre' (the United States, Japan, Western

2. The dependency theorists reflected not the interests of the business or working classes, but the nationalist sentiments of the intellectual (and professional) groups that expanded so rapidly after the war. It is significant that early analyses of obstacles to Latin American economic development generally stressed internal factors (e.g. A.O. Hirschman, 'The Political Economy of Import Substituting in Latin America'), while the role of external economic influences was regarded as positive more often than not. Thus, Argentine Communists welcomed the British economic role in the Argentinian economy in the 1920s (E. Laclau, 'Argentina — Imperialist Strategy and the May Crisis'). ECLA and the Dependentistas mark the growing predominance of nationalist mythology in thinking about Latin America's economic development, with a resulting narrowing of the intellectual imagination and a concentration upon sterile variations on empty formulae.

3. A genuinely Marxist analysis would have required that the analyst take some distance from the immediate practical problems of development. To begin from the standpoint of developmental policy inevitably prejudges answers to crucial analytical questions about the underlying dynamics of the societies concerned, and disorients political practice. Hence the extreme

Europe) and the Latin American countries of the 'periphery' such that the movements and structure of the former decisively determine those of the latter in a fashion somehow detrimental to the economic progress of the Latin American societies. The conceptual problem then arises of what is meant by 'detrimental'. This problem, of course, originates in the nationalist policy orientation of the dependency school itself, with its utopian criteria of 'national development', which have proved able to produce a wide variety of conclusions, depending on the analyst's subjective conception of nationalist development.[4] One effect of this has been a continuing effort — especially on the part of the more perceptive dependency theorists, such as Cardoso and Furtado — to define dependency sufficiently generally to divorce it from specific 'theories of under-development' and to emphasize its character as a 'framework for analysis', or an 'approach'.[5] These attempts to conceptualize dependency in a *general* fashion provide useful material for identifying and thus assessing the assumptions on which the theory is based — and also the hypotheses the theory has ruled out of court.

At the risk of doing violence to particular authorities and of imparting to the dependency school more coherence than it actually possesses, its major contentions may be summarized in six points.

---

degree of confusion among the Dependentistas over what social force is to be the instrument of the desired social change: the national bourgeoisie is ruled out as comprador or non-hegemomic, the working class as incorporated by the multinational corporations, the military and civilian bureaucracy as imperialist collaborators. All that is left is the political mobilization of the marginals (plus, presumably, the intellectuals).

4. It is particularly ironic that the Dependentistas, who make so strong a point of decrying the 'diffusionist' assumption that Latin American societies will modernize in the same fashion as did the European/North American societies in the eighteenth and nineteenth centuries, themselves so often have an idyllic picture of that industrialization as the criterion by which Latin American attempts are judged and found wanting.

5. It may be suspected that the characteristic introspection of the dependency school is also related to a desire to justify its existence as an intellectual current, distinct from the standard anti-imperialist position on the Third World.

1. Dependency is 'the conditioning structure of poverty' (Dos Santos).[6]

2. Poverty is the result of (or is equated with) underdevelopment.

3. 'Development and underdevelopment are partial, interdependent structures of one global system.'[7] The development of the core countries is the consequence of the underdevelopment of the periphery; the underdevelopment of the periphery is the consequence of the development of the core (Dos Santos).

4. In other words, the global system is such that the development of part of the system occurs at the expense of other parts.

5. Underdevelopment is not simply *non-development*, but is a unique type of socio-economic structure brought about by the integration of the society concerned into the sphere of the advanced capitalist countries (Frank).

6. Thus: 'Dependence is a conditioning situation in which the economies of one group of countries are conditioned by the development and expansion of others. A relationship of interdependence between two or more economies or between such economies and the world trading system becomes a dependent relationship when some countries can expand through self-impulsion while others, being in a dependent position, can only expand as a reflection of the expansion of the dominant countries, which may have positive or negative effects on their immediate development.'[8]

6. Cited in P.K. O'Brien, 'A Critique of Latin American Theories of Dependency', chapter in ed. Oxaal et al., *Beyond the Sociology of Development, Economy and Society in Latin America*, London, 1975, p. 24.

7. O'Brien, p. 12. He describes this thesis as the basic hypothesis of the theory of dependency.

8. Dos Santos, cited in O'Brien, p. 12.

The dual theme taken up in the sixth point — namely that the dependent countries lack an autonomous capacity for development (cannot expand through self-impulsion), but can expand only as a consequence of the self-impelled expansion of the core economies — is shared by most Dependentistas.[9] Cardoso stands somewhat apart from other theorists in that while retaining the dependency approach, he imparts a substantially more dynamic emphasis to it. He states explicitly that dependence and a 'structural dynamism of industrialization' are not incompatible but are linked in practice. He characterizes this as 'dependent development' or 'dependent-associated-development'. This dynamic emphasis is related to, and is in part the logical corollary of, a dimension of his approach that argues that dependency is not mechanistically determined by external forces but rather arises when external forces become internalized in the struggles and contradictions of indigenous social forces.[10] He explicitly attacks Frank's

9. Thus, Sunkel and Ray: 'development is a global, structural process of change, and underdeveloped countries are those countries which lack an autonomous capacity for change and growth and are dependent for these on the centre.' (O. Sunkel and P. Ray, *El Subdesarollo Latino-Americano y la Teoria del Desarollo*, Siglo XXI Editores, Mexico, 1970, cited in O'Brien). 'The objectives, intensity, instruments and efficiency of development policy are limited within certain margins of flexibility.' (See O. Sunkel, 'National Development Policy and External Dependence in Latin America.') Or the same two themes adumbrated slightly differently in Furtado: 'we could define the autonomous development process as that in which the ordering of the primary motivating factors would be as follows: technological progress-capital accumulation-structural modification due to demand profile changes. At the opposite extreme we would have the essentially dependent development process in which the sequence is inverted: modifications in the composition of demand-capital accumulation-technical progress.' (C. Furtado, *Obstacles to Development in Latin America*, 1970, page 134.) It should be noted that some of the other propositions of the Dependentistas, for example points 1, 2, and 4, are by no means logically connected to the dual theme of point 6, as we shall see.

10. Kahl summarizes Cardoso's view as follows: 'The new concept of *dependency* is more flexible. It tries to separate analytically the political from the economic forces and suggests that although the modernizing limits are indeed set by the external world, by imperialism, the range of possible responses to a given situation depends upon internal political alliances and creativity. Because the history of each country gives it a

slogan of the 'development of underdevelopment', contrasting it with his own emphasis on the possibilities of a dynamic process of industrialization within dependent situations. As O'Brien points out, however, it is not clear that Frank would deny the *possibility* of such industrialization — only that it could be autonomous (independent). Moreover, since Cardoso himself accepts the underdevelopment concept and conceives of it as the obverse of the development of the core countries and a consequence of their domination of the periphery, it seems that Cardoso's substantive difference of emphasis as regards the dynamic character of Latin American development is not matched by an emancipation from the same theoretical framework.

3. Limiting Assumptions and Some Alternative Hypotheses

O'Brien has posed the question: 'How successful is it (dependency theory) in establishing a framework for analysing the dynamics of Latin American society?' Cardoso has asked: 'Have dependency studies been able to whet the imagination so that discussion is opened on themes and forms of comprehending reality compatible with the contemporary historical process?'[11]

Consideration of the concepts listed above suggests that these questions must be answered in the negative. The dependency approach, while not formally excluding

---

peculiar mix of possible action, the response cannot be predicted by general theory alone and requires careful study of historical trends and the realities of power in each instance. The key to an understanding of these realities is a focus on the internal response to external dependency.' J.A. Kahl, *Modernization, Exploitation and Dependency in Latin America*, 1976, page 136. See also F.H. Cardoso, 'The Consumption of Dependency Theory in the United States', mimeo (1976), pp. 8-11.

11. O'Brien, p. 7; Cardoso, p. 16. It should be noted that not all Dependentistas are interested in this question. They are concerned to inquire why Latin American society has allegedly acquired a number of characteristics they dislike.

alternative answers, has effectively narrowed the intellectual focus of analysis of the dynamics of Latin American society and has foreclosed the posing of critical questions in the name of an irrelevant antithesis between diffusionist (or structural-functionalist) and dependency approaches.[12] Specifically, the following criticisms may be advanced.

1. Dependency theory is static not in the sense that it precludes possibilities of dynamic development, but in the sense that it takes dependency, however defined, as *given*, only its form changing;[13] it conjures away the possibility that dependency may be a declining phenomenon.

2. The centre-periphery paradigm on which the entire theoretical structure rests therefore remains largely unexamined. The shifting geographical distribution of world economic power (in favour of the less developed countries) is simply assumed to unfold under the control of the centre; but even at the most superficial level, the impact of nationalism and the competitive tensions aroused by the growth of Third World manufacturing require empirical investigation of this assumption.

3. Static assumptions about the continuing validity of the centre-periphery paradigm preclude further questions about the forms of reciprocal influence the 'peripheral' economies may exert (or have already exerted) on the core countries as the former become relatively more powerful economically than they were previously.[14]

4. The assumptions implicit in the view that the shifting geographical location of world economic power represents merely an extension of the power of the centre, and the

12. R.H. Chilcote and J.C. Edelstein, *Latin America: The Struggle with Dependency and Beyond*, p. 30.
13. Thus, Cardoso (pp. 8-9) considers the merits of the approach as developed by the original Dependentistas (before vulgarization set in), as the analysis of new forms of dependency.
14. The centre economies may be becoming more 'dependent' on those of the periphery, for markets or raw materials, for example.

further assumption that legal ownership of productive facilities translates directly and immediately into political or even economic power evince the sort of vulgar economic determinism that Cardoso in particular set out to combat. Neither the present nor prospective investments of multinational corporations in Latin America can simply be assumed to command economic or political power.[15] The national state concerned wields considerable bargaining power because of the opportunity cost to the multinational of *not* investing there — a cost that may be high if the market has good expansion prospects. Existent investments may be hostages to fortune more than bargaining counters from the standpoint of the multinationals. A strong state may increasingly become capable of integrating multinational investments into its national priorities.

5. The Dependentista approach incorrectly assumes that imperialism is a monolithic structure. This empirically and historically incorrect contention enables dependency theorists, for example, to minimize the widening range of options open to Latin American societies and strengthens the deterministic-economistic tendency to translate economic ownership (of production facilities) into economic or political power.[16]

6. Dependency theorists generally equate imperialism with the world market. They thus exclude by definition the possibility of any non-dependent capitalist Third World progress. This makes it impossible to distinguish between historical stages of the relationships between Third World and advanced capitalist countries, reducing a real historical

15, The ITT-Chile incident was probably a final outburst, distinct in principle from commercial bribery (Lockheed style) and politically marginal to the downfall of the Allende regime, which seemed determined not only to make the maximum number of enemies but also, having done so, to expose itself to them as ostentatiously as possible.

16. For example, the relocation and restructuring of Latin American manufacturing industry is stated to take place 'under the control of the multinationals', which are thus presumed to act as a *group*.

process to a lifeless abstraction. In particular, the adaptation of an economy to the world market and to subsequent changes in the world market cannot be equated with subordination to imperialism, unless this term is rendered meaningless and the important distinction between the differing ways in which, for instance, Nigeria and Pakistan have adapted to the world market is obliterated.

7. The characterization of dependency as a 'conditioning situation' (Dos Santos) is meaningless as it stands, since *all* phases of the development of any society in the modern period are conditioned by external areas in various ways (and conditioning operates both ways). The formulation can have meaning only if it specifies the mechanism or effects (or direction of effects) of the conditioning, or both. Otherwise the definition becomes either tautological or says simply that some economies have a more powerful effect on other economies than these do on them.[17] Dos Santos's definition qualifies as both tautology and truism. His second sentence (intended to impart some substance to the meaningless first sentence about 'conditioning') states that 'a relationship of interdependence between two or more economies and the world trading system becomes a dependent relationship when some countries can expand through self-impulsion while others, *being in a dependent position,* can only expand as a reflection of the expansion of the dominant countries *which may have positive or negative effects on their immediate development*' (emphasis added). The first emphasized phrase leaves the definition of dependency tautological, while the second leaves open the possibility that dependency may have beneficial effects from the standpoint of the advance of the productive forces (or even of 'national development'!) Indeed, the possibility that

17. This is the sense in which I use the term 'dependency' when not characterizing the approach of others. I am aware, however, that this definition does not correspond to popular usage, and especially to the emotive usage of those who employ it politically.

dependency may be the best situation for the development of the productive forces is implicit in the assertion that some economies 'can *only* expand as a reflection of the dominant countries'.[18]

8. Moreover, if dependency may accelerate the development of the productive forces, then the possibility more strongly suggests itself that a correspondingly wider range of economic policy options may be available in the future as a result of an initial period of 'dependency' (see point 5).

9. The peripheral economy, moreover, precisely as a result of its relationship with the core economies, may gradually develop an increased capacity for self-impulsion (e.g. the industrialization of São Paulo as a result of the coffee boom).

10. The expansion of the peripheral economies in response to impetus from the centre cannot be automatic, nor identical in all countries. The capacity for response will vary, and this variation will illustrate the role of policy *choices* in determining actual development. Indeed, foreign influence and domestic social forces may complement each other in determining the responsive capacity. It may well be that the greater the previous experience of imperialist penetration, the greater the subsequent ability to respond to new demands from the world market.

11. Dependency theory assumes: a) that there is a latent, suppressed historical alternative to the development that actually took place; b) that the failure of this alternative to

18. Cf. Kahl's summary of part of Cardoso's analysis, which suggests the same positive evaluation of dependency: 'There was another type of development in some countries, namely "the enclave" or direct investment by foreign powers in certain areas of production in which the local elite seemed unable to generate either the capital or the technology adequate to the task' (Kahl, p. 160). It should be noted, however, that Cardoso does not appear to suggest (except by accident) that dependency may be the *best* situation for peripheral development — only that it is *compatible* with *some* development. He appears to believe, however, that such development is inferior to autonomous development.

materialize was the result primarily of external *imposition* — even if mediated through internal social forces — and not of the *choice* of the internal directing groups; c) that the latent (suppressed) alternative would have been more autonomous and therefore would have achieved more rapid development. Without such assumptions, the dependency theory amounts to no more than the assertion that the modern development of Latin American economies was influenced by the impersonal forces of the world market.

But these unstated premises of dependency theory require empirical grounding. In particular, it is certainly insufficient simply to assume that indigenous elites whose material interests are bound up with external trade or foreign investment in the domestic economy are essentially the local embodiment of world-market forces by virtue of this relationship.[19] Their initial controlling position may have been the *cause* of their command over the material gains of external connection. More important, the ruling elite's dominant position cannot originate solely from external sources, since there must obviously be an internal dimension to trade and foreign investment. If their dominance in the society concerned results from their control of trade, which makes them wealthy, then this domination cannot be considered externally imposed unless some additional political element injected by the trading partners is specified. All this implies that the historical course of development of the Latin American economies may have been the result of choice and not of domination. Further, it cannot be taken for granted that social forces capable of embodying the allegedly suppressed alternative actually exist. Even more important, it cannot be assumed a priori — and it is justified neither by economic theory nor by historical experience (nor by mechanical or biological analogy, for those who favour such procedures) — that autonomous development is always more rapid, or even

19. Bodenheimir classifies local elites in enclave economies as the political agents of foreign firms. May it not be equally realistic to regard the foreign firm as the economic partner of the local elites?

more 'balanced', than dependent development.[20]

12. The superiority of the 'autonomous' path is often assumed on the view that 'dependent' development restricts freedom of choice by closing other options. But *any* path of development necessarily forecloses other options or combinations of options; this is as true of 'autonomous' as of world-market oriented development. The term 'autonomous' can be quite misleading. An 'inward-centred' path may indeed offer indigenous rulers more policy options in numerical terms. But at the same time, retardation of the development of the economy through the restriction of the impact of dynamic external forces may reduce the absolute range of choices available to the society concerned, quite apart from the possibility that a more rapidly expanded economy, even if brought into being by dependent policies, may eventually create both the social forces and economic conditions for a much more soundly based policy of greater domestic control. Sunkel's statement[21] that in a dependency situation 'the objectives, intensity, instruments and efficiency of development policy are limited within certain margins of flexibility' well illustrates the odd assumption that any development policy can be found that is *not* limited within certain margins of flexibility. This meaningless formulation could be made meaningful only by specifying the margins of flexibility. To do this, however, presents considerable difficulty, since the more concrete the formulation (or the more meaningful, in this case), the more easily it can be empirically refuted when rapid economic change takes place. For example, the formulation that alleged that it is impossible to move beyond import-substitution industrialization based on luxury consumer goods has turned out to be

20. Thus nationalist economic policies may retard capitalist development by creating excessive obstacles and restrictions on direct foreign private investment, or by mobilizing populist sentiment on the basis of economic welfare policies destructive of long-term accumulation (Sri Lanka, Chile). Autonomous decision-making does not mean decision-making in a vacuum.
21. Cited in O'Brien, p. 12.

decisively contradicted by the readily observable speed and nature of the industrialization process in the countries concerned.

13. It is the normative, a-historical approach of the Dependentistas that underlies their assumption that alternative 'paths of development' actually existed and were suppressed by external imposition. This assumption in turn induces an ineluctable theoretical reliance on the concept of 'underdevelopment', hardly ever defined. Dependency theorists vigorously deny that underdevelopment is identical to 'non-development' and assert equally vigorously that it is the obverse of development in the imperialist countries. All we are ever offered by way of definition or characterization is a description that generally amounts to a catalogue of the evils of large numbers of people living longer. The joint assertion that underdevelopment is not non-development and that underdevelopment is the Siamese-twin of development in the centre, combined with the failure to define 'underdevelopment', forges a conceptual construction that: a) excludes by definition the possibility that the less developed countries have been becoming progressively more developed, in terms both of the expansion of the productive forces and of material welfare, as a result of their rising integration into the world market, partially because of imperialism; b) affords an empty concept into which any subjective-normative criteria may be fitted so as to expound an apparent historical alternative, or even more important, a *better* alternative.[22] There is no reason to abandon the view that underdevelopment is *non*-development, measured in terms of poverty relative to the advanced capitalist countries. The substitution of some other concept of underdevelopment, structurally rooted and therefore resistant to change, has served only to divert

22. The Dependentistas are not concerned solely, or even mainly, to postulate the historical actuality of an alternative, but rather of a better alternative. The former can readily be granted, at least if one is not a determinist.

attention from the dynamic elements of change in the Third World societies and to fuel nationalist mythology.[23]

It may be added that the notion of 'the development of underdevelopment' is even less definable than that of underdevelopment itself, even more difficult to substantiate without resorting ever more crudely to normative-utopian criteria.[24]

4. Structural Changes: Relations Between Poor and Rich Countries

It will now be argued that all the normal indicators of 'dependence' point to *increasingly* non-subordinate economic relations between poor and rich countries as regards trade diversification (geographically or by commodities), control of foreign investment, structural change (in both inter-sectoral and intra-sectoral terms), and balance of payments accounts. Technological dependence remains, but in increasingly competitive conditions this should be viewed dynamically as a necessary, if not sufficient, condition for greater 'independence'. The distribution of world economic power is becoming less concentrated and more dispersed, and the countries of Asia, Africa, and Latin America are playing ever more independent roles, both economically and politically.

Political independence must be counted among the major achievements of the countries of the Third World. Paradoxically, failure to recognize the magnitude of this achievement — a failure symbolized by the popularity of

23. It has also hampered understanding by discouraging the necessary dissolution of aggregate analysis of Third World countries and the recognition of their differences.

24. The subjective-normative character of the redefined term 'underdevelopment' is most clearly illustrated by one alleged dimension of underdevelopment — 'marginalization' — which, both economically and politically, presumes a totally idealized picture of what was allegedly the case previously. Here again definitions are difficult to come by.

'neo-colonialist' and 'dependence' theories — has itself fostered a psychological slavery to the past, characterized by international beggary, moral hypocrisy, and the use of foreign scapegoats to excuse domestic failures. Moreover, the effect of such theories on the working-class and socialist movement has been to subordinate them to ideologies of nationalist, anti-imperialist unity, to prevent their independent political development, and to induce them to bow to undemocratic regimes. The doctrines of dependence and neo-colonialism have also had detrimental effects on economic policy; these, however, would have been far more serious had the governments prominent in denouncing foreign economic contacts really believed what they were saying and acted accordingly.

Does experience corroborate the neo-colonial thesis that political independence has meant only marginal changes in the economic ties between ex-colonies and their former masters and that whatever more significant changes have occurred have merely altered the form of dependence?

By whatever standard it may be judged, the view that economic relations between rich and poor countries have changed only marginally since independence must be rejected.[25] The case for dependence must therefore rest on the claim that a new type, or 'form', of dependent relationship has taken root. The ex-colonies have, for example, significantly diversified their market outlets and sources of supply in a remarkably short time,[26] thus reducing

25. Most of the points that follow are relevant to the Latin American countries, although they achieved independence much earlier, as is obviously reflected in most of the indicators of structural change and welfare. But the international economic and political changes since the Second World War, including rising nationalism and mass social pressures for change, have produced similar developments in Asia and Africa. On the basis of cross-sectional estimates, Kleiman concludes that 'the effects of decolonization were quite rapid: the metropolitan shares in trade in countries independent for four to six years were about one-third lower than in the colonies. And in those independent for some two decades, they amounted to about one-quarter of their colonial level. The indices suggest that the metropolitan share declines exponentially, at an annual rate of nearly 8% in exports and 6.5% in imports'.

26. On the basis of time-series estimates, the annual rate of decline of the

monopolistic and monopsonistic market factors acting to their disadvantage. To a substantial degree they have diversified their exports into manufactured goods, which by 1970 accounted for more than 25 per cent of the value of their exports. They have exercised mounting control over foreign-owned or -controlled economic activity within their borders, including rather widespread nationalization,[27] especially but not exclusively of resource-based foreign-owned enterprises.[28] Among the more positive effects of this control have been improved division of rent (gross profits, interest charges, royalties, and licence fees) especially from resource-based industries,[29] by taxation and other means; an already

metropolitan share of ex-colonies' trade tends to be somewhat less than the cross-section estimates, but still substantial: about 5-5.5% for exports and 3% for imports. E. Kleiman, 'Trade and the Decline of Colonialism'. Note that more than one-third of the manufactured exports of developing countries in 1970 were sold to other developing countries. A.H. Amsden, 'Trade in Manufactures between Developing Countries'.

27. Or reservation of specific areas of economic activity for local enterprise, for example in Ghana and Nigeria.

28. Examples are so numerous that it would be tedious to cite them. For a general survey see M.L. Williams, *The Extent and Significance of the Nationalizations of Foreign Owned Assets in Developing Countries*, Oxford Economic Papers (July 1975). Where nationalization, especially of resource-based industries, has not taken place, this is generally not a reflection of 'dependence', but of the rational calculation of a government with the power to nationalize that it has more to gain by refraining. Of course, rational calculations can be mistaken. But that is different from irrationally based decisions.

29. For example, the LDCs raised their share of profits on crude oil from 10-15% in the 1920s to about 85% in the early 1970s (*before* the OPEC price increase of 1973, which represented a vast gain to the oil-exporting countries mainly at the expense of the consumers rather than the companies). UNCTAD *Restrictive Business Practices: The Operations of United States Enterprise in Developing Countries: Their Role in Trade and Development*, by Raymond Vernon, UN, New York, 1972, p. 11. Similarly for copper, the second most important field for US foreign resource investment. In Chile, taxes paid by the large copper companies increased from well below 10% of the value of the product in the 1920s to about 30% in 1964. Taxes imposed on the Zambian copper industry in 1965 have significantly reduced the net outflow of factor payments, and by the late 1960s domestic factor payments were about 80% of the international value of the product. (R. Mikesell, ed., *Foreign Investment in the Petroleum and Mineral Industries*, p. 7 and UN, *World Economic Survey 1969-70: The Developing Countries in the 1960s: the Problem of Appraising Progress*, pp. 14-15.) The growing success of the

substantial and steadily rising training of indigenous personnel; a constant increase in the local content of non-labour (as well as labour) inputs, which is rapidly reducing 'enclave' features of foreign-owned or -controlled manufacturing enterprises,[30] a process that has gone quite far in Latin America (Table 5); the spread of shareholding and investment in manufacturing enterprises in countries previously inexperienced in these activities;[31] the expansion of exports of manufactures;[32] and the transfer of modern

Indian government in eroding the power of the foreign petroleum companies in the 1950s and 1960s has been documented by R. Vedavalli: 'The situation now, unlike that in the fifties, is that the government knows how the oil industry works and that the oil companies have sensed the improved bargaining strength of the government over two decades.' (*Private Foreign Investment and Economic Development. A Case Study of Petroleum in India*, p. 185.) Summing up the findings of several case studies of individual resource industries in a number of countries (petroleum in Argentina, Venezuela, Saudi Arabia, and Iran, sulphur in Mexico, iron ore in Venezuela and Brazil, copper in Chile, and manganese in Brazil), Mikesell concludes that, for most of the studies, retained value — i.e. the direct contribution of the foreign companies to the host country, tax payments and local expenditures for goods and services, or net foreign-exchange contributions — has been about 60-70% of export value of the product in recent years, with 50-75% of this usually in various forms of payments to the host governments (p. 428). This represents a very remarkable change since the early days, which demonstrates the extraordinary lack of perspective and empirical grounding of the dependency thesis.

30. Enclave characteristics refer mainly to the lack of backward linkages in the local economy, to minimal multiplier-accelerator effects, and to small or even negative external economies (e.g. the diffusion of skills and stimulus to new methods by example). For some evidence of the degree to which the petroleum industry created a pool of trained labour that benefited the public sector in India, see Vedavalli, pp. 179-180.

31. Nigeria and Ghana, for example. The mobilization of local capital by foreign-owned or -controlled enterprises is not necessarily, or even probably, a diversion of resources from local enterprise, since what is involved is often the mobilization of *latent* savings that would otherwise have remained unused. This is an aspect of the interdependence of savings and investment decisions, and is in principle distinct from direct backward and forward linkages.

32. In retrospect, it can be seen that whatever the wastes involved in the process of import substitution in many countries, it has nevertheless served as preparation for the expansion of export manufacturing, notably in Brazil, but also elsewhere. The significance of this expansion cannot be dismissed on the grounds that the multinational corporations dominate the

174

technology. Many, even most, of these achievements are largely the result of the operation of economic processes per se, but it is important to note that all have been strengthened and their advance accelerated by deliberate policy.

Table 5

Payments of US-Controlled Manufacturing Subsidiaries in Latin America, 1957

Payments	Amount (millions of $)	Percentage of Total Sales
Local Payments,[1] of which	1,868	81.7
Materials,[2] supplies, services	1,212	53.0
Wages and Salaries	354	15.5
Income Taxes	149	6.5
Other Local Payments	153	6.7
Foreign Payments, of which	308	13.5
Materials and Services	246	10.8
Remitted Profits	62	2.7

1. The sum of local payments and foreign payments is less than total sales because of the exclusion of retained earnings and depreciation from payments.
2. Local payments for materials are not invariably payments for locally produced materials. Nevertheless, as Vernon notes, the figures are suggestive of heavy involvement of these enterprises in the local economies.

Source: Department of Commerce censuses and Council for Latin America Inc., *The Effects of United States and other Foreign Investment in Latin America*, New York, 1970, cited in Vernon, p. 14.

National control of foreign enterprise has been most important in increasing rent share for resource-based enterprises and in widening linkages of foreign manufacturing enterprises with the rest of the economy. But there has

production of manufactured goods for export in LCDs, since the multinationals share in these exports is currently only on the order of 15 % In the case of Latin America, the share of majority-owned US affiliates in total exports has clearly been *declining* since the mid-1960s. See D. Nayyar, 'Transnational Corporations and Manufactured Exports From Poor Countries', pp. 78 and 65.

also been considerable progress in improving the linkages forward and backward of the resource-based enterprises; processing of minerals and the development of refineries and petroleum-based industries have become increasingly widespread.

The lack of any significant trend towards a reduction in profit shares of expatriate manufacturing enterprise is the result of a rational desire to obtain the benefits of advanced technology and organization. It reflects the fact that the governments of less developed countries (LDCs) are realistic enough not to take seriously the ridiculous notion that because the outflow of profits and dividends exceeds the original investment, the host country has lost.[33] In any case, since the secular trend is towards stiffening competition of manufacturing multinationals in LDCs,[34] the problems of monopoly rent encountered with resource-based enterprises in the past[35] are largely absent with regard to manufacturing.[36] Furthermore, since total GNP (as distinct from GNP per capita) in the LDCs is increasing considerably faster than in the DMEs, the importance of the former as markets will rise, and forward-looking multinational manufacturers will be prepared to accept various initial risks, inconveniences, and even losses in order to establish a stake in the future.[37] For

33. If the outflow of rent, interest, and profits did not exceed the original investment, resources of both the host country and the investing firm would have been wasted and further investment prejudiced.

34. UN, *Economic Survey of Latin America 1970*, New York, 1972, Part Two. Special Studies, Chapter 1, 'The Expansion of International Enterprises and Their Influence on Development in Latin America', pp. 30-34.

35. Internationally, oligopolistic concentration and restrictions on competition were and are much more significant in fuel and minerals than in manufacturing enterprises.

36. Although the problem also exists for manufacturing in small economies with highly protected domestic markets.

37. For comparative figures on rates of growth of GNP see page 196. The importance of LDC markets for manufactures is illustrated by the fact that in 1978 about 28% of the total of manufactured goods exported from developed countries were going to LDCs. (World Bank, *Annual Report 1978*). Recent estimates have projected a doubling of the share of developing countries in total world GDP by the end of the century. (Leontieff, et al., p. 32.)

this reason alone, most of the negative effects of rising LDC-control of foreign enterprise (resulting from nationalistic excesses or primitive economic policies and measures tending to reduce the flow of foreign private investment) will have only a relatively minor impact; the *net* effect of the increasing ability of LDCs to control foreign enterprise in their territories is likely to be distinctly favourable in the main.

It is implicit in this discussion that private foreign investment in the LDCs is economically beneficial irrespective of measures of government control. This should come as no surprise to Marxists — Lenin attempted to attract foreign investment in the early years of the Soviet republic, Vietnam is currently welcoming foreign investment, and it is an elementary principle of Marxism that under capitalism exploitation presupposes the advance of the productive forces. To the extent that political independence is real, private foreign investment must normally be regarded not as a cause of dependence but rather as a means of fortification and diversification of the economies of the host countries. It thereby reduces 'dependence', in the long run.

Substantial trade and investment relationships with the advanced capitalist countries are widely held to augment dependence in the LDCs,[38] most generally by preventing such structural change as a truly independent economy requires and by causing constant balance of payments deficits and mountainous debt.

That the trade and investment relationships of developed to underdeveloped countries inherently tend to cause chronic balance of payments and debt problems for the latter (especially if they aim for rapid growth) is incorrect in

38. Aid is frequently cited as another major device for augmenting dependence. Cf. Teresa Hayter, *Aid as Imperialism*, or Susan George, *How the Other Half Dies. The Real Reasons for World Hunger*, especially chapter 8. But since the real value of aid has not been rising significantly and has declined substantially as a proportion of the national income of donors (OECD, *Development Co-operation: 1978 Review,* Paris, November 1978), opponents of dependence may sleep a little more peacefully.

principle;[39] in practice it has been frequently disproven,[40] and the recurrent payments problems of many countries can be shown to be due to specific (incorrect) policies rather than inherent tendencies. It is now widely recognized that the trade policies pursued by many LDCs were not only not dictated by intrinsic features of their relationship with the developed countries, but were in some respects harmful both to the interests of the advanced countries and to themselves — particularly policies whose effect was to reduce potential production and/or raise the relative prices of some primary products for various countries.[41] The neglect of agricultural production for export was in many cases partly the result of the mistaken belief that there has been a secular trend towards a downward movement in the terms of trade for primary relative to manufactured products.[42] The rapid global development of manufactured exports by the Third

39. Cf. I.M.D. Little, 'Economic Relations With the Third World: Old Myths and New Prospects', *Scottish Journal of Political Economy*, November 1975, pp. 227-8. The two-gap model, which provides a theoretical basis for this view, amounts to saying that if the state concerned is not prepared to enact the necessary policies to ensure appropriate exchange rates, relative costs of specific exports and import-competing goods, money income flows and mobility of resources, then rapid development means a foreign-exchange gap. This is undoubtedly true, but it does not follow that rapid development *must* mean a foreign-exchange gap. When used as a justification for aid, the two-gap model implies the possibility that the aid will be obtained at the cost of the more fundamental policy and structural changes. This is not to say that aid is necessarily harmful.

40. For example, Nigeria, the Gold Coast, Malaya, and many others at various periods.

41. Low producer prices (compared to costs and the price levels of producer purchases) for palm products in Nigeria and for cocoa in Ghana and initial neglect of sugar in Cuba after the revolution are striking examples of such harmful policies.

42. This view has been refuted time and again, but a mighty edifice of vested interest stands behind it, including, in a sense, the entire personnel of UNCTAD. For some of the latest refutations, see Bairoch, chapter 6, and G.F. Ray, 'The "Real" Price of Primary Commodities', *National Institute Economic Review* (1977). Sri Lanka in the 1970s provides an excellent example both of the neglect of agricultural exports and of the widespread acceptance within planning circles of the theories of declining terms of trade. The result was that by 1977, while real tea prices were as high as at any time since independence, output was 10 per cent lower than in 1972, and the persistent failure to invest was resulting in the lowest yields since 1962.

World (albeit relatively highly concentrated in a few countries), together with the bias against such efforts until recently, strongly suggest an unrealized potential that has been stunted by policy. Similar remarks apply to the compounding of payments problems by rising food imports. Here again policy has played a crucial role in the related problems of resource allocation and incentives to producers.

In spite of these policy mistakes, now widely recognized, the payments performance of the LDCs as a whole improved during the 1960s, the fastest decade of growth for the LDCs in this century. Taken as a whole, the real purchasing power of their exports rose at the same rate as their real GDP— 5.5 per cent per annum[43] (with approximately stable terms of trade); exports rose more rapidly than imports in the 1960s, unlike in the 1950s.[44] The result was that the trade balance, payments balance, and reserves improved, especially in the second half of the 1960s.[45] These favourable trends have continued into the 1970s.[46]

The quadrupling of oil prices in less than a year after late 1973 has of course improved the payments position of the LDCs as a statistical aggregate. It is therefore commonly argued that the petroleum-exporting countries should be treated as a separate group, their success effectively ignored in assessing the trade, payment performance, prospects, and

43. Little, p. 223. The performance was even more impressive in the 1970s; the annual average increase in the purchasing power of developing-country exports between 1971 and 1976 was 12 per cent. (UN, *World Economic Survey*, p. 6).
44. In the 1960s the value of exports rose 7.2% per annum, the value of imports 6.4%. In the 1950s the corresponding figures had been 2.9% for exports and 4.1% for imports. UNCTAD, *Handbook of Trade and Development Statistics*, Geneva, 1972, pp. 22 and 26.
45. Although the Third World still had an overall visible trade deficit in 1970, it had been declining. IMF, *1971 Annual Report*, p. 20 and Table 5.1 of UNCTAD 1972 *Handbook*, p. 22. Balance of payments figures are given in IMF, *Annual Report 1970,* Washington DC,p. 105; IMF,*Annual Report 1971*, p. 71. Figures for reserves are given in UN, *Statistical Yearbook 1972*, New York, 1973, p. 40.
46. UNCTAD, *Handbook*, Supplement 1977, New York, 1978. Foreign exchange reserves of LDCs represented 3.8 months of imports in 1960; by 1976 their reserves were equivalent to 6.1 months of imports.

growth rates of the LDCs. But this procedure is illogical for those who accept the thesis of growing polarization. It amounts to claiming that the LDCs are all doing badly except for those that are doing well. For those who do not accept the thesis of growing polarization, the successes of the oil producers signify merely a dramatic demonstration of the rapidly disintegrating and inherently transitory validity of the polarization perspective. In any case, the improvement for the LDCs, as a global aggregate, of trade, payments, and reserves was already quite marked before the increase in oil prices. And the oil-price increase benefited the inhabitants not only of a handful of desert sheikhdoms with tiny populations, but of states whose total population in 1978 amounted to more than 250 million. In what sense is it valid to detach Indonesia and Nigeria from other LDCs and put them in a special, presumably 'privileged' group? If typological distinctions are to be made within the less developed world, far more significant criteria are available than membership of OPEC.

Nor can the dependency thesis be sustained by reference to an alleged new type of dependence based on the technological superiority of the West[47] or on a new international division of labour enabling the Western multinationals to exploit the cheap labour of the LDCs for assembly industries or the manufacture of components. Third World exports of manufactures may indeed primarily reflect the location by multinationals of productive units in LDCs in order to avoid rising domestic labour costs; but if so, the dependence is two-way — it is interdependence.[48]

47. As attempted by Cardoso, for example, or by Sanjaya Lall, 'Multinationals and Development: A New Look', National Westminster Bank, *Quarterly Review*, February 1975.
48. In any case, the empirical evidence is now quite clear that industries that start off as assembly industries or simply component manufactures tend, before long, to develop further stages in the manufacture of the final article, as well as developing strong backward linkages to other industries, e.g. in Taiwan and South Korea. In the period 1963 to 1976 there was a substantial diversification in the pattern of manufactured exports from LDCs; the share of semi-manufactures in total manufactured exports declined from 60% to 35%, while the share of engineering products rose from

Dependence on Western technology flows logically from a perfectly sensible desire to make use of that technology, and the amazing achievements of some of the LDCs in the twentieth century would have been inconceivable without this technological transfer. Any LDC, of course, can terminate its dependence on Western technology by doing without it. But a moment's contemplation of the implications — in terms of massively higher disease rates alone, for example[49] — is sufficient to illustrate the distorted outlook of the many development economists who refer to the advanced technology of the industrialized countries almost as if it were a disaster for the Third World. Here as elsewhere, dependence is two-way. Technology can be purchased, and competition among sellers ensures that the only serious limitations on its availability to the LDCs are their capacities to use it. These capacities rise irreversibly and almost automatically as an integral dimension of the advance of commercialization and industrialization, and of the mushrooming of education and the acquisition of experience, including bargaining experience. It is by no means clear that the purchase of technology should necessarily imply economic, military, or political dependence.

The allegedly peculiar character of 'know-how' — that its heavy costs to the purchaser reflect various forms of monopoly power rather than real cost, to a much greater extent than is the case with other commodities[50] — is misleading, for it neglects the corresponding benefits. Further, although the costs of 'know-how' may include

13% to 30%. GATT, *Adjustment, Trade and Growth in Developed and Developing Countries*, Geneva (September 1978), pp. 13-16.

49. The example provided by the banning of DDT under conservationist influence in Ceylon is instructive. This ban was part of the reason for a rapid rise in the number of clinically confirmed cases of malaria, which had previously almost been eliminated. See W. Beckerman, *In Defence of Economic Growth*, p. 116, and R.H. Grey, 'The Decline of Mortality in Ceylon and the Demographic Effects of Malaria Control', *Population Studies*, Volume 28, No. 2, July, 1974.

50. See S.J. Patel, 'Transfer of Technology and Developing Countries', *Foreign Trade Review*, Annual Number (Jan-March 1972), Indian Institute of Foreign Trade.

elements of monopoly rent, this component of the cost is likely to decline as the bargaining power of the LDCs rises. Perhaps even more important, the indirect or external benefits of technology cannot be monopolized by those who have incurred the costs of its production, a point that is particularly obvious and important in the long run. It is never very clear exactly what is meant by indigenous technology (often considered essential for independent development), but one must not lose sight of the time element, for as Japan has shown, initial acquisition of foreign technology, however costly, can lead eventually (without undue subordination) to great economic power, itself the basis for substantial independent technological innovation.[51] Western technology has already brought about considerable economic achievements in Africa, Asia, and Latin America. The process of 'borrowing' technology can be regarded as creating dependence only if it is viewed statically.

Dependence is frequently supposed to be the result of a non-diversified economic structure, characterized in particular by the limited development of manufacturing industry (especially capital goods)[52] and reliance on primary products for the generation of foreign exchange. In an analysis of particular interest because it has almost broken free of the whole dependency approach, Cardoso summarizes the basic characteristics of dependency as follows:

'Basically, the dependency situation is maintained because, in addition to the already stated factors of direct

51. Certainly, the borrowed technology was modified, but the fact still significantly undermines generalization about the alleged necessity of independent technology for non-dependent development. It should be noted that the Japanese method of acquiring specific technologies or elements of technology, for example buying patents rather than encouraging foreign investment as such, is not necessarily the best policy in societies such as Zambia or Indonesia, with less sophisticated business, technical, and other traditions. It may not have been appropriate in all circumstances even in Japan.

52. Cf. Bob Sutcliffe, 'Imperialism and Industrialization in the Third World', in Roger Owen and Bob Sutcliffe, eds., *Studies in the Theory of Imperialism.*

control by the multinationals and dependence on the external market, the *industrial sector* develops in an incomplete form. The production goods sector (Department 1), which is the centre-pin of accumulation in a central economy, does not develop fully. Ordinarily, economists refer to "technological dependency", and it means that the economy has to import machines and industrial inputs, and consequently has to stimulate exports (expecially of primary goods) to generate the necessary foreign exchange.'[53]

No doubt there is an element of truth in this, although its validity was closely related to lack of sovereignty, since an independent state might well even intensify its reliance on a single commodity in order to improve exchange earnings as a preliminary to diversification. In any event, significant diversification of the economic structure has been occurring in the Third World, and growth rates of output during the past twenty-five years have been higher for heavy than for light industries in developing countries.

The concept of dependence has always been imprecise; such significance as it has relates almost entirely to *political* control of one society by another.[54] Since national economies are becoming increasingly *interdependent*, the meaning of dependence is ever more elusive, not to say mystical.[55] Every multinational with a branch or subsidiary in an under-developed country is dependent on the continued goodwill (economic reasoning being an element of goodwill) of that country to ensure that its investment pays off, or possibly to

53. F.H. Cardoso, 'Some New Mistaken Theses on Latin American Development and Dependency', mimeo, October 1973, p. 29, n. 13.

54. Although borderline cases occur in which informal political control may be exercised (as in some prewar Latin American countries by the US), this is not the same as informal economic control, which is largely impossible in postwar circumstances of intense political and economic competition, as indeed is now the case with informal political control.

55. The trend towards interdependence has been accelerating since the Second World War. For most countries, developed and underdeveloped, the value of foreign trade is rising faster than GDP. (The postwar average growth rate in the volume of international trade was about 8% up to 1973. F. Cripps, 'Causes of Growth and Recession in World Trade', *Economic Policy Review*, No. 4, March 1978, p. 37.)

ensure that it establishes an early stake in a potentially large and rapidly expanding market. The host country may be dependent on the firm for the organizational skills and technology to establish a new industry. If all the multinationals or the advanced capitalist countries as a group acted in concert, their bargaining power would undoubtedly be superior to that of the LDCs taken singly or as a group; but they do not, and their superior economic power (as individual economies or firms, compared to less developed economies or indigenous businesses) is often used in competitive battles against one another.[56] But there is more. In general, the LDCs are neither particularly trade nor foreign-investment dependent.[57] More to the point, the more

56. Cf. *UN Survey of Latin America, 1970*, p. 304: 'A first effect of this increased competition between subsidiaries of international companies may possibly be to weaken the position of the individual companies in the countries in which they wish to operate. Up to now, the market for foreign investment has been characterized by the fact that international enterprises could take their pick of the countries, selecting whichever offered them the greatest tax incentives, while governments vied with each other in furnishing ways of attracting more foreign investment. Because of the growing need for firms to invest abroad, the consolidation of regional groupings in which efforts are made to equalize conditions for entry of foreign capital, and the governments' increasing concern about the gradual takeover of their industries (by US concerns), it may well be that the balance in the foreign capital market will gradually incline in favour of the governments of the countries in which the enterprises operate. The strengthening of the countries' bargaining position would force firms to adopt a more and more flexible attitude to the terms imposed by countries or regional groupings. There are already signs of greater flexibility among the international enterprises in both the extractive and the manufacturing sectors. Firms are agreeing to being minority shareholders and to much more restrictive conditions than in the past. They are entering into associations with public, semi-public and private enterprises in countries with different economic systems. This means that firms are more and more willing to fulfil the positions that the countries assign them according to the development model they have adopted.'

57. Little notes that Third World countries are much less trade dependent than the developed countries. Only a quarter of LDCs had trade dependence (measured in terms of exports as a proportion of GDP) greater than 30% in 1972. The corresponding figure for the DMEs was 40%. Not much more than 10% of the Third World's population live in countries with trade dependence greater than 20%; the corresponding figure for DMEs is 30%. About 90% of the population of LDCs in 1967 lived in countries whose foreign-owned assets per head were less than $40. (Little, p. 226.) Furthermore, it should be noted that

184 of 298

trade or investment dependent they are, the more prosperous they tend to be. The cross-sectional relationship between trade dependence and per capita income in the Third World is positive; the wealthier countries are those most dependent on foreign investment.[58] This does not mean that dependence is the price that must be paid for prosperity. But it does mean that the concept of dependence is totally misleading in present world circumstances, because it is one-sided, unidirectional, and static in its approach to international economic relationships. The advent of genuine equality among interdependent economies requires to a large extent increasingly fruitful contact between the poor and rich countries. As with technology, it is only by a static view that reliance on foreign trade, capital, skills, and example can be regarded as intensifying dependence. It follows from the argument in this chapter that the idea of 'neo-colonialism' — that the formal political independence of almost all the former colonies has not significantly modified the previous domination and exploitation of the great majority of humanity in Asia, Africa, and Latin America by the advanced capitalist world — is highly

highly advanced economies like the US and Japan are extremely dependent on LDC markets, since LDCs account for 28.6% and 43.5% of their total exports respectively. (UNCTAD, Handbook 1979, pp. 130 and 136; figures are for 1975).

58. Little, p. 226. Summarizing the most recently available data on non-concessional financial flows from the Development Assistance Committee countries, the *Economic and Political Weekly*, February 3-10, 1979, p. 197, notes: 'The patterns of direct foreign investment in developing countries have changed in recent years. There has been a shift away from the traditional concept of full or majority ownership and control towards more flexible forms of co-operation, including agreements on joint ventures, production-sharing, management and licensing. These changes are not reflected adequately in the data available, which thus are not a full measure of the implications of investment for production and productivity growth. As regards the allocation of investments to income groups of "non-oil" host countries, recipients in higher income brackets obtain the bulk of foreign direct investment. The major destinations in 1976, in order of magnitude, were Brazil, Indonesia, Bermuda, Bahamas, Zaire, Argentina, Netherlands Antilles, Peru and the Philippines.' R. Vengroff, reviewing the empirical literature, notes that 'economic dependency and performance are positively associated on many measures'. 'Dependency and Development in Black Africa: An Empirical Test', *Journal of Modern African Studies*, 15, 5 (1979), p. 624.

misleading and affords an assessment of postwar world capitalism that omits most new developments. The theory of neo-colonialism is also having, and has had, serious negative political consequences. [59] It does, however, have some merit.

Clearly there was a lag between the achievement of formal independence and the ability of underdeveloped countries to exert their bargaining power. (This was in part due to inexperience, shortages of skilled personnel, and delays in the creation of an effective state machine and the achievement of adequate representation on international bodies.) More important, the theory of neo-colonialism served a valid social function in the underdeveloped world, providing powerful ideological support for Third World bourgeois nationalism and lending it an internationally acceptable rationale, which in turn helped the Third World to improve its international bargaining power in the critical matters of commodity prices and control of markets. More generally, bourgeois nationalism is a fundamental ideological condition for the creation of modern nation-states out of states previously characterized by feudal particularism, religious and communal division, and all varieties of patriarchal backwardness.

But the fact that the theory of neo-colonialism helped bourgeois nationalism to sweep away many retarding influences impeding the development of capitalism and to forge modern nation-states does not eliminate its crucial weakness. The crux of the theory is to deny the importance of political independence in stimulating indigenous capitalism in the Third World. But any serious examination of the underdeveloped countries since independence demonstrates that these countries have made important gains in a context in which nationalism has forced the pace of economic development.

59. Most important, the domination of working-class movements in the Third World by populist nationalism has been reinforced by the ideological outlook of 'neo-colonialism', which tends to divert and dampen internal class struggles by orienting discontent towards external alleged enemies.

8

The Illusion of Underdevelopment: Facts of Post-War Progress

Earlier chapters have analysed the origins and some of the inadequacies and consequences of the current world-view of the majority of the left, an important element of which is the belief that the postwar record of economic development in the Third World has been one of failure drifting inexorably towards catastrophe. The central components of this view can be summarized as follows.[1]

1. The material record of the LDCs, as measured by the (formerly) standard indicator of per capita GNP, has been disappointingly poor, sometimes even negative. One of the results has been a widening gap, absolute and relative, between developed and underdeveloped countries.

2. More important, the absolute rise in per capita GNP in the LDCs has not been reflected in rising absolute standards of welfare for the majority of the population. There are many reasons for this,[2] among the most critical of which are

1. There are infinite variations, elaborations, and combinations, and differing approaches may be conflated. But the general feeling of disappointment about Third World development cannot be doubted.
2. The causes are interrelated and overlap in a logically unsatisfactory fashion; but they suffice to draw attention to some of the principal arguments of the proponents of this view.

regressive income-distribution and patterns of output irrelevant to basic social needs, as well as forms of economic development tending towards increasing marginalization of ever-wider sections of the population. Indeed, postwar Third World economic development has been characterized by negligible improvement, or even worsening material misery for the majority, only a small minority benefiting from development.

3. Even when material standards have improved, the result has been growth without development, a process whereby average purchasing power over goods and services rises, but without an improvement, and perhaps even with a decline, in the quality of life for the majority. Growth without development entails unjust income distribution, demolition of traditional values and communities without constructing worthwhile alternatives, rising crime rates, the loss of human dignity owing to worsening unemployment and underemployment, and, in general, the imposition of Western capitalist industrial culture, including unsuitable consumption patterns, on Third World societies.

4. In any case, such disappointingly small material progress as has been achieved is likely to be ephemeral, for it is threatened by starvation, ever-rising mass unemployment, and dwindling resources.[3]

5. The menace of starvation results from rapidly accelerating population growth, the pattern of international trade (which favours cash-crop production by the LDCs), and a political system dominated by privileged elites whose interests and consumption patterns are not directed towards the development of domestic food production. The reality of this threat is demonstrated by the failure of Third World agriculture throughout the postwar period.

3. The fourth horseman of the Apocalypse is, of course, war. The other disasters, together with the rich world/poor world gap, may confidently be expected to bring this in their train.

6. Third World countries are already racked by mass unemployment, including large-scale urban and rural underemployment unprecedented since the localized experience of the advanced capitalist countries in the 1930s; and currently accelerating rates of population growth, the capital-intensive character of modern industry, and a host of other factors (not least of which is uneven income distribution) make it probable that by 1990 overall unemployment in the Third World will range between 58 and 73 per cent.[4]

7. Dwindling resources pose a threat to the whole of humanity unless there is a fundamental change in the way of life of the rich minority in the advanced industrial countries. Currently known and estimated reserves of a range of commonly used and indispensable raw materials are likely, at current prospective rates of consumption, to last for comparatively short periods. The threat posed by this problem is greatest for the LDCs, since the superior political, military, and economic power of the Western countries affords them a powerful advantage in securing the greatest share of these dwindling resources. Moreover, because of the need, in the face of these scarcities, for a change in life-style, it is all the more imperative for the LDCs to leave the path of growth without development.

8. Internationally, the old pattern of direct colonial rule has given way to one of indirect dependence based on the West's monopoly of advanced technology. The international division of labour has changed, but not in a fashion that permits autonomous Third World development; on the contrary, it perpetuates and even tightens the ties of dependence and accentuates the immoral and potentially politically disruptive division between rich and poor nations.

4. Cf. Hans Singer, 'Brief Note on Unemployment Rates in Developing Countries', p. 2. The likely range for 1980 is given as between 34% and 52%.

Insofar as it can be distinguished from this liberal-populist view, the specifically Marxist or neo-Marxist version of this outlook[5] emphasizes that the alleged failure of postwar Third World development is evidence of the socially retrogressive character of capitalism in the age of imperialism and of the consequent inability of this system to match the material achievements of early, non-imperialist capitalism in the West. One influential conceptualization of this neo-Marxist approach relies heavily on the concept of the 'development of underdevelopment'; it postulates that underdevelopment is a *sui generis* state of distorted development caused by Western imperialism. A corollary of this view is that capitalism in Third World countries, being externally introduced (and generally forcibly imposed), has no healthy internal roots or vigorous dynamic of its own.

In what follows I shall argue that the empirical data belie this picture and that substantial, accelerating, and even historically unprecedented improvements in the growth of productive capacity[6] and the material welfare of the mass of the population have occurred in the Third World in the postwar period. Moreover, the developing capitalist societies of Asia, Africa, and Latin America have proved themselves increasingly capable of generating powerful internal sources of economic expansion and of achieving an ever more independent economic and political status. This progress has been highly uneven among states, classes, regions, and ethnic groups, and has been accompanied by new and varied tensions both between societies and within social groups. This latter point relates to a wide range of phenomena that lie beyond the scope of the discussion in this chapter. But this strikingly uneven development, together with the more general heterogeneity of the societies of the Third World (far greater than that of the advanced capitalist countries taken as a group), raises the question of

5. As a Marxist myself, I obviously do not consider the dominant trend of most Marxist thinking in this field to be in the scientific tradition of Marxism.
6. Understood in the widest sense, to include human attitudes, skills, etc.

whether it is appropriate to treat these societies in aggregate, and of whether the related conceptual division of the world into developed and underdeveloped countries is at all accurate. International economic change has been so rapid and sweeping that the kernel of truth in this division of the world is rapidly dissolving. The present situation could more appropriately be conceptualized as a spectrum of varying levels, rates, and structures of national development, one in which the positions of individual countries are constantly shifting. Nevertheless, the Third World countries do retain sufficient common features to justify aggregate treatment,[7] provided the elements of change qualifying such treatment are duly taken into account.

1. Rising Per Capita GNP

Comparisons between the poor and rich countries in terms of per capita GNP, infant mortality, calorie intake per capita, etc., are frequently used to argue or suggest that Third World development efforts have failed. Yet such comparisons throw no light on the performance of the poor countries in their efforts to change, since they take no account of the position before the effort to improve began, nor of the time that has since elapsed. Indeed, we shall see that the relevant data actually present a relatively cheerful picture with respect to progress over time.

In terms of the standard measure of economic progress, GNP per capita,[8] the postwar record of the Third World has been reasonably, perhaps even outstandingly, successful as compared *either* with their prewar performance *or* with

7. Above all, it must be recalled that despite the heterogeneity, all LDCs, without exception, have in the postwar period been part of the great upsurge combining nationalism and the demand for a better life, which is bringing the great majority of humanity, formerly quiescent, into the forefront of history and into the modern world.

8. We shall argue below that despite the undoubted defects of this measure as an indicator of material welfare, the cross-temporal picture it suggests is broadly accurate.

whatever past period of growth in the developed market economies (DMEs) may be taken as relevant for comparison. *Any argument that the postwar economic growth of the LDCs has been a relative or absolute failure must therefore rest on other grounds.*[9]

Postwar economic growth in terms of GDP per capita has in general been faster than prewar for the LDCs. Kuznets's summary of the evidence for seven underdeveloped countries for which long-term records are available is given in Table 6. Of the four (or perhaps five) countries for which the data permit prewar and postwar comparisons (Jamaica, Philippines, United Arab Republic, India, and perhaps Ghana), all show markedly accelerated growth rates of real product per capita postwar, with the possible exception of Ghana, where there was probably very little change on average. Aggregate data for Latin America over a more limited period show a similar postwar acceleration. According to the Economic Commission for Latin America, GNP for the Latin American countries increased at 4.2% per annum from 1935 to 1953, GNP per capita at 2% per annum, while in the period 1945 to 1955 total output rose at an annual rate of about 4.9% and output per capita by 2.4%.[10] Bairoch's aggregate estimates of annual rates of change of GDP per capita for all non-communist LDCs and for Latin America and Asia taken separately for the period 1900 to 1970 (Table 7) also unequivocally show an acceleration of per capita growth postwar. These results are all the more impressive in that the prewar- postwar comparisons show an acceleration compared with a period (about 1900-1945) that itself probably witnessed unprecedented growth rates as compared with any earlier period in the history of LDCs,[11]

9. Other grounds may exist, of course. We shall consider these below.
10. United Nations, Department of Economic and Social Affairs, *Analyses and Projections of Economic Development, 1. An Introduction to the Technique of Programming* (New York, 1955), p. 10; and United Nations, Department of Economic and Social Affairs, *Economic Survey of Latin America 1955* (New York, 1956), p. 3, cited in P.T. Bauer, *Dissent on Development*, p. 34.
11. Ibid., pp. 35-7. Bauer discusses some of the abundant but scattered

Table 6

*Rates of GDP Growth per Capita per Decade Before and
After the Second World War for Selected Countries*

Country	Period (no. of years in parentheses)		Rates of Growth of Product per Capita per Decade
Argentina	1. 1900-04 to 1925-29	(25)	12.0
	2. 1925-29 to 1963-67	(38)	8.9
	3. Lines 1-2	(63)	10.1
Mexico	4. 1895-99 to 1925-29	(30)	13.3
	5. 1925-29 to 1963-67	(38)	22.3 (38.5)[1]
	6. Lines 4-5	(68)	18.2 (26.8)[1]
Jamaica	7. 1832 to 1930	(98)	0.0
	8. 1929-31 to 1950-52	(21)	8.9
	9. 1950-52 to 1963-66	(13.5)	77.7
Ghana	10. 1891 to 1911	(20)	20.0
	11. 1911 to 1950-54	(41)	13.9
	12. 1950-54 to 1963-67	(13)	14.2
	13. Lines 10-12	(74)	15.6
Philippines	14. 1902 to 1938	(36)	9.6
	15. 1938 to 1950-54	(14)	-3.9
	16. 1950-54 to 1963-67	(13)	30.0
	17. Lines 14-16	(63)	10.3
United Arab	18. 1895 to 1945-49	(50)	-2.2
Republic (Egypt)	19. 1945-49 to 1963-66	(17.5)	29.8
India	20. 1861-69 to 1881-89	(20)	13.1
	21. 1881-89 to 1901-09	(20)	-3.1
	22. 1901-09 to 1952-58	(50)	6.3
	23. 1952-58 (F) to 1963-67 (F)[2]	(10)	12.2
	24. Lines 20-23	(100)	6.2

1. Alternative estimate.
2. Fiscal year beginning 1 April.

Source: Simon Kuznets, *Economic Growth of Nations: Total Output and Production Statistics*, Harvard University Press, 1971, pp. 30-31.

with the exception of some countries (such as Ghana) in the closing decades of the nineteenth and first decades of the twentieth centuries.

evidence for this, especially in connection with West Africa and Southeast Asia. This growth was of course patchy. It was only as the economic contact of the poor countries with the advanced capitalist world became generalized in the twentieth century, and especially after the Second World War, that Third World economic growth too became generalized. However, it is difficult to know what weight to attach to these figures.

Table 7

Annual Rates of Change in GDP per Capita (at constant prices)
for Non-Communist LDCs by Region

| | All non-communist less-developed countries | | Latin America | | Asia (excluding communist countries) | |
	Total	Per Capita	Total	Per Capita	Total	Per Capita
1900-1913	2.1	1.2	2.1	0.3	2.2	1.5
1913-1929	1.9	0.9	2.8	1.0	1.3	0.8
1929-1952/54	2.2	0.6	3.5	1.4	1.1	-0.3
1950-1960	4.8	2.4	5.4	2.5	4.1	2.0
1960-1970	5.1	2.4	5.5	2.5	4.8	2.1

Source: Bairoch, p. 184.

Comparison of the recent development experience of the Third World with that of the developed capitalist economies at an earlier stage of their growth (generally the period of their industrialization) is not legitimate, since the industrialization of the developed countries was the culmination of a process of modern socio-economic change that lasted several centuries, the rise of capitalism coinciding with the long period of the dissolution of feudalism. Since most of the LDCs have started the process of development from a far more backward position in this respect, the comparison would be bound to minimize the achievements of the LDCs, *if other things were equal.* Despite this, the LDCs do rather well in such a comparison. Their postwar growth rates of product per capita have generally exceeded those of the industrializing capitalist countries of the eighteenth and nineteenth centuries. Summarizing the evidence for all the non-communist developed countries for which long-term records exist, and excluding countries with populations of less than 2 million, Kuznets notes that the rate of increase of per capita product for the long period covering the modern economic growth of the fourteen countries concerned ranges from 1-1.2% per annum for Australia, the Netherlands, and

Britain, to 2.9-3.2% for Sweden and Japan.[12] The rates for the remaining nine countries cluster between 1.4% and 2.3% per annum.[13] This compares with average postwar per capita growth rates in the Third World ranging from 2.4% per annum in the 1950s to 2.6% per annum in the 1960s and 3.8% per annum in the early 1970s;[14] the average per annum in the years 1963 to 1973 was 2.8%.[15]

Limited as the value of these comparisons may be, they do suggest *the extent to which other things were actually not equal*: the most significant difference being the capacity for material advance, and in particular the degree to which new elements have improved the prospects of more rapid material advance from a domestic base considerably less appropriate than that of the countries of Western Europe, North America, Australasia, and Japan in the eighteenth and nineteenth centuries. Broadly speaking, the 'advantages of backwardness' thesis appears to be more relevant to contemporary Third World economic growth than has often been supposed — as regards both technology and the increased opportunities and impetus provided by the expansion of the world market.[16]

12. Kuznets, p. 22, gives the figures as growth rates per decade.
13. France, Belgium, Germany, Switzerland, Denmark, Norway, Italy, Canada, and Australia. Ibid., p. 41. Utilization of the long-term rates of increase of per capita product is appropriate, since for the periods after the beginning of modern economic growth no significant acceleration or deceleration is found. Specifically, Kuznets's data provide no support for Rostow's 'take-off' theory - postulating an initial acceleration of the growth rate of per capita product followed by constant sustained growth at a high rate.
14. UNCTAD, *Handbook of International Trade and Development Statistics* (New York, 1976), p. 341. Real growth in GDP was higher in developing than developed countries during 1974-77. World Bank, *Annual Report, 1978*.
15. United Nations, Department of Economic and Social Affairs, *1974 Report on the World Social Situation*, New York, 1975, p. 6.
16. On the other hand, the combination of a comparatively late start and extremely rapid growth, often with a comparatively unsuitable cultural environment, may create tensions of a highly ambiguous character, contributing to forward-looking change, but simultaneously raising new spectres of irrationalism, especially of xenophobic nationalism, following Europe's own catastrophic example.

Table 8

*Annual Percentage Growth Rates of Per Capita GDP
1950-74, Developed and Developing Market Economies*

	1950-60	*1960-70*	*1970-74*
Developed Market Economies	2.8	4.1	3.2
Developing Market Economies	2.4	2.6	3.8

Source: UNCTAD, *Handbook*, 1976, p. 341.

Table 9

*Index of Per Capita GDP 1960-75, Developed
and Developing Market Economies*

1970 = 100

Year	Developed Market Economies	Developing Market Economies
1960	69	76
1961	72	78
1962	75	78
1963	77	81
1964	81	84
1965	84	85
1966	88	86
1967	91	88
1968	95	93
1969	98	96
1970	100	100
1971	103	103
1972	107	106
1973	113	111
1974	112	116
1975	110	117

Source: *Yearbook of National Accounts Statistics 1976,* Vol. II, International Tables, UN Department of Economic and Social Affairs, New York, 1977, pp. 255-6.

Because of the less appropriate technological, institutional, and cultural base for modern economic development from which today's LDCs start, the comparison of their growth rates with those of the developed countries is so ahistorical as to possess limited value as a measure of economic

Table 10

Growth in Real Terms of GDP Per Capita of Countries With More Than One Million Inhabitants, 1960-1973

Country	Annual Growth Rate in Real Terms of GNP Per Capita (%)	Population (in millions)	Country	Annual Growth Rate in Real Terms of GNP Per Capita (%)	Population (in millions)
Libya	10.5	2.16	Costa Rica	2.7	1.87
Japan	9.4	108.35	Dominican Republic	2.7	4.43
Saudi Arabia	8.7	7.75	Zaire	2.6	23.44
Portugal	7.4	8.99	Bolivia	2.5	5.33
Greece	7.3	8.93	United Kingdom	2.4	56.00
Singapore	7.1	2.19	Colombia	2.4	22.50
Republic of Korea	7.1	32.91	Indonesia	2.4	124.42
Hong Kong	7.0	4.16	Ethiopia	2.4	26.55
Taiwan	6.9	15.42	Philippines	2.3	40.22
Iran	6.4	32.14	New Zealand	2.2	2.96
Spain	5.8	34.74	Liberia	2.2	1.45
Puerto Rico	5.7	2.95	Trinidad & Tobago	2.1	1.06
Israel	5.6	3.21	Peru	2.1	14.53
Thailand	4.8	39.40	Uganda	2.1	10.83
France	4.7	52.16	Venezuela	2.0	11.28
Papua, New Guinea	4.6	2.60	Sri Lanka	2.0	13.18
Finland	4.5	4.66	Paraguay	1.9	2.42
Austria	4.4	7.53	Ecuador	1.9	6.79
Panama	4.4	1.57	El Salvador	1.9	3.77
Togo	4.4	2.12	Laos	1.9	3.18
Belgium	4.3	9.76	Chile	1.7	10.23
Italy	4.3	54.89	Algeria	1.7	14.70
Netherlands	4.1	13.43	Zambia	1.7	4.65
Mauritania	4.1	1.26	Rhodesia	1.7	5.90
Norway	4.0	3.96	People's Republic of Congo	1.7	1.20
Denmark	3.9	5.02			

Country		
Turkey	3.9	37.93
Malaysia	3.9	11.30
Angola	3.8	5.72
Syria	3.8	6.95
Lesotho	3.8	1.17
Canada	3.7	22.13
Federal Republic of Germany	3.7	61.97
Ireland	3.6	3.03
Jamaica	3.6	1.97
Brazil	3.6	101.05
Nigeria	3.6	71.26
Malawi	3.5	4.83
Tunisia	3.4	5.46
Pakistan	3.4	66.23
Mexico	3.3	56.05
Nicaragua	3.3	1.97
Guatemala	3.3	5.18
Mozambique	3.3	8.28
Cameroon	3.2	6.21
USA	3.1	210.40
Australia	3.1	13.13
Ivory Coast	3.1	5.89
Kenya	3.1	12.48
Switzerland	3.0	6.43
Sweden	3.0	8.14
Lebanon	3.0	2.98
Iraq	2.9	10.41
Tanzania Mainland	2.8	13.97
Argentina	2.7	24.28
Morocco	1.6	15.90
Sierra Leone	1.6	2.79
Egypt	1.5	35.62
Jordan	1.3	2.54
Honduras	1.3	2.78
India	1.3	581.91
Burundi	1.0	3.58
Benin	1.0	2.95
Mali	0.7	5.37
Burma	0.6	29.51
South Vietnam	0.4	19.87
Central African Republic		1.71
Nepal	0.4	12.02
Malagasy Republic	0.3	8.30
Afghanistan	0.3	16.63
Rwanda	0.3	3.98
Guinea	0.1	5.24
Ghana	0.0	9.31
Uruguay	-0.2	3.00
Bangladesh	-0.2	74.00
Somalia	-0.2	3.04
Haiti	-0.3	4.45
Bhutan	-0.3	1.12
Upper Volta	-0.4	5.71
Sudan	-0.9	17.05
Senegal	-1.8	4.07
Cambodia	-1.8	7.57
Niger	-1.9	4.36
Chad	-2.1	3.87

Note: The centrally planned economies and South Africa have been omitted.

achievement. A substantial divergence in favour of the developed countries would not in itself suggest poor Third World performance, particularly in view of the differences in rates of population growth. An alleged divergence of this type, however, has been taken as a reasonable criterion of performance, and specific economic and political conclusions drawn from it.[17] Although I do not at all subscribe to this approach, it may nevertheless be noted that *'depolarization'* occurred in the 1970s, the *per capita* growth rates of the LDCs rising faster than those of the DMEs (Table 8), a development that began in the late 1960s (Table 9).[18]

More fundamentally, however, the notion of a 'widening gap' between rich and poor countries implies a marked discontinuity in the range of growth rates, with all or most of the countries commonly classed as less developed at the lower end of the range, and most of the developed market economies bracketed at the upper end. If this is not the case, and particularly if the second condition is not fulfilled, then the thesis of growing polarization must be discarded. The evidence, indeed, points to a continuous spectrum of growth rates with no marked discontinuities (Table 10). Further, although most of the LDCs are bunched in the lower ranges of the growth spectrum for the period 1960-73, some one-quarter to one-third were in the upper and middle ranges.[19]

17. In particular, it has been concluded that the Third World has been becoming more and more subordinate to and dependent on the developed capitalist world and that the political result has been the growing importance of international economic polarization as the greatest single menace to world peace and harmonious international political relations.

18. This does not, of course, deny a growing absolute gap.

19. The range of growth rates of GNP per capita for all market economies (developed and undeveloped) was 12.6 percentage points, from +10.5 % per annum to -2.1 % per annum. Taking five equal percentage intervals between the lowest and highest growth rates and allotting the countries to their appropriate range, we get the crude results above. Weighting of the countries according to population would tend to suggest greater polarization owing to the relatively slower growth of some of the largest LDCs. On the other hand, Israel and the southern European countries (Greece, Spain, and Portugal) have been counted as DMEs, which rather minimizes the suggestion of depolarization. Turkey has been counted among the LDCs.

Only about a quarter of the developed market economies fell within the higher growth-rate ranges; the vast majority were in the middle range, a few even in the lower ranges. While this evidence indicates uneven development and continuing polarization, at least up to the late 1960s, it certainly does not indicate economic stagnation or growing polarization.

2. Growing Inequality?

Has the rapid expansion of output in thé Third World been counterbalanced by aggravated inequality and marginalization such that the mass of the population — or the lowest 20%[20] — is worse off than before? Has the 'type of growth' pursued in most LDCs itself been a cause of growing inequality?

20. The majority and the poorest *x* % are often treated as interchangeable. In fact, the majority may be getting better off relative to the upper income classes, while the poorest 20% may not — or *vice versa*. Moreover, policies to improve the relative position of the poorest 20 % may conflict with policies to improve the relative and absolute position of the mass of the population (perhaps the poorest 60%). This is quite likely to be the case, since poverty is highly correlated with location (especially in isolated, rural areas) and recent empirical evidence supports the view that increasing urbanization is economically more efficient than a more even urban/rural allocation of resources, subject to the constraint that agricultural output growth is not neglected. A summary of the evidence on this point is given by Koichi Mera, 'On the Urban Agglomeration and Economic Efficiency', *Economic Development and Cultural Change* (January, 1973). Further, the fact that the poorest quartile is getting statistically worse off may be no indication of the deterioration of the position of a particular poor group, since the constituent individual or household membership or social composition of the lowest 20% may be changing significantly over a comparatively brief time period, as is likely to be the case in periods of rapid overall socio-economic change, and particularly when commercialization and industrialization are making an impact on predominantly agrarian societies where social demarcations are not rigid and kinship and patron-client relationships are important, as in much of Asia and Africa. A discussion of this and other aspects of the complex process of multi-directional mobility of households may be found in T. Shanin, *The Awkward Class*, p. 71 et. seq. This crucial aspect of modernization is generally overlooked in the literature of 'redistribution with growth'. The implications are potentially damaging to the efficiency, logic, and morality of the redistribution approach.

The widespread belief that the rapid economic progress in the Third World since the Second World War has generally been associated with worsening aggregate inequality is not borne out by the (admittedly scanty and unreliable) time-series data or by the more plentiful cross-section data. Summarizing time-series data for eighteen countries on a graph depicting the annual growth rate of the income of the poorest 40% of the population relative to the rate of growth of GNP, Ahluwalia notes that 'the scatter suggests considerable diversity of experience in terms of relative equality. Several countries show a deterioration in relative equality, but others show improvement'.[21]

21. M.S. Ahluwalia, 'Income Inequality: Some Dimensions of the Problem', Hollis Chenery, p. 13. Thirteen of the countries are underdeveloped: Taiwan, South Korea, Sri Lanka, Mexico, Brazil, India, Venezuela, Peru, Panama, El Salvador, Colombia, Iran, and the Philippines. The exclusion of the five non-Third World countries does not affect the validity of Ahuwalia's conclusions. His work is the most comprehensive reliable summary of the evidence on the relationship between postwar redistribution and growth. Its general findings may be taken as definitive of the current state of knowledge on the subject. Individual time-series studies of income distribution also show no clear pattern. Tanzania appears to have reduced income inequality between 1967 and 1972, but the sources of data and methods of estimation are unclear. (Reginald H. Green, 'Tanzania', in H. Chenery et al., pp. 268-75.) Sri Lanka witnessed substantial equalizing redistribution between 1953 and 1973. (Lal Jayawardena, 'Sri Lanka', ibid., pp. 273-280.) South Korea apparently witnessed a substantial decline in income inequality throughout the postwar period, although the data are fragmentary. (Irma Adelman, 'South Korea', ibid., pp. 280-285.) There appears to have been a substantial reduction in inequality in Taiwan between 1960 and 1970, although here again the evidence is shaky. It does appear fairly certain, however, that some sort of decline in inequality did take place. (Gustav Ranis, 'Taiwan', ibid., pp. 285-290). Between 1960 and 1970, income distribution in Mexico became increasingly unequal as measured by the Gini coefficient for the years 1950, 1958, 1963, 1968 and 1969, according to Gunter van Ginneken. (*Mexican Income Distribution within and between Rural and Urban Areas*, World Employment Programme Research, Working Papers, ILO, Geneva, 1974, pp. 98-99.) On the other hand, Richard Weiskoff's study ('Income Distribution and Economic Growth in Puerto Rico, Argentina and Mexico', in Alejandro Foxley, ed., *Income Distribution in Latin America*, Cambridge University Press, 1976) of changes in Mexico between the years 1950, 1957 and 1963 shows the Gini coefficient *declining* from 1950 to 1957 and rising only from 1957 to 1963. His coefficient of variation suggests that distribution grew more equal throughout the period, while the moments of

Ahluwalia's cross-section evidence covers sixty-six countries and examines the statistical relationship between
distribution and per capita income on the one hand and
between distribution and GDP growth at given levels of per
capita income on the other,[22] the former taken as an
indicator of the secular influence of growth on distribution,
the latter as an indicator of the short-term impact of

logs of income show that despite the decline in skewness, the variance
increased during the entire period. Size distribution of personal income
(income shares received by deciles of families) demonstrates that the
'middle classes' have gained at the expense of the top 5% and the bottom
60%. Almost exactly the same picture holds for Puerto Rico between 1953
and 1963, where the different measures show contradictory results;
although the Gini coefficient is unequivocally rising, the ordinal shares
again show the middle groups gaining as compared to the top 5% and the
bottom 60%. The picture for Argentina for the years 1953, 1959, and 1961 is
of rising inequality between 1953 and 1959 with a decline between 1959 and
1961, leaving, according to all measures except the coefficient of variation,
income more unevenly distributed in 1961 than in 1953. In Brazil income
inequality rose between 1960 and 1970 as measured by the Gini coefficient.
(Albert Fishlow, 'Brazilian Size Distribution of Income', in Foxley, ed.,
Income Distribution in Latin America.) In Peru, the redistributive effect of
the reforms between 1968 and 1972 appears to have been minimal. (Adolfo
Figueroa, 'The Impact of Current Reforms on Income Distribution in Peru',
ibid.) In Western Malaysia between 1957 and 1970 (with observations also
for 1960 and 1967) the Gini coefficient rises between 1957 and 1960,
falling thereafter through 1967 to 1970, but with income still more unequal
in 1970 than in 1957. (Linn Lin Lean, *The Pattern of Income Distribution in
West Malaysia 1957-70,* World Employment Programme Research, ILO,
Geneva, 1976.) For Ghana, between 1956 and 1968, all measures of change
in inequality of monetary income distribution agree (coefficient of
variation, standard deviation of log of income, Pareto coefficient, the Gini
coefficient ratio, and the Gini coefficent), showing growing inequality.
(Kodwo Ewusi, 'The Distribution of Monetary Incomes in Ghana',
Technical Publication Series No. 18, Institute of Statistical, Social and
Economic Research, University of Ghana, Legon, 1971). Non-monetary
incomes are extremely unlikely to move independently. In India, the size
distribution of income appears to have widened over the period 1951-60.
(Subramanian Swamy, 'Structural Changes and the Distribution of Income
by Size: The Case of India', *Review of Income and Wealth* (June 1967).) If we
exclude the countries for which the different measures give conflicting
results (Puerto Rico, Mexico and Argentina), and which in fact by cross-
national comparisons with other LDCs already have relatively equal income
distribution, no obvious general predominance of decreasing or increasing
inequality is discernible.
22. As measured by per capita GNP at factor cost in constant 1971 US
dollars.

economic growth on income distribution. Concerning the *secular* relationship of economic growth and inequality, Ahluwalia finds that 'there is some confirmation that income inequality first increases and then decreases with development'.[23] Elsewhere, discussing the same data, he argues that 'there is no strong pattern relating changes in the distribution of income to the rate of growth of GNP. In both high-growth and low-growth countries there are some which have experienced improvements and others that have experienced deteriorations in relative equality. The absence of any marked relationship between income growth and changes in income shares is important for policy purposes. It suggests that there is little firm empirical basis for the view that higher rates of growth inevitably generate greater inequality' (p. 13).

23. These statistical findings are regarded by Ahluwalia as providing some confirmation for the following scenario: 'On the one hand, the process of development gives economic impetus to the modern high-income sectors and dislocates traditional low-income sectors, thus promoting relative inequality and perhaps even absolute impoverishment. On the other hand, development also promotes the demand for skilled labour, raising real wages and employment levels in the modern sector, thus enabling low-income groups to share in the benefits of growth. Under some optimistic assumptions about the trend in wage share, this may lead to a reduction in relative inequality. These conflicting influences are usually reconciled by treating them as sequential, i.e. income inequality increases in the early stages of development but then declines as development continues.' (Ibid., p. 27.) H.T. Oshima presents evidence to the same effect for several Asian countries in 'The International Comparison of Size Distribution of Family Incomes with Special Reference to Asia', *Review of Economics and Statistics,* Vol. 44 (1962). Kuznets argues that inequality probably first increased and then declined in Britain, Germany, and the United States ('Economic Growth and Income Inequality', *American Economic Review,* March 1955.) Adelman and Morris, however, come to the conclusion from their cross-sectional evidence that 'the results do not support the hypothesis that economic growth raises the share of income of the poorest segments of the population. On the contrary.' (I. Adelman and C.T. Morris, *Economic Growth and Social Equity in Developing Countries,* Stanford University Press, California, 1973, pp. 160-161.) But their judgement is dependent on an idiosyncratic system of classification and not, like Ahluwalia's, on a non-selective approach. The allegedly disappointing performance of the first development decade of the 1960s appears to have resulted from a retrospective change in expectations rather than genuinely poor economic performance.

Table 11

Distribution of Income for Countries Grouped by Level of GDP Per Capita

Gross Domestic Product Per Capita (in US$)	No. of Countries	Income Shares Received by Quintiles of Recipients (Percentages)					Gini Coefficient
		Q.1	Q.2	Q.3	Q.4	Q.5 (Highest 5%)	
Below 100	9	7.0	10.0	13.1	50.4	29.1	0.42
101-200	8	5.3	8.6	12.0	56.5	24.9	0.47
201-300	11	4.8	8.0	11.3	57.7	32.0	0.50
301-500	9	4.5	7.9	12.3	57.4	30.0	0.49
501-1,000	6	5.1	8.9	13.9	50.1	25.4	0.44
1,001-2,000	10	4.7	10.5	15.9	46.6	20.9	0.40
2,000 & above	3	5.0	10.9	17.3	42.7	16.4	0.36

Source: UN, *Report on the World Social Situation 1974,* based on Felix Paukert, 'Income Distribution at Different Levels of Development: a Survey of Evidence', *International Labour Review,* Aug.-Sept. 1973, p. 118.

There is now a considerable body of cross-sectional evidence supporting the view that the earlier stages of growth are likely to be characterized by rising inequality, but that the trend is reversed as higher levels of development are reached. The turning-point towards the emergence of substantial middle-income groups and the stabilization and improvement of the lower quartiles appears to occur at about the $500 level (Table 11). It is of interest to note that of the eighty-odd LDCs shown in Table 4, well more than one-fourth had already passed that level by 1973.[24]

Furthermore, Ahluwalia notes concerning the short-term relationship between growth and distribution: the 'cross-section evidence does not support the view that a high rate of economic growth has an adverse effect upon relative equality. Quite the contrary, the rate of growth of GDP in our

24. The twenty-six countries with GNP above the $500 level compares with nearly half that number only four years before (*Finance and Development,* No. 1, 1972, p. 1.), a difference which cannot be accounted for solely by inflation.

sample was positively related to the share of the lower 40%, suggesting that the objectives of growth and equity may not be in conflict' (p. 17).

The evidence, then, does not corroborate the hypothesis that income distribution tends towards greater equality as soon as modern growth commences. Nor, more specifically, does it suggest that steady and increasing equality has been achieved in the majority of Third World countries that have registered significant growth postwar (there are a few that may have suffered negative growth rates during the last three decades). The overall picture in this respect certainly does not correspond to the utopian itinerary that 'the community of development economists' (Irma Adelman's felicitously chummy phrase) seem to have expected.[25] On the other hand, one searches in vain for the data stimulating the current concern that the upper-income groups may be garnering all the gains of growth. In the first place, solid evidence is scanty; second, such evidence as does exist shows no clear trend, and most certainly does not at all suggest widespread and disastrous deterioration of income distribution. Indeed, the outlook on the basis of past performance may reasonably be described as mildly hopeful if we regard more nearly equal income distribution as positive.[26]

The secular scenario of rising inequality at the outset of rapid growth followed by declining inequality is quite hopeful in itself. Moreover, when allied with the postwar tendency towards accelerated growth in Third World countries, it suggests that if growth continues the turning

25. It is difficult to identify the economists who did expect a trend towards equality or that growth would be accompanied by no income redistribution one way or the other for most economies except in a secular sense. Arthur Lewis's famous model (*Economic Development with Unlimited Supplies of Labour,* Manchester School, May 1954), which has commanded and still commands widespread support among development economists, clearly implied the reverse during at least part of the period of development, prior to the absorption of the agricultural labour surplus.

26. The present writer does so regard it, within limits and subject to the constraint (to which we shall turn shortly) that its achievement should not be at the cost of absolute improvement for the mass of the population.

point for stable and eventually improved income distribution is likely to arrive sooner than was the case in the now developed countries. In other words, the sequential incidence of initially rising and subsequently falling income concentration, which is caused, according to Ahluwalia, by counteracting aspects of modern development operating first one way and then the other, is likely to be compressed such that the initial period is foreshortened. In some cases — perhaps postwar Taiwan, for example — it may well be that the equalizing aspects of modern development were strong enough to outweigh the initial concentration aspects almost from the start, so that the sequential *aggregate* evolution of income redistribution did not occur and there was no initial concentration of overall distribution.[27] This kind of compression would explain Ahluwalia's findings, somewhat contradictory at first sight, that early development (considered secularly) shows initially rising concentration, while rates of short-term economic growth correlate positively with the shares of the lowest 40% in the postwar period.[28]

This apparent paradox may also be related to the great heterogeneity within and between these societies, which is bound to reduce the value of cross-sectional correlations as indicators of change over time, particularly in the earlier stages of growth, when societies are most heterogeneous. In societies with fragmented social structures, changes in the Gini coefficient may be the net result of shifts in disparate social groups within the same national territory, together

27. In the case of Taiwan, account must be taken of pre-1945 development. Nevertheless, this invalidates neither the principle nor the illustrative relevance of the example. It should be emphasized that I am not proposing a new utopian picture of continuously improving distribution once the turning-point has been passed, without limit and without reversals. In a market economy there are limits to such a trend (indeed in a socialist economy too, but here the limits are set further out), and a secular trend is consistent with significant and even prolonged reverse shifts in distribution, as some of the evidence cited above suggests.

28. This could be explained by the conjecture that Ahluwalia's sample consists predominantly of countries with an already high level of per capita income, but this is not the case.

with changes in the relative importance within society (in income terms and in terms of numbers) of these component social groups — all this aggravated by the incomparability of the purchasing power of groups with radically different life-styles. In effect, these considerations would tend to render less certain the initial phase of *overall* increasing concentration, while not invalidating the secular tendency towards stabilization and a measure of reduction of inequalities. We repeat, then: there is no implication of general, widespread, early, or continuous 'improvements' in distribution. On the contrary, traumatic disruptions in previously accepted relative incomes within and between sectors are highly likely, particularly in the case of the development of social differentiation in agriculture as commercialization penetrates, although in some areas this will lead not to increased concentration but to the replacement of one type of social differentiation by another.[29]

Nevertheless, the rejection of a Panglossian approach should not blur the logical implications of the empirical data. Far from curtailing growth to improve income distribution (the 'basic needs' approach), policy ought to accelerate growth to bring more rapidly into play the economic and institutional forces[30] that tend to ensure that the more advanced societies are also the more egalitarian, and at higher absolute standards of living.[31]

29. Corresponding, for example, to the change from latifundia to large-scale commercial farming.

30. The fact that institutional factors play a part in improving income distribution as growth proceeds implies that changing *policies* can and ought to be a relevant part of the process. But this does not prejudice the claims of growth to priority. However, improving equality in income does not logically or causally imply increasing political participation. The reverse may hold, i.e. control of society by a small revolutionary elite may be a necessary condition for greater income equality in some cases. Equally, there can be no presumption that more rapid economic growth automatically promotes democracy, even if it promotes greater income equality.

31. It is only too easy to envisage policies of substantial egalitarian redistribution that lower the potential or actual welfare of the poorest

It has sometimes been argued that since the evidence does not demonstrate that rapid growth is incompatible with more equal income distribution, extensive egalitarian policy measures are justified.[32] But this ignores the fact that the move towards more equal income distribution is generally the by-product of high levels of economic achievement (and of growth-promoting measures) rather than the reverse. Land reform is a partial exception to this rule, but it promotes economic development mainly to the extent that it is aimed at growth rather than equality. (Mexico may be an exception in this respect.) A recent study on Latin America suggests that as capitalist development increasingly pervades agriculture and latifundistas become more akin to large-scale commercial farmers (Lenin's 'Russian way'), land reform becomes less important, if not completely irrelevant and economically disastrous.[33] Distribution, of course, is much less unequal in Asia and Africa, where land redistribution is therefore even more likely to have damaging effects on output and greater concentration may be the precondition for rapidly expanding output.

The view that growing inequality is detrimental to material welfare is rooted in neo-classical assumptions of declining marginal utility of consumption with given tastes (so that transference of income from the rich to the poor leads to an absolute rise in total utility). But such a static analysis can suggest no presumption of declining welfare with growing inequality in a growing economy, especially since tastes are changing rapidly and the situation is not a zero-sum game. This analysis is purely consumption-

groups (as compared to alternative policies and outcomes), but in conditions of great poverty we consider this an immoral approach, and therefore cannot agree with Dudley Seers ('What Are We Trying to Measure', in N. Baster, ed. *Measuring Development*, London, 1972, p. 23) that in the context of severe underdevelopment equality should be regarded as an aim in itself.

32. ILO, *Report of the Director-General to the Tripartite World Conference on Employment, Income Distribution and Social Progress and the International Division of Labour*, Geneva, 1976.

33. David Lehmann, *A Theory of Agrarian Structure: Typology and Paths of Transformation in Latin America*, Centre of Latin American Studies, University of Cambridge Working Papers, No. 25.

oriented. It ignores both the effects of real or anticipated differences in income on the growth of output through incentives to capital and labour and the crucial role of such differences in resource reallocation during periods of rapid structural change, when barriers to the mobility of labour and capital are formidable.[34]

Changing, and probably rising, income differences are therefore likely to contribute to economic growth in various ways: by promoting the necessary diversification of skills and occupations; by mobilizing energies previously relatively dormant in partially commercialized sectors of the economy, in which custom and habit had prevailed; by mobilizing scarce or underutilized entrepreneurial talents; by promoting rapid changes in resource allocation at a much lower cost than could be achieved by bureaucratic methods. These disequalizing aspects of economic growth are likely to be most severe in the earliest stages, as the expansion of the nascent high-productivity sector generates sectoral inequalities, while commercialization of agriculture and the expansion of the urban informal sector causes mounting inequality as social differentiation proceeds and as entrepreneurs emerge. Within the modern sector, too, there may be increasing initial differentiation as new skills and industries emerge, while trade unions are not yet powerful enough to counteract this trend. Such processes, although they aggravate income inequality, are likely eventually, and perhaps immediately, to enhance material welfare for the majority, creating conditions for raising the standards of those who have failed to acquire new skills or to respond to new opportunities, or who had no new opportunities to respond to.[35] These unequalizing forces will

34. I am indebted to Peter Ayre for this latter point.

35. The establishment of a railway system in the Sudan created a relatively well-paid group of railway workers and benefited well-off contractors and traders, while increasing absolute rewards to poor, former subsistence farmers now able to sell food to the towns and to low-paid casual labour in cotton picking (by increasing their mobility). Locational differences, combined with the inefficiency of allocating scarce complementary resources too thinly, inevitably means that the spread of opportunities is an uneven process.

tend to decline as the proportion of the labour force employed in the modern sector rises, as productivity levels in the agricultural and urban informal sectors increase in relative terms, and as trade unions become stronger and barriers to resource mobility weaker. This highly stylized picture is lent support not only by the cross-sectional evidence, but also by analyses of causes of income differentials, which shows them to be closely correlated with geographical and sectoral location[36] and with education.

It is certainly true that widening income differences do not always promote economic growth. But the business and professional classes required for capitalist economic development will also transmit from generation to generation experience, traditions, and cultural traits appropriate to their calling, and socio-economic positions in competitive societies which, especially in the case of businessmen, demand that they keep advancing if they are to maintain their position. In the long run, the stabilization of a substantial capitalist class promotes the institutionalization of economic innovation and accumulation on a continuous and cumulative basis.[37] The claim that rising inequality coincides with declining welfare thus cannot be sustained by restricting the concept of inequality to that arising from ownership structures or structures of political authority (classes and elites), since the development of ownership and power structures in a capitalist society is inseparable from the acquisition of new skills and behavioural traits adapted to the requirements of this type of economy. Even where economic inequalities arise from morally unjust and/or economically irrelevant factors, the attempt to discriminate carefully between such inequalities

36. For example, distance from towns and railheads or cash-crop producing areas, or whether one is a subsistence farmer or a car-assembly worker.

37. The separation of ownership from direction and management implicit in this process eventually begins to create one of the major conditions making a change towards a socialist system appropriate. But this is another story, which in any case relates to an advanced stage of economic and cultural development.

and those arising from economically functional income differences may be very difficult in practice, sometimes impossible. Even when possible, it is likely to mean an immense strain on weak administrative apparatuses and an enormous cost in terms of alternative uses of such apparatuses, and especially of wastefully used skilled labour. In general, the consumption-oriented egalitarian approach ignores the economic costs of egalitarian policies, both direct and indirect.[38] These costs are likely to be quite high if some of the policies now being advocated are implemented.[39]

Moreover, the pursuit of income equality for its own sake is both unjust and undemocratic. It is unjust in that it would tend to equally reward different groups and individuals with different value judgements about consumption, leisure, intensity of work, acquisition of new skills, and the desirability of altering long-held customs and beliefs. The separation of reward from individual effort in societies characterized by extreme poverty would unjustly prevent individuals from fulfilling their social and personal obligations. It is undemocratic in that it is exceedingly unlikely that the current preoccupation of development economists with equality reflects the value judgements of the majority of the inhabitants of the Third World currently emerging into or adapting to the exchange economy. An aspiration to keep up with the Joneses, or even to avoid

38. It should not be forgotten that several decades of civil war were necessary for the establishment of an egalitarian regime in China, with all that implied in terms of economic loss. This in no way means that the Chinese Communist struggle was unjust or its outcome undesirable, but it does call attention to the glibness of those who call for similar egalitarian results in breathlessly short time periods and without experienced and realistic communist political leaderships.

39. Thus Charles Elliott views with disfavour the market selection and allocation of resources to Zambian farmers on the basis of their economic efficiency as an unfortunate case of increasing inequality (see Baster, p. 43) while C.L.G. Bell and John H. Dulay solemnly discuss how to restrict (!) the spillover benefits of rural feeder roads so that they do not also benefit richer farmers, traders, and contractors, but only the poor farmers. (C.L.G. Bell and John H. Dulay, 'Rural Target Groups', in Chenery et. al.)

starvation, logically implies neither a desire for an egalitarian economic policy, nor support for equality for those worse off than oneself.[40] Yet increased 'participation' by the population in government is illogically assumed to be consistent with egalitarian policies.[41]

In sum, such increasing income inequalities as are manifest in the Third World — and the evidence does not support the view that they dominate over trends towards greater equality — cannot be assumed to be detrimental to the poorest sections of the community,[42] except in a strictly arithmetical sense (i.e. the top 5 per cent have gained 'at the expense of' the bottom 40 per cent), since there are strong grounds for arguing that these inequalities are as much a cause as a consequence of economic growth and therefore of an eventual absolute improvement in the living standards of the majority.

3. Marginalization

The term 'marginalization' generally refers to the rising unemployment or underemployment of the labour force; it may be applied to situations in which workers are working short hours (or are employed for only a small number of working days in the year) or are engaged in comparatively unproductive or low-paying occupations.[43] The latter

40. There is a discussion relating to this point in W.G. Runciman, *Relative Deprivation and Social Justice*, part one.
41. Anybody acquainted with Nigeria would quickly see the point.
42. Although they may be so in particular cases.
43. The various definitions of underemployment in agriculture centring on zero marginal productivity or real incomes in excess of marginal productivity are irrelevant to the urban informal sector, since it must operate according to market criteria. Frequently stated views to the effect that this sector has little connection with the market ignore the fact that unlike its rural counterpart, it cannot provide subsistence and its practitioners must buy to live. One recent discussion of marginalization has defined the *marginal pole* as 'an attempt to conceptualize what, in some bourgeois literature, is characterized as the *informal sector*'. (M. Legassick and H. Wolpe, 'The Bantustans and Capital Accumulation in South Africa', *Review of African Political Economy*, No. 7, 1976.

conception of underemployment is often inaccurately applied to conditions in which a rising proportion of the work force is engaged in activities like crime or beggary, which effectively amount to obtaining a share of the productively earned income of the rest of the labour force.

The misleading impression has often been given that unemployment rates in the LDCs are extremely high and even rising, especially in urban areas. This picture is usually based on employment-exchange statistics. The only worthwhile evidence, however, is derived from census or sample survey data, and it actually shows that open unemployment in the urban areas of the LDCs is considerably less than has generally been supposed, often comparable to rates in the DMEs.

A recent ILO estimate of aggregate open unemployment in the Third World (based on such 'hard' data) puts the figure as low as 5 per cent in 1976.[44] This is consistent with a number of studies that have revealed unexpectedly low rates in individual countries.[45] It is difficult to establish long-term trends for the poor countries as a whole on the basis of hard data of this type, but the limited evidence available lends no support to the view that unemployment rates have been rising; it rather suggests the contrary (Table 12). The FAO *Report on the State of Food and Agriculture 1973* noted that of the thirteen LDCs that conducted regular sample surveys of the labour force in the 1960s, five showed a downward trend in the rate of open unemployment and one an upward

44. *Report of the Director-General.*
45. For example, J. Krishnamurty found an open unemployment rate, from National Sample Survey data, of only 2.6 percent for all India for 1966-67 ('Some Aspects of Unemployment in Urban India', in *Journal of Development Studies*, January, 1975, p. 13), while Adolfo Figueroa notes that in Peru the 1961 Census gave a national open unemployment percentage of only 2.8 percent while the 1967 survey of Lima's labour market gave a figure of 4.2 percent. ('Income Distribution, Demand Structure and Employment: The Case of Peru', *The Journal of Development Studies*, January, 1975, p. 21.). A. Berry and R.H. Sabot have summarized recent measures of open unemployment rates, and their average figure for Asia is 3.9%, for Latin America 5.1%, and for Africa 7.1%. (*Labour Market Performance in Developing Countries: A Survey*, World Development, Vol. 6 (1978), p. 1212).

Table 12

Labour Force Surveys For Selected Developing Countries 1964-1977
(Rate of Unemployment in %)

Country	1964	1965	1966	1967	1968	1969	1970	1971	1972	1973	1974	1975	1976	1977
Egypt	—	—	—	—	3.1	2.7	2.4	1.8	1.5	1.6	2.3	2.5	—	—
Argentina (Gran Buenos Aires)	5.7	5.3	5.6	6.4	5.0	4.3	4.8	6.0	6.6	5.6	3.4	2.3	—	—
Chile	—	—	5.7	4.7	4.8	4.7	3.4	3.8	3.1	—	—	6.1	6.5	—
Panama	7.4	7.6	5.1	6.2	7.0	6.6	7.1	7.6	6.8	7.0	5.8	4.9	5.2	—
Peru	—	—	—	—	—	5.9	4.7	4.4	4.2	4.2	4.0	—	—	—
Trinidad and Tobago	—	14.0	14.0	15.0	15.0	13.5	12.5	12.6	—	15.4	15.3	15.0	3.9	3.0
South Korea	—	—	—	6.2	5.1	4.8	4.5	4.5	4.5	4.0	4.1	4.1	—	—
Philippines	6.4	8.2	7.2	8.0	7.8	6.7	5.2	5.2	6.3	4.8	4.0	3.9	—	—
Syria	11.4	7.4	5.5	5.3	7.4	4.3	6.4	7.5	4.7	4.5	5.1	4.8	6.2	—

Source: ILO, Yearbook of Labour Statistics 1977 and 1974, Table 10, Geneva (1974 and 1977).

trend; in the others the trend was unclear (p. 133). It does not seem likely that this can be explained principally by shifting participation rates (as potential job-seekers withdrew from or failed to enter the labour market),[46] since the decline in crude participation rates that actually occurred in developing market economies in the 1960s was mainly due to a reduction in the proportion of the population of working age, together with a widespread tendency towards decreasing activity rates for males in the youngest and oldest brackets. There was little variation in activity rates for men in the central age groups, who provide most of the labour supply in most countries.[47]

The case for such remarkable suggestions as those of Singer (unemployment rates of up to 50 per cent by 1980) must therefore rest upon underemployment. If we adopt the short-hours approach to underemployment — the only non-tautological and measurable approach for the urban labour force — a survey of the available evidence shows that average hours worked by the total urban labour force are generally high, that those wishing to work longer hours are frequently doing so already, that there is no particular relationship between time worked and extra time wanted, that estimates of the extra work demanded as an equivalent percentage of full-time unemployment tends to be only about 2 or 3 per cent, and that those working short hours tend to be concentrated at the extremes of the age range of the labour force. Moreover, average hours worked are high despite genuine short-time working and despite the fact that some groups (such as teachers) have short hours by agreement.[48] Turnham has advanced the important suggestion that since the gap between 'hours worked' and 'hours available for work' does not seem particularly wide, especially among

46. Although this does appear to have happened in individual cases at certain times, e.g. in Egypt and India. (United Nations Department of Economic and Social Affairs, *The Determinants and Consequences of Population Trends*, Vol. I, 1973, pp. 309-310.)

47. Ibid., pp. 295-6, p. 315.

48. David Turnham and Ingelies Jaeger, *The Employment Problem in Less Developed Countries: A Review of Evidence*, OECD, Paris, 1971, p. 59.

those working few hours, the application of conventional unemployment methodology (as in the developed economies) may be quite appropriate to the LDCs.[49] This, of course, would enhance the significance of the evidence for comparatively low and probably declining open unemployment rates.

Attention has accordingly been focused increasingly on the use of poverty (low income, absolute or relative) or low productivity as measures of underemployment, for the emotional resonance of the term 'unemployment', with all its overtones of the 1930s, must be preserved at all costs. Quite often the simple assumption is that the portion of the urban work force not employed in the 'modern' sector must be substantially underemployed. But since poverty and low productivity have many causes other than unemployment or involuntary short hours, they can be measures of underemployment only by definition; as such, they cannot in themselves indicate a large marginal population, unless the enterprises of the urban informal sector can be shown to be 'marginal' by some criterion other than productivity or income.

It is now clear from recent research[50] that it cannot be

49. Ibid., p. 60. Unfortunately, Turnham then fudges his point by advocating the poverty approach to underemployment.

50. For example, *Employment and Equality: A Strategy for Increasing Productive Employment in Kenya*, ILO, Geneva, 1972, ch. 12; C.J. Fapohunda, *Development of Urban Infrastructure in Greater Lagos*, World Employment Programme Research, ILO, Geneva, 1974, p. 54; J. Weeks, 'Introduction', Manpower and Unemployment Research in Africa (November, 1973), p. 5 (on Ghana); Kalmann Schaefer and Cheywa R. Spindel, *Urban Development and Employment in São Paulo*, World Employment Programme Research, ILO, Geneva, 1974, pp. 4-5; S.V. Sethuraman, *Urbanization and Employment in Jakarta*, World Employment Programme Research, ILO, Geneva, 1974; Heather Joshi, Harold Lubell, and Jean Mouly, *Urban Development and Employment in Abidjan*, World Employment Programme Research, ILO, Geneva, 1974, chapter 4; Dr. A.N. Bose, *The Informal Sector in the Calcutta Metropolitan Economy*, World Employment Programme Research, ILO, Geneva, 1974; K. King, *Kenya's Informal Machine Makers; A Study of Small Scale Industry in Kenya's Emergent Artisan Society*, Centre of African Studies, Edinburgh University (March, 1974); M.A. Bienefeld, *The Self-Employed of Urban Tanzania*, I.D.S. Sussex, Discussion Paper, No. 54 (May 1974).

assumed automatically that the activities of the urban informal sector are primarily of a time-filling, redistributive (e.g. beggars and thieves),[51] or duplicatory (e.g. hawkers) character.[52] The relative importance of such parasitic activities within the informal sector is unknown, but the least that can be said is that in most of the large cities of the Third World a wide variety of essential goods and services are provided at relatively low cost to a substantial proportion of the population by the informal sector.[53] There is disagreement as to whether the informal sector is basically residual and stagnant or whether it comprises significant elements of internal dynamism in terms of innovation, accumulation, and the upward mobility of the more successful operators. A strong case can be made for the latter view,[54] which implies the existence of an expanding wage-labour force in the informal sector[55] and suggests that

51. Prostitutes are often classified with beggars and thieves, but their occupation must be regarded as socially beneficial in cities with large male immigrant populations.

52. Biplap das Gupta's analysis of the informal sector in Calcutta is an exception. He concludes that the Calcutta urban informal sector makes little contribution to the national economy and creates innumerable economic and social problems which cannot be easily solved. ('Calcutta's Informal Sector', *Institute of Development Studies Bulletin*, October 1973, pp. 72-3.).

53. One observer has argued that 'the majority of the urban population in black Africa obtains its housing, transport, services, fuel, food and clothing through the non-enumerated sector'. John Weeks, 'An Exploration into the Nature of the Problem of Urban Imbalance in Africa', Manpower and Unemployment Research in Africa, November 1973, p. 17.

54. Particularly positive verdicts on the economic contribution of the informal sector are given in ILO, *Employment and Equality,* in Fapohunda, in Weeks's 'Introduction', in Schaefer and Spindel, and in Joshi, Lubell, and Mouly for Kenya, Ghana, São Paulo (Brazil), and Abidjan (Ivory Coast) respectively. See also K.C. Zachariah, 'Bombay Migration Study: A Pilot Analysis of Migration to an Asian Metropolis', in *Demography* (1966).

55. All the studies cited in note 50 (except the ILO Kenya study) give evidence of the importance of wage labour in the informal sector, with in addition many transitional forms between self-employment and wage employment. The ILO Kenya Report's characterization of the informal sector as consisting primarily of self-employed has been strongly contested. Cf. C. Leys, 'Interpreting African Underdevelopment: Reflections on the ILO Report on Kenya', Manpower and Unemployment Research in Africa, November 1974. A recent study of employment in small-scale industry in

the dichotomy between formal and informal sector may be excessively rigid. A wide range of service activities often taken as prima facie evidence of underemployment appear actually to be functional to the general growth of the urban economy; many of them are linked directly to the needs and growth of the secondary sector.[56] The proliferation of various types of traders has been convincingly presented as an economically efficient adaptation to the structure of the economy.[57] These traders undertake modern and traditional occupations involving the use of modern technologies, from photography and cab-driving to small-scale engineering,[58] and profit maximization is found even among the self-employed and craftsmen. Thriving 'informal' apprenticeship systems testify indirectly to the non-ephemeral, productive, and expansive character of some important informal-sector activities.[59] Scattered but mounting evi-

rural Sri Lanka found that the role of unpaid family workers was small and that, on the other hand, the rate of growth of employment in these rural enterprises was on the order of 6 % per annum. ILO, *Rural Small-Scale Industries and Employment in Sri Lanka*, World Employment Programme, Geneva (October 1978), Part I, p. 4 and Part II, p. 9.

56. It is estimated, for example, that jobs in the production services sub-sector of São Paulo account for about 50 % of total services jobs. The growth of such activities is a direct function of the economic development of the area and covers such activities as merchandizing, wholesale and retail trade, transport, communications, real estate, and banking services. Productivity levels are probably comparable to those in the secondary sector. Schaefer and Spindel, p.4.

57. Due to the economies of breaking bulk arising from the character of the market, consisting as it does of large numbers of very low-income purchasers, and from the credit economies thereby attained. Cf. P.T. Bauer, *West African Trade*, chapter 2, and Barry Lamont Isaac, *Traders in Pendembu, Sierra Leone, A Case Study in Entrepreneurship*, University of Oregon: Ph. D. thesis, 1969, cited in Weeks, 'Urban Imbalance', p. 17.

58. Weeks's path-breaking discussion ('Urban Imbalance') is excellent on this point but tends to over-emphasize self-employment and the competitive as opposed to the complementary relationships of the formal and informal sectors. A good description of their complementary characteristics on the supply side is given in Kenneth King, 'Skill Acquisition in the Informal Sector of an African Economy: The Kenya Case', *Journal of Development Studies*, January 1975. Complementarity on the demand side needs no argument for the informal sector in general, but competitive relations may be more important in specific cases.

59. For Ghana, for example, see Planungsgruppe Ritter (Koenigstein,

dence of a spectrum of earnings, numbers employed, and productivity suggest dynamic processes leading to the emergence and enrichment of the more efficient entrepreneurs.[60] It thus remains to be established that those working in the informal sector are marginal — except in the tautological sense that underemployment is equated with relatively low levels of productivity or income.[61] The view that the existence of the informal sector reflects widespread underemployment thus appears to be a distorted reflection of the fact that the range of productivity and earnings levels within and between occupations and industries is much greater in LDCs than in DMEs.[62]

It is widely held that underemployment is growing in the Third World as the urban work force expands faster than employment in the formal sector, and that this implies a secular trend towards declining average levels of produc-

F.R. of Germany), *Project on Urbanization, Employment and Development in Ghana: Report on Two Surveys,* World Employment Programme Research, ILO (Geneva 1974), pp. 52 ff.; and for Kenya, Kenneth King. Examples could be multiplied.

60. For example W.J. Steel, *Empirical Measurement of the Relative Size and Productivity of Intermediate Sector Employment: Some Estimates from Ghana,* MURA (April, 1976), pp. 23-31; A. Peace, 'The Lagos Proletariat: Labour Aristocrats or Populist Militants', in *The Development of an African Working Class,* edited by R. Sandbrook and R. Cohen, London, 1975, pp. 281-302. Stuart W. Sinclair draws attention to the dynamic implications of these studies for processes of capital accumulation in the informal sector, *The Intermediate Sector in the Economy,* MURA (November 1976). D. Mazumdar presents findings from Malaysia, Peru, and Tanzania showing a wide diversity of earnings among the self-employed, suggesting that a substantial proportion of this group perform *better* than the wage earners. ('The Urban Informal Sector', *World Development,* Vol. 4, 1976, p. 666).

61. The integrated character of the urban economy (which indeed is what defines it) is such that relatively low productivity or income cannot define marginal activity in any accepted sense of the term 'marginal'. Night-soil removers or petty traders, although by conventional measurement with low productivity or remuneration, are likely to be *essential* to the effective functioning of the economy.

62. See G. Myrdal, *Asian Drama,* p. 2182. If this is the case, it suggests that the conceptualization in the literature of a specific informal sector, presumably with its own characteristics that separately or in combination distinguish it from other sectors, may obscure more than it illuminates. Weeks's term 'non-enumerated sector' largely avoids this problem, which has already laid numerous false trails.

tivity and remuneration. But it is not clear that the work force in the informal sector is rising proportionately to the urban labour force, nor that productivity in the informal sector is declining.

The *1974 Report on the World Social Situation*, by the United Nations, points out, for example, that in Latin America, the birthplace of 'marginalization', 'the available occupational statistics do not indicate a disproportionate relative increase in those forms of self-employment and tertiary-sector labour which are most likely to contain disguised unemployment and poverty' (p. 40, n. 29).

Table 13 illustrates these points for six Latin American countries, and also shows that the proportion of the urban labour force accounted for by the self-employed is comparatively small. In addition, there is evidence from a number of other developing countries that the wage-labour force is expanding at the expense of other types of employment (family or self-employment).[63] Thus, Table 14 shows that in the majority of developing economies for which data is available, the proportion of wage-earners as a percentage of the economically active population rose between 1960 and 1970.[64]

63. The fact that a sizeable proportion of the wage labour force is initially employed in the state sector does not affect the fundamentally capitalist character of the development: since the overall orientation is generally towards an increasingly market economy; since initial development of the state sector is often a historical interlude serving to stimulate the private sector (Turkey is the classic case); and since the relative importance of state-sector wage employment is generally much exaggerated, as the figures almost invariably understate the extensive development, especially in agriculture, of a wide variety of transitional forms of wage labour (including various types of migrant and seasonal labour), which although frequently neglected in the literature because of statistical difficulties arising from incomplete specialization, are nevertheless economically vital and indicate even further the extent and intensity of the capitalist transformation of society at the most fundamental levels.

64. Ramos's research in Latin America showed a rising share of salaried employment for 13 countries during the period since the Second World War and led him to conclude that disguised urban unemployment was decreasing over the period of the 1950s and 1960s. J. Ramos, 'A Heterodoxical Interpretation of the Employment Problem in Latin America', *World Development*, Vol. 2 (1974), cited in Bery and Sabot.

Table 13

Latin America: Distribution of the Economically Active Population in Selected Countries by Occupational Strata, 1960-1973 (in %)

	National Coverage						Urban Coverage					
	Brazil		Chile		Venezuela		Costa Rica		Ecuador		Uruguay	
	1960	1972	1960	1972	1960	1973	1963	1970	1962	1968	1963	1970
I. Middle & upper strata (other than primary sector)	15.0	23.3	20.3	27.8	23.9	36.8	33.6	46.2	25.0	39.8	50.9	45.8
a) Employers	1.9	4.1	1.5	2.4	1.8	3.6	3.0	6.0	1.7	4.1	8.4	5.6
b) Self-employed with own commercial establishment	0.2	1.6	3.7	4.9	5.4	7.0	4.4	3.1	9.1	12.1	3.0	3.8
c) Independent professionals & semi-professionals	0.7	0.5	0.6	0.6	0.4	0.6	0.5	0.3	0.7	1.3	2.5	1.5
d) Dependent professionals	2.6	4.3	4.0	6.2	4.8	8.2	9.4	11.0	5.3	7.2	7.5	7.3
e) Managerial personnel	2.6		1.4	1.2	1.0	1.3	1.9	3.4	0.4	1.1	1.3	0.8
f) Clerks, sales personnel & other employees	7.0	12.8	9.2	12.5	10.5	16.1	14.4	22.4	7.8	14.0	28.2	26.8
II. Lower strata (secondary sector)	22.7	20.1	32.4	31.3	26.0	30.2	32.4	31.3	38.2	34.7	30.1	36.1
a) Wage workers	15.2	14.6	26.1	25.2	19.3	22.5	25.1	26.1	19.2	22.5	25.0	29.5
b) Own account & unpaid family workers	7.5	5.5	6.3	6.1	6.7	7.7	7.3	5.2	19.0	12.2	5.1	6.6
III. Lower strata (tertiary sector)	7.1	7.9	13.4	12.0	11.4	12.6	16.5	15.7	14.8	17.7	14.9	14.3
a) Wage workers	6.7	6.5	12.3	10.9	10.0	10.7	15.2	15.0	12.4	13.9	13.9	12.7
b) Own account and unpaid family workers	0.4	1.4	1.1	1.1	1.4	1.9	1.3	0.7	2.4	3.9	1.0	1.6
IV. Middle & upper (primary sector) Employers in agriculture & extraction	0.0	0.0	1.1	0.8	0.9	1.0	1.3	1.1	1.2	1.0	0.3	0.6
V. Lower strata (primary sector)	50.9	40.2	29.9	24.4	32.7	19.1	12.6	4.8	18.9	6.1	0.5	1.4
a) Rural wage workers	14.2	11.8	21.7	16.5	11.6	7.1	8.3	3.9	10.6	3.9	0.4	0.5
b) Own account & unpaid family workers	36.7	28.4	8.2	7.9	21.1	12.0	4.3	0.9	8.3	2.2	0.1	0.9
VI. Unclassified	4.3	8.4	3.2	3.7	5.1	0.3	3.6	0.9	1.9	0.7	3.3	1.8

Source: UN 1974 Report on the World Social Situation, p. 53.

Table 14

Salaried and Wage Earners as Per Cent of the Economically Active
Population — Some Developing Market Economies[1] — 1960 and 1970[2]

Country	1960	1970
Ghana	18.10	22.50
Morocco	34.70	37.20
Dominican Republic	44.10	38.20
El Salvador	50.00	51.70
Mexico	64.10	62.30
Panama	42.50	55.30
Puerto Rico	80.20	84.50
Argentina	69.20	70.80
Brazil	48.00	54.80
Chile	72.80	70.20
Syria	49.10	41.70
Turkey	18.80	25.80
Hong Kong	79.00	83.00
India	12.80	17.00
South Korea	21.30	38.00
Philippines	27.20	39.90
Thailand	11.80	15.60

1. All market LDCs covered (except Israel) for which data available.
2. 1960-1970 comparison 'relatively good'.

Source: UNRISD, *Development Indicators, 1960-1970*, Comparisons, p. 102.

Little or nothing is known about the trends of productivity and real earnings in the urban informal sector, but it has generally been found that per capita remuneration there is higher than for the openings available in the rural sector;[65] the possibility of obtaining a job in the formal sector is therefore not the only economic reason for rural-urban migration. This, however, leaves open the possibility that average informal urban-sector earnings may be declining if average earnings are declining in the rural sector. Very little

65. For São Paulo, for example, see Schaefer and Spindel, pp. 4-5; for Jakarta, Sethuraman, pp. 6.31 and 6.39; for Abidjan, Joshi, Lubell and Mouly, p. 5.15; for Kenya, ILO, *Employment Incomes and Equality*, p. 5; for Peru, Mazumdar, who cites research to the effect that 'the common assumption that urban workers (except for a lucky few placed in modern establishments) are no better off than the rural poor, is an erroneous generalization derived from the case of the urban fringe: the poorest (and most visible) 5 - 10 %'(p. 671).

is known about the trend of real earnings in agriculture and other rural activities, and generalization about the Third World is even more dubious on these issues than on others. There is a slight presumption that average real earnings in agriculture may have risen somewhat throughout the Third World postwar, since both overall agricultural output per capita and food output per capita have risen slightly, while the proportion of the total labour force employed in agriculture has declined substantially: from 73.3% in 1950 to 60% in 1970.[66] Surveying the evidence on employment in agriculture, Turnham remarks that there is no empirical basis for the widely held view that agriculture is racked by unemployment and underemployment, particularly that labour has little to do for four to six months of the year.[67] But changing terms of trade between manufactured and agricultural products, shifting income distribution in the countryside, government fiscal policies, and other factors will all have affected the situation, as well as the fact that in particular cases there will be no alternative openings in agriculture, i.e. there will be open unemployment. It is pertinent here, however, that the spectrum of earnings within the informal sector and the overlap between formal- and informal-sector earnings,[68] together with the fact that length of residence tends to be positively correlated with the urban immigrants' average earnings,[69] imply an upward mobility that would ensure that average earnings in the informal sector would not be rigidly tied to the trends in rural income.

66. P. Bairoch, p. 160. Agricultural output per capita in developing countries was slightly higher in 1977 than in 1970, and between 1970 and 1977 there was a fairly substantial decline in the percentage of the active population in the developing countries engaged in agriculture. (FAO, *Production Yearbook 1977*, Rome (1978), pp. 70 and 80.)

67. P. 62. For evidence on *declining* rural unemployment trends in India, see K. Bardhan, 'Rural Employment, Wages and Labour Markets in India, A Survey of Research', *Economic and Political Weekly*, Vol. XII, No. 27, 1977, p. 1067.

68. This point is brought out in most of the World Employment Programme Research studies, and in Mazumdar.

69. For example, Sethuraman on Jakarta, p. 6.31.

The interpretation of rising urban underemployment in terms of shifts from more to less productive and remunerative occupations is consistent with the concept of 'disguised unemployment' from which the underemployment approach originated.[70] In the original conception this move from occupations of higher to lower productivity was supposed to be due to a decline in effective demand. It is more likely that what is called underemployment in the Third World, at least in the urban areas, is the result of a shift from less to more remunerative occupations, at least for the bulk of rural-urban migrants. The principal basis for characterizing them as 'underemployed' is that they fall below some arbitrary dividing line demarcating the superior productivity or earnings of the rest of the urban labour force, even if the incomes of the 'underemployed' have actually improved over time.

The concept of marginalization implies the effective disruption or weakening of the linkages of a growing number of the (generally urban) population with the central activities of the economy. As is common in development economics, a term that arose with a valid descriptive function (referring to shanty towns on the outskirts of Third World cities) has acquired a sophisticated, conceptual superstructure.[71] In fact, so-called marginalization is a way of referring to the anarchic, chaotic, unplanned, sometimes brutal, but nevertheless vigorous fashion in which urbanization expands the market, stimulates commercialization of the whole of society (especially the agricultural sector), and thereby increases the division of labour and thus the *integration* of society, as Adam Smith noted long ago. The real process is just the opposite of that implied by the word; it is one of increasing *integration*. The shanty towns, unlike slums, are not the result of deterioration, but represent improvements over rural conditions,[72] and many

70. J. Robinson, *Essays in the Theory of Employment*, 1937, p. 84.
71. Analogous to 'dependence' and 'underemployment', not to mention 'underdevelopment' itself.
72. Although there are also, of course, slums of the traditional type in the

are improved over time.[73] The rural-urban migration, together with the return flows to the villages, is a progressive force in breaking up subsistence activities, institutions, and attitudes that held up material progress; rural life in general and agricultural practice in particular are consequently transformed. The growth of towns undermines relatively self-sufficient communities and leads to specialization and reintegration of separate economic activities through the market, breaking down the economic isolation characteristic of precapitalist societies.[74]

4. Output, Consumption, and Welfare

Indices Measuring Improvements in Welfare

The thesis that the rising volume of goods and services available in the Third World since the Second World War is not oriented towards the 'basic needs' of the majority of the population (food, health care, housing, education) often forms a dimension of the marginalization approach[75]' and a major source of the dissatisfaction of development economists with the first development decade.

This position is often phrased in terms of 'distortions' from some usually unstated 'norms' that seldom (if ever) existed

Third World. The UN *1974 World Social Situation Report* distinguishes between slums and squatter settlements and notes that comparisons between rural and urban areas almost always show greater overcrowding in the former than the latter (pp. 235-6).

73. Ibid., p. 233. Certainly in Brazil there may well have been a greater urban surplus population in the late nineteenth and early twentieth century than later in the capital-intensive stages of industrialization. B. Roberts, *Cities of Peasants, The Political Economy of Urbanization in the Third World*, p. 170.

74. Cf. Zachariah, also J.C. Caldwell, *African Rural-Urban Migration.* The empirical basis of the 'over-urbanization' case has recently been seriously questioned, e.g. by Koichi Mera.

75. In the sense that not only occupational and participatory patterns but also consumption patterns will show an increasing divergence between marginal participants and those thoroughly integrated into the economy and society.

historically, or alternatively from consumption patterns that allegedly would have existed but for the artifical wants created by advertising and exposure to Western-type consumption patterns.[76]

This argument is closely related to another point: that GNP per capita is an inadequate proxy for 'welfare' or 'development' if those terms are taken to refer in some sense to the needs of the great majority of the population rather than the privileged few. Uneven distribution alone ensures that GNP per capita is a value-loaded proxy, since market valuations are inherently biased to afford greater weight to consumption by the rich. Moreover, the incomplete development of the market in LDCs and the high degree of market imperfections undermine the validity of GNP calculations even on their own terms. Finally, the statistical basis of such calculations in many, perhaps most, LDCs is so weak that measures of GNP per capita are liable to errors as great as several hundred per cent.

All these points are valid to a great extent,[77] but they leave open the *extent* to which figures on GNP per capita give a misleading impression both of shifts in the level and pace of development and welfare over time and of comparisons between countries.

76. All consumption patterns are culturally determined to some extent, and cultural contact between different civilizations has generally been regarded as an enriching element and an important stimulus to human progress. Can it be assumed that Third World consumers are acting irrationally or in a vulgar, grossly materialist fashion in emulating Western consumption patterns? Such assumptions would be not only condescending, but also, if incorporated in policy aims, undemocratic. The shift in taste from rice towards bread, for instance, should not be seen as an unmitigated disaster for South Asian countries; at least from the point of view of women, the consequent reduction in meal preparation time must be regarded as a bonus. From a purely economic point of view, such attempted emulation need not necessarily result in excessive consumption. It may encourage greater production to obtain the desired goods.

77. It should be noted, however, that the fact that monetary GNP is a value-loaded indicator does not make it subjective insofar as it reflects the objectively effective values of the society concerned. Knowledge of the fact does not of course imply moral or political acceptance of it, but neither does moral rejection make it any less a fact.

The large element of statistical error, for example, is far less serious for rates of change than for absolute levels of GNP per capita; the measure of relative progress in one country over time by this statistic may therefore be much more nearly accurate than its measure of national differences. More fundamentally, however, composite measures of development or welfare on the basis of physical indicators show a close association between per capita GNP and the living- or development-index. A 1966 study by the United Nations Research Institute for Social Development covering twenty countries[78] around 1960 and based principally on physical indicators was designed to gauge 'the level of satisfaction of the needs of the population assured by the flow of goods and services enjoyed in a unit of time'. The seven components of the index consisted of six physical indicators covering nutrition, education, housing, leisure and recreation, health, and security, plus a monetary indicator for surplus, covering higher needs. A distributional component was also incorporated into the index. Spearman rank-coefficient correlation of the level-of-living indices for per capita consumption expenditures and for per capita GNP were (with sliding weights). 0.889 and 0.923 respectively (p. 63). Product-moment coefficients of the level-of-living index on consumption per capita and GNP per capita with sliding weights were 0.919 and 0.930 (p. 64). The authors remark, after examining divergences in relative positions for individual countries as given by the level-of-living index and the per capita GNP index, that these divergences are wide enough to justify use of the former (or of some similar measure) rather than per capita GNP in assessing the pace of development (p. 65). This view is acceptable, but the fact remains that the close correlations between GNP per capita and the level-of-living index must imply that if the latter provides a reliable indication of welfare, then so should GNP

78. UNRISD, *The Level of Living Index,* by Jan Drewnowski and Wolf Scott, Geneva, 1966. The countries are: Ghana, Mauritius, Morocco, UAR Uganda, Argentina, Chile, Equador, Jamaica, USA, India, Israel, Japan Thailand, Belgium, Denmark, Greece, Spain and Yugoslavia (p. 59).

per capita, on the average.

UNRISD has since produced a more ambitious Development Index.[79] It is based on the years 1959/61 and covers fifty-eight countries, twenty-seven of them underdeveloped. It differs from the 1966 level-of-living index in that the old index was basically normative, whereas the new eschews any attempt to measure the level of culture, civilization, human welfare, happiness, or the 'better life'. Essentially it measures those characteristics that distinguish developed from less developed countries insofar as they are interdependent components, i.e. both outputs and inputs of the development process.[80] It is based on eighteen core physical indicators[81] of both levels of living and structural features associated with development that are not in themselves welfare components or proxies for welfare components. No distributive component is incorporated explicitly, but some of the indicators do reflect the general level of living (and the authors argue that in the broadest sense income distribution means distribution of levels of living): percentage of children in school, literacy rate, percentage of dwellings with electricity, life expectation rate, all of which reflect the spread of socially favourable

79. UNRISD, *Contents and Measurement of Socio-Economic Development: An Empirical Enquiry*, prepared by D. McGranahan, C. Richard-Proust, N.V. Sovani, M. Subramamian. Report No. 70.10, Geneva, 1970.

80. Ibid., p. 143.

81. They are: expectation of life at birth; population in localities of 20,000 persons and over as a proportion of the total population; consumption of animal proteins per capita per day; combined primary and secondary enrolment as a percentage of the 5-19 age group; vocational enrolment as a percentage of the 15-19 age group; average number of persons per room; circulation of daily newspapers of general interest per 1,000 of the population; telephones per 1,000 of the population; radio receivers per 1,000 of the population; percentage of the economically active population in electricity, gas, water, sanitary services, transport, storage and communications; production per male agricultural worker in 1960 (in US dollars); adult male labour in agriculture as a percentage of the total male labour force; electricity consumption in kwh per capita; steel consumption in kg per capita; energy consumption in kg of coal per capita; GDP derived from manufacturing as a percentage of total GDP; foreign trade (sum of imports and exports) per capita in 1960 US dollars; and salaried and wage-earners as a percentage of the total economically active population.

conditions and can be contrasted with the accumulation of benefits where they are already high.[82] Similar results to those noted for UNRISD's index emerge from this study, despite the differences between the two indices. Discrepancies between the development and per capita GNP indices for individual countries appear to be sufficient to justify use of the former instead of the latter as a measure of development as defined.[83] The correlation of the two indices is high for all fifty-eight countries (.86), but lower (though still respectable) for the LDCs alone (.67).[84] The level-of-living index and the development index (compared with the GNP-per-capita index) for the individual countries is given in Tables 15 and 16. It is worth noting that the *range* of the two new indices is very much lower than that of per capita GNP, which is consistent with the recent ILO re-estimates of the DME/LDC per capita GNP gap, the effect of which is to reduce average income differences between rich and poor countries from about 13:1 to 4:1.[85] These results, especially those based on the level-of-living index, must be regarded as highly tentative (as the authors themselves emphasize), but they do at least suggest that GNP per capita, although it may well yield wild results for individual countries, may not, after all, be so bad a guide in assessing the pace of *development*[86] for LDCs in general. The more narrow range of the development and level-of-living indices than the per capita GNP index, together with the ILO re-estimates of rich-poor per capita income gaps, *may* imply faster development of LDCs relative to DMEs than is generally supposed. Although the development index is emphatically *not* a normative index, insofar as it does reflect the advance of LDCs towards the characteristics of the developed countries it necessarily incorporates progress towards the eradication of poverty,

82. Ibid., p. 15.
83. The development index is also more closely correlated with the individual indicators than is per capita GNP; ibid., p. 41.
84. Ibid., Tables 14 and 15.
85. *Report of the Director-General*, 1976.
86. In the sense in which it is distinguished from growth.

unemployment, and inequality, the basic normative elements of development as defined, for example, by Dudley Seers; these values are widely accepted by development economists. It is therefore up to critics to show that rises in monetary per capita GNP do not exhibit at least a rough and ready correlation with welfare and development.[87]

Table 15

Level of Living Index & GNP Per Capita for Twenty Countries, ca. 1960

Country	Level of Living Index (sliding weights) Value	Rank	GNP Per Capita (US$) Value	Rank
Ghana	38.1	19	290	14
Mauritius	61.1	11	410	13
Morocco	39.4	17	230	17
United Arab Republic	47.9	14	240	16
Uganda	37.3	20	120	20
Argentina	83.9	7	860	5
Chile	69.5	10	750	6
Ecuador	44.7	15	250	15
Jamaica	50.2	13	510	11
USA	171.3	1	2,790	1
Venezuela	52.7	12	570	9
India	42.0	16	160	19
Israel	126.6	4	950	4
Japan	85.3	5	700	7
Thailand	39.0	18	200	18
Belgium	129.7	3	1,690	3
Denmark	130.4	2	1,760	2
Greece	84.1	6	620	8
Spain	75.9	9	540	10
Yugoslavia	80.6	8	480	12

Notes: (i) GDP for Uganda; (ii) Mauritius GNP figure is for 1961; (iii) GNP figure for Yugoslavia for 1962.

Source: UNRISD, *The Level of Living Index*, 1966, p. 70.

87. Seers remarks: 'Egalitarians like myself face a theoretical paradox. If we argue that the national income is an inappropriate measure of a nation's development, we weaken the significance of a growing per capita income "gap" between rich nations and poor.' (Ibid., p. 34.) Actually, we have here not a theoretical paradox but a classic example of wishing to have one's cake and eat it.

Table 16

Development Index and Per Capita GNP for 1960 for Fifty-Eight Countries

Country	Development Index	Per Capita GNP for 1959/61 (US$)	Country	Development Index	Per Capita GNP for 1959/61 (US$)
USA	111	2828	Portugal	52	300
United Kingdom	104	1369	Yugoslavia	51	—
Canada	103	2092	Costa Rica	50	352
New Zealand	103	1515	Panama	48	385
Sweden	103	1696	Taiwan	46	249
Australia	98	1542	Colombia	46	253
Norway	98	1274	Jamaica	45	396
Belgium	96	1247	Mexico	44	348
Netherlands	96	965	Brazil	38	267
Switzerland	96	1591	Peru	37	198
Denmark	95	1300	United Arab Republic	34	158
West Germany	94	1327	El Salvador	32	321
France	88	1303	Jordan	32	196
Austria	86	867	Nicaragua	32	238
Finland	85	1085	Syria	32	—
Israel	81	1220	Ecuador	31	202
Hungary	75	—	Dominican Republic	30	228
Hong Kong	74	—	Libya	29	283
Ireland	74	653	Paraguay	29	160
Japan	74	463	Turkey	27	202
Uruguay	74	494	Iran	26	210
Argentina	73	551	Morocco	26	154
Poland	73	—	South Korea	25	149
Italy	71	684	Philippines	24	206
Venezuela	63	958	Honduras	23	209
South Africa	62	453	Guatemala	21	269
Chile	61	604	Ceylon	18	139
Spain	58	344	Ghana	16	195
Greece	52	432	Thailand	10	96

Changes in various basic individual indicators of welfare in recent years are also consistent with the view that there has been considerable progress in material welfare for the populations as a whole and not simply for the privileged few. Calorie intake as a percentage of requirements in developing market economies, for example, rose from 93% in 1961 to 97% in 1969-71,[88] following a much steeper improvement during the previous period, 1948-52 to 1957-58.[89]

Truly remarkable advances have also been achieved in education, especially primary but also secondary (Tables 17, 18, and 19). Equally spectacular results are evident in the field of health, the two most significant indicators — infant mortality and life expectation at birth — showing marked improvements (Table 20). Data on changes in housing conditions are rather scarce. Table 21 presents three indicators for all LDCs (unfortunately excluding those defined by the IBRD as 'capital surplus oil exporters'), covering the dates 1960, 1970, and 'most recent' (which refers

Table 17

Proportion of Children in the Age Group 5-14 Receiving Primary Education in Africa, Asia and Latin America, 1950 and 1959

	1950(%)	1959(%)
Africa	17	28
Asia	25	42
Latin America	38	49

Source: UN, *Report on the World Social Situation*, 1963, p. 64.

88. FAO, *The State of Food and Agriculture 1975*, Rome, 1976, p. 76. An improvement in these aggregate terms is, of course, quite consistent with the existence of widespread malnutrition. However, the proportion of the population of developing countries that suffers from malnutrition has frequently been overestimated. P.V. Sukhatme, 'Assessment of Adequacy of Diets and Different Income Levels', *Economic and Political Weekly*, Special Number (1978).

89. Figure III.3. in FAO, *The State of Food and Agriculture 1970*. Those developing countries which the World Bank defines as 'Low Income', 'Lower Middle Income', and 'Intermediate Middle Income' all show continued improvements between 1970 and 1976 in the index of calorie supply as a percentage of requirement. World Bank, *World Economic and Social Indicators*, p. 36.

Table 18

Proportion of Children of Primary School Age Attending School (at any level) in Africa, Asia and Latin America, 1960, 1970 and 1975

	1960 (%)	1970 (%)	1975 (%)*
Africa	34	48	51
Asia	50	59	64
Latin America	60	78	78

Source: UN, *Report on the World Social Situation*, 1974, p. 225.

*This column contains *enrolment ratios* for the age-group 6-11 years extracted from UNESCO *Statistical Yearbook 1976*, Paris (1977), Table 2.9.

Table 19

Proportion of Children of Secondary School Age Attending School (at any level) in Africa, Asia and Latin America, 1960, 1970 and 1975

	1960 (%)	1970 (%)	1975 (%*)
Africa	12	25	31
Asia	22	44	35
Latin America	26	49	56.5

Source: UN, *Report on the World Social Situation*, 1974, p. 225.

*This column contains *enrolment ratios* for the age-group 12-17 years extracted from UNESCO *Statistical Yearbook 1976*, Paris (1977), Table 2.9.

to the period between 1973 and 1976). The majority of developing countries show substantial improvements by all three measures, even though there has been deterioration for some of the 'low income' countries.

The improvement in general welfare suggested by the physical indicators for nutrition, health, housing, and education (and strongly suggested by the correlation of level-of-living and development indices with GNP per capita) is further supported for the period 1963-72 by ILO estimates of the proportion of those classed as 'poor', 'seriously poor', and 'destitute'. The percentage of the total population falling into each of these categories was on the decline in the developing economies taken in aggregate and for Asia, Africa, and Latin America taken separately (Table 22). The sole exception was the category of those below the highest

Table 20

Health Indicators: Infant Mortality Rate and Expectation of Life at Birth for Some Undeveloped Market Economies, 1960, 1970 and 1975

Country	Infant Mortality Rate per 1,000 Live Births[1]			Life Expectancy at Birth[2]		
	1960	*1970*	*1975[3]*	*1960*	*1970*	*1975[3]*
Costa Rica	80.30	61.50	38	61.70	66.80	68
El Salvador	76.30	66.60	58	49.30	56.40	58
Guatemala	91.90	87.10	75	45.70	51.60	53
Haiti	171.60	146.90	150	—	—	
Mexico	74.20	68.50	50	57.90	61.40	63
Panama	70.20	40.50	36	61.60	65.80	67
Argentina	62.40	63.30	59	65.50	67.90	68
Chile	125.10	79.20	79	57.00	61.70	63
Colombia	83.30	80.60	56	55.70	59.80	61
Ecuador	100.00	76.60	70	52.60	58.40	60
Uruguay	47.50	42.60	48	68.50	69.90	70
Hong Kong	57.00	19.60	15	64.60	71.40	70
Pakistan	130.00	128.40	113	—	—	—
Philippines	121.00	96.90	72	52.50	57.10	58
Singapore	34.80	20.50	14	64.50	67.60	70
Sri Lanka	56.80	53.00	45	62.00	66.80	68
Venezuela	—	—	—	58.70	65.30	65
Turkey	—	—	—	50.00	55.70	57
Malaysia	—	—	—	55.00	58.10	59
Thailand	—	—	—	56.70	56.90	58

1. The comparability of the 1960 with the 1970 data for infant mortality rates is described as 'relatively good' and that for life expectancy at birth as 'moderate'.
2. These are all the LDCs for which data are given, except Israel.
3. 1975 Data abstracted from IBRD, *World Development Report 1978*, Table 17.

Source: UNRISD, Report No. 73/3, *Research Bank of Development Indicators*, Vol. III, *1960-1970 Comparisons*, pp. 8 and 12.

poverty line in Asia; the relative size of this group remained constant. The rise in the *absolute* number of people below the highest povery line (now estimated to be 208 million) is in any case a result of past improvements in general welfare, since the increasing numbers are associated with rising life expectancy at birth, which in turn is the best single indicator of health conditions. Since health is affected by such factors

Table 21

Indicators Of Housing Conditions for Three Categories in LDCs, 1960 to 1973/6

	Low Income			Lower Middle Income		
	1960	1970	Most Recent Data	1960	1970	Most Recent Data
Persons per Room (urban)	2.5	2.0	2.8*	2.6	2.5	2.2
Occupied Dwellings Without Piped Water (%)	62.2	69.8	n.a.	68.7	64.6	67.8
Access to Electricity (%)						
— All	n.a.	n.a.	n.a.	17.3	23.3	40.4
— Rural	n.a.	n.a.	n.a.	n.a.	n.a.	n.a.

	Intermediate Middle Income			Upper Middle Income		
	1960	1970	Most Recent Data	1960	1970	Most Recent Data
Persons per Room (urban)	2.3	2.2	1.6	1.4	1.2	n.a.
Occupied Dwellings Without Piped Water (%)	74.6	64.2	58.9	59.1	75.3	67.1*
Access to Electricity (%)						
— All	28.4	49.6	71.9	50.6	47.4	59.8
— Rural	5.6	26.7	34.1	26.9	n.a.	n.a.

	High Income		
	1960	1970	Most Recent Data
Persons per Room	1.1	n.a.	n.a.
Occupied Dwellings Without Piped Water (%)	57.1	20.0	n.a.
Access to Electricity (%)			
— All	79.3	91.0	n.a.
— Rural	57.0	58.0	n.a.

* Denotes a declining trend.

Source: *World Economic and Social Indicators* (April, 1978).

as food consumption, literacy, housing, water supply, and personal income as much as or more than by direct health services, and since it in turn affects all these variables, there is a close correlation between life expectancy at birth and the

Table 22
The Poor, the Seriously Poor and the Destitute by Regions, 1963 and 1972
(in %)

	Poor		Seriously Poor		Destitute	
	1963	1972	1963	1972	1963	1972
Asia	88	88	76	71	46	42
Africa	88	69	77	69	46	39
Latin America	73	43	55	43	33	27
Plain Regions	86	67	73	67	44	39

Sources: Peter Richards, 'Poverty and Underemployment', Background Papers, Tripartite World Conference on Employment Income Distribution and Social Progress and the Distribution of Labour, Geneva, 1976, Vol. I, tables III & IV, pp. 3 & 4.

infant mortality rate on the one hand and forty-one other selected development indicators on the other.[90] This points to a strong causal link between rising welfare and rapid population growth, the latter implying the former, and suggests that the relevant indicators are relatively free of distributional bias. Thus, far from basic needs being neglected, the accelerating population growth, which many consider the underlying cause of underdevelopment, arises precisely from increasing attention to basic needs in the most fundamental sense of the word 'basic'.[91]

Agricultural Performance

The relative neglect of agriculture — indeed, the promotion of policies whose effect has often been to militate against a growth of agricultural output adequate to the needs of the expanding economies of Africa, Asia, and Latin America — has caused real food prices to rise in recent years and has left signficant numbers of people in the Third World in danger of

90. Donald McGranahan, 'Development Indicators and Development Models', in Baster, p. 94. The correlations are 0.72 for infant mortality rate and 0.77 for life expectancy at birth.
91. 'The most acceptable explanation of the large reduction of mortality and growth of population which preceded advances in hygiene is an improvement in nutrition due to greater food supplies.' T. McKeown, *The Modern Rise of Population*, p.15.

starvation in the event of a conjuncture of unfavourable circumstances. The increases in calorie intake per capita throughout the 1950s and 1960s were in part dependent on mounting food imports, which rose at a rate of 3.5 per cent per annum for the LDCs as a whole from 1961-63 to 1972.[92]

Alone, of course, rising food imports are no indication of economic inefficiency, since they may reflect a comparative advantage in exporting minerals, non-food cash-crops, and manufactures. But other considerations, such as the rise in relative food prices, strongly suggest major misallocation of resources and other mistaken policies, which retarded agricultural production and restricted productivity increases, especially in the 1960s. The agricultural sector has thus acted as a serious drag on the overall development of Third World economies.[93] The sluggishness of this sector has retarded the developing independence of these countries both directly, contributing to balance of payments problems,[94] and indirectly, acting as a fetter on the entire economy by limiting the growth of markets and of complementary inputs for the non-agricultural sectors.

Agriculture has failed not only in responding inadequately to the needs of the rest of the economy, but also relative to its technical-economic potential. Every sector always lags behind its potential to some extent in all countries, but the

92. Note that this represents a slackening compared with the period 1955-66, when such imports almost doubled; indeed, between 1966 and 1969-71 the number of food-surplus countries in the developing world rose from twenty to thirty-eight, while the number of food-deficit countries fell from seventy-two to fifty-five. (FAO, *State of Food and Agriculture 1974*, pp. 100, 101, 105.) However, the period since 1972 has witnessed a rather large increase in the volume and value of food imports into LDCs. (FAO, *Trade Year Book 1976*, Vol. 30, Rome, 1977, p. 34.)

93. One clear index of the failure of aggregate agricultural production in developing countries is that per capita agricultural production has hardly increased at all since the early 1960s, and has declined quite considerably in some regions, Africa for example. See FAO, *Production Yearbook 1977*, Table 7.

94. An inadequate growth of agricultural output and productivity will prejudice the growth of manufactured exports as it pushes up costs to industry. This is quite apart from the balance of payments effects of rising food imports.

gap for much of Third World agriculture is not only relatively much wider than that of other sectors but, more important, is also narrowing far more slowly.[95] Moreover, the slow growth of agricultural output relative to population growth and rising incomes persisted into the first half of the 1970s, Africa performing particularly badly: the 1977 FAO per capita food production index for Africa was 10 per cent below the level of the period 1961-65.[96]

One of the major reasons for the relative failure of agriculture is that it is much easier to erect a modern industrial structure on a backward rural base than to transform the rural base itself. But a gradual social revolution in agriculture has been under way, which is steadily creating a social framework within which the already advanced technical revolution can realize its potential. This social revolution consists of the displacement and/or transformation of subsistence and semi-commercial, small-scale family farming by capitalist farming, plus rising social differentiation within capitalist farming, which tends to concentrate advantages on the richer farmers. There is considerable evidence of the rapid spread of capitalist social relations of production in agriculture throughout the Third World: very rapid increase in the proportion of the agricultural output that is marketed; swift development of a market for hired labour unconstrained by non-economic ties and obligations; substantial expansion of domestic markets for agricultural means of production, both land and produced means of production; rising social differentation among rural producers.[97] A recent detailed

95. The gap between potential and actual agricultural performance is impossible to quantify. Crude proxies are available such as cross-national comparisons of yield per acre for various crops or agricultural product per man-year, although the more significant comparison is between the actual yields achieved by different types of farm within the same region in particular LDCs. Reputable authorities argue that 'the doubling and trebling of land productivity is a realistic technical and organizational possibility'. Leontieff et al., p. 5.

96. Cited in World Bank, *Annual Report 1978*, p. 20.

97. For some general references to this evidence, see D. McEachern, 'The Mode of Production in India', *Journal of Contemporary Asia*, Vol. 6, No. 4,

survey of the available evidence for India shows a strong, positive, reciprocal relationship between the advance of capitalist social relations in agriculture and the fuller realization of the technical potential of the green revolution, within existing socio-economic constraints.[98] The point at which this social revolution becomes sufficiently widespread to generate a self-sustaining accelerated growth of agricultural output and production cannot be guessed, but the combination of accumulating relatively easily used technical potential and a major shift towards capitalist farming is bound to have lasting favourable effects on agricultural productivity.

A number of more immediate and prosaic factors also suggest that the prospect for agriculture is not unfavourable. Relative failure in this domain is not inevitable, but is largely the result of mistaken policy, lack of suitable incentives, and allocation of insufficient resources to agriculture. These policy errors are now being rectified. Development plans are recognizing the desirability of allotting greater proportions of resources to agriculture. International financial support for agricultural projects has risen significantly.[99] The shortage of fertilizer in Third World countries is expected to ease during coming years,[100] and the volume of research devoted to agricultural problems

1976, and Sender. On the growth of wage labour (generally a reliable indicator) in Indian agriculture see K.N. Raj, 'Trends in Rural Unemployment', *Economic and Political Weekly,* Special No. (August 1976).

98. Biplap Das Gupta, *Agrarian Change and the New Technology in India,* UNRISD, 1976, especially chapter IV.

99. Lending for agricultural projects by the IBRD and the IDA, for example, rose from $400 million in 1970-71 to more than $900 million in 1973-74 and nearly $2,000 million in 1975. *World Economic Survey 1975,* p. 128. In the period 1974-8 Bank and IDA lending for agricultural projects amounted to more than $10,000 million. World Bank, *Annual Report 1978,* p. 18.

100. *World Economic Survey 1975,* pp. 130-131. Imports of fertilizers by developing countries have been increasing very rapidly in the 1970s, as have imports of pesticides and tractors. For example, between 1973 and 1975 the number of tractors imported annually by developing countries rose from about 85,000 to about 131,000. (FAO, *1976 Trade Yearbook,* Vol. 30, pp. 282-291.)

in developing countries has expanded remarkably in recent years. It is expected that the area of arable land will soon increase by about 1.5% a year, the area under irrigation by about 6% a year.[101] The scope for improvement in productivity through further use of higher-yield cereals on a commercial scale remains enormous.[102] These short- and medium-term factors are likely significantly to accelerate the trend towards capitalist (and ever larger-scale) farming, thus in turn increasing the effectiveness of individual policies.

It does not appear, therefore, that long-term institutional and social trends, technical limitations, the general direction of policy, or the availability of cultivable land need retard improvements in agricultural performance, except perhaps in the short run. It is also clear that substantial progress in capitalist industrialization and in acceleration of the growth of manufactured exports has already been achieved in a significant number of important under-developed countries, as we shall see in the following section. But what of the threat of the exhaustion of non-renewable resources? It is impossible to deal with this enormous question within the compass of a brief, already impression-istic survey of the postwar economic record of the Third World. Its relevance, however, is considerable, and a pessimistic outlook on Third World economic progress is often closely linked, especially as regards future prospects, to a pessimistic outlook in this domain as well. A bald statement of my position may therefore be appropriate here, if only to lend formal coherence to the fundamentally optimistic outlook of this chapter.

I do not consider the problem of the exhaustion of non-renewable resources any more intractable now than it has

101. The increase in recent years in the acreage of irrigated agricultural land in developing countries has been very rapid, the area increasing by about 25% between 1966 and 1976. (FAO, *Production Yearbook 1977*, p. 57.) On the potential for future increases in the area of arable land in developing countries, see Leontieff et al., p. 5.
102. *World Economic Survey 1975*, p. 127.

been in the past. To begin with, non-renewable resources have always been on the road to exhaustion. This was so for known and estimated reserves of coal, for example, from the moment the first lump was burned. What must be shown is that some critical point is approaching. The evidence of relative prices (abstracting from the effects of producer cartels and similar factors) is that there is no clear trend.[103] Moreover, resources are not fixed but are a function of changing technology and economic efficiency; innovation renders resources available where none previously existed: at one time neither oil nor uranium were resources. The sum total of physical resources is therefore always expanding.[104] Finally, historical perspective suggests that the innovatory-economic capacity to remove specific supply bottlenecks is unlikely to lessen. Indeed, innovation and its incorporation into economic processes have been advancing at an accelerating pace, often well ahead of specific bottlenecks, as innovation becomes an ever more autonomous process. If there has been a good deal of technical inefficiency in the use of fuel and materials, this is because it was not economic to devote real resources to reducing this inefficiency; in other words, it was not inefficiency in *economic* terms. There is no clear evidence that it has even yet become more economic to devote greater resources to economizing in the use of exhaustible resources (perhaps by developing new ones).[105] But if the necessity does arise, nothing in historical experience suggests that modern industrial society will be unable to rise to the challenge. On the contrary, the capacity of the human species to master such problems has nearly always surpassed expectations. Here the conventional wisdom of yesterday remains wisdom today. The real problem is man's ability to master himself and his society, and not his ability to bend nature to his will.

103. Little, p. 231. If there were secular trends of rising relative prices for minerals, this would presumably improve the terms of trade for LDCs in any case.
104. Natural elements that are not used in the productive processes cannot be considered resources.
105. Although there may be strategic reasons for doing so.

5. Industrialization

Growth of Manufacturing Output

Despite assertions and predictions to the contrary, the underdeveloped world as a whole has made considerable progress in industrialization during the postwar period. By the 1950s, the Third World already accounted for a higher proportion of the world's manufacturing output than it had before the war. Whereas in 1937 the manufacturing output of the developed capitalist countries was about nine times that of Latin America, Africa, and Asia, by 1959 the ratio had been reduced to seven-to-one.[106] Moreover, this tendency for manufacturing output to rise faster in the under-developed than in the developed world has continued: Third World manufacturing output grew at about 7 per cent per annum between 1960 and 1968, while that of the advanced capitalist world grew at about 6 per cent per annum.[107] In the period 1971-76 both light and heavy manufacturing output in developing countries rose at an average annual rate more than twice that achieved in the developed capitalist countries,[108] even though industrial growth in the developed capitalist world during the 1960s was exceptionally high by

106. A. Maizels, *Growth and Trade*, NIESR Students Edition 1, 1970, p. 22. The exclusion of Japan from the Asian figures makes little difference to the overall developed/underdeveloped ratios (Table 1). 'In the less developed continents considerable progress has been made since before the war in Latin America and in many countries elsewhere   Manufacturing production in Latin America almost doubled from 1937 to 1950. In Asia, excluding Japan, production in 1950 was only marginally above the prewar level, but from 1950 to 1959 it rose by about one and a half times. Indeed, over this last decade, the rise in manufacturing output in Asian countries (excluding Japan) accounted for about half the total expansion in the less developed areas' (p. 24).

107. UN, *World Economic Survey, 1969-70: the Developing Countries in the 1960s: the Problem of Appraising Progress*, New York, 1971, p. 24. The authors of the survey note that since the countries without relevant data are likely to be those with the smallest manufacturing sectors, which will tend to grow especially fast initially, the estimate of Third World manufacturing growth is likely to be too low (p. 25).

108. UN, *World Economic Survey 1976. Current Trends in the World Economy*, 1977, Table 5, p. 58.

historical standards, with overall GNP growth easily exceeding the OECD 'growth target' of 50 per cent over the decade.

It may be argued that this apparent success is merely a reflection of the high statistical growth rates associated with small industrial bases and is therefore illusory; or that the record of the underdeveloped countries compared with that of the developed capitalist countries is rather poor in terms of output per head. Inspection of the figures for individual countries over a rather long period, however, shows that many underdeveloped countries are able to maintain faster rates of growth of manufacturing output than the industrialized economies (Table 23). Moreover, the really unusual feature of postwar industrialization in the

Table 23

Annual Average Rates of Growth of Manufacturing,
1951-69 and 1965-74, for Selected Countries

	1951-69	1965-74		1951-69	1965-74
Brazil	7.8	11.2	Panama	14.2	8.5
Costa Rica	9.7	—	Peru	7.5	7.8
Iran	11.2	13.3	Philippines	8.5	5.8
Iraq	6.8	7.6	Puerto Rico	6.5	—
Jamaica	5.0	—	Singapore	14.8	15.3
Jordan	15.2	—	Taiwan	16.1	—
Korea			Thailand	8.7	—
(Rep of)	16.9	24.4	Trinidad &		
Malaysia	6.4	9.6	Tobago	10.0	—
Mexico	7.4	7.6	Turkey	11.5	—
Nicaragua	7.6	—	Venezuela	10.5	5.0
Pakistan	15.0	—	Zambia	13.8	7.4

Note: Countries selected by Chenery from 75 countries for which International Bank had compiled fairly complete statistics. Chenery chose 29 of the fastest growing countries, from which Israel, Greece, Japan, Yougoslavia, Bulgaria, and Spain have been removed (there are no data for the Ivory Coast).

Source: H. B. Chenery, 'Growth and Structural Change', *Finance and Development,* Vol. 8, No. 3 (September 1971), pp. 25-63 and UN, *Yearbook of Industrial Statistics, 1975,* Vol. I, Dept. of Social and Economic Affairs, New York (1977).

Third World as a whole is its sustained momentum over a period longer than any previously recorded.[109] Finally, this industrialization has occurred in a period when neither war nor world depression have 'cut off' the Third World from the advanced capitalist countries, though it is precisely this cutting off that Gunder Frank considers critical in explaining such industrial progress as has been registered (in partial exception of his theses of 'developing underdevelopment' and 'increasing polarization').[110]

Although the figures of Table 23 are likely to be slanted somewhat upwards since they refer to high-growth countries (average growth rates of per capita income of 5.5 per cent per annum or more in nearly all cases), it should be recalled that we are concerned only to make the point for a substantial proportion of underdeveloped countries. I do not claim that sustained industrialization has been universal (nor even that sustained industrialization over a long period is inconsistent with intermittent periods of stagnation, deceleration, or decline). But since some of the figures cover more than two decades, the growth rates they show cannot be ascribed solely to initial fast starts.

The growth of per capita manufacturing output in the underdeveloped countries has undoubtedly lagged behind that of some developed countries, in part because of the unprecedented rates of population increase in the Third World since the war. But to take the growth of per capita manufacturing output as a basis of comparison is to apply an extremely demanding criterion. A similar remark applies to the growth of per capita total output. From the standpoint of living standards, per capita growth rates are clearly the most relevant criterion. But from the standpoint of the distribution of world industrial power and the total growth of the market, growth rates are the central issue.

109. On this, see UNIDO, *Industrial Development Survey,* Volume I, New York, 1969, pp. 5-6.
110. A.G. Frank, *Capitalism and Underdevelopment in Latin America,* p. 52.

Share of Manufacturing in GDP

If the advance of modern manufacturing is crucial to the elimination of underdevelopment, then the proportion of gross domestic product in the underdeveloped countries accounted for by manufacturing is a useful, if only approximate, comparative indicator.[111] The figures are rather impressive. For the LDCs as a whole, manufacturing accounted for 14.5 per cent of gross domestic product in 1950-4; the figure rose to 17.9 per cent in 1960 and 20.4 per cent in 1973. In the developed capitalist countries manufacturing contributed 28.4 per cent to GDP in 1973.[112] *The difference is therefore becoming rather small.*

Aggregate figures, however, can be misleading if we are concerned with the rise of alternative centres of economic power in the Third World rather than with overall changes. Indeed, the very concept of a Third World separated by a gap from the developed world as a whole implies a polarity that is not always real. Table 24 shows quite clearly that in a number of large and medium-size underdeveloped economies (in addition to some small ones, like Hong Kong and Malta) manufacturing already makes a contribution to gross domestic product comparable or even superior to that of some of the developed capitalist economies. In Mexico, Argentina, Chile, Brazil, Korea, and Taiwan, for example, manufacturing accounts for a proportion of GDP similar to that in the developed market economies as a whole; indeed, in some of these countries it contributes more to gross domestic product than it does in Canada, Denmark, Australia, Norway, Sweden, Finland, New Zealand, and the United States.

A number of other countries are also approaching the position of the developed capitalist economies in this

111. It may be misleading as a short-term indicator, since a rational strategy for many economies may be an initial development of mineral or cash crops before using the resources so gained for manufacturing progress.

112. World Bank, *World Tables, 1976,* John Hopkins Press, 1976, Table 4, p. 416.

Table 24

Selected Countries' Manufacturing as a Percent of Gross Domestic Product at Current Factor Cost (1973) and Percentage of Active Labour Force Employed in Manufacturing (latest estimates)

Country	Manufacturing as % of GDP (a)	% of Active Labour Force Employed in Manufacturing (b)
Egypt	21.6	12.9
Taiwan	29.8	n.a.
South Korea	24.3	20.5
Argentina	38.3	19.7
Brazil	24.6	11.0
Chile	25.9	15.9
Costa Rica	21.9	11.9
Mexico	25.4	17.8
Peru	21.4	12.5
Uruguay	23.0	18.8
	average = 25.6	average = 15.7
Australia	26.6	24.8
Canada	20.1	18.0
Denmark	26.6	23.1
Norway	25.4	24.4
Sweden	24.8	26.5
United States	24.7	22.4
	average = 24.7	average = 23.2
Greece	20.4	17.1
Spain	26.7	25.7
Malta	26.5	27.8
Hong Kong	32.1	44.4
Singapore	26.1	25.6

Sources: (a) World Bank, *World Tables*, 1976.
(b) ILO, *International Yearbook of Labour Statistics, 1977*, Geneva (1977), Table 2, p. 52, *et seq.*

respect. Costa Rica, Uruguay, and Peru now fall in the same range as Canada, New Zealand, Spain, Norway, Finland, and Australia.

The most relevant single indicator of the degree to which a large or medium-size economy is building modern productive forces, however, is the percentage of the active population employed in manufacturing. A high contribution to GDP by manufacturing may simply reflect the primitive character of agriculture. Occupational comparisons are therefore better guides to the degree of development of productive forces than sectoral output comparisons; for an occupational comparison will show whether a large proportion of the population is engaged in low-productivity labour or whether there is a spread of high-productivity employment through the active population, as in developed countries. The figures listed in column (b) of Table 24 give a much less cheerful picture of the relative extent of industrialization. They show a proportion of the active population engaged in modern manufacturing in the developed capitalist economies considerably higher than the corresponding contribution of manufacturing output to GDP. But here again the progress registered in some important Third World countries must be noted; thanks to very substantial industrialization, they now have features far from typical of underdeveloped economies.

The Elitist Pattern of Manufacturing Output

It may, however, be argued that much, if not most, of this industrial growth is oriented towards consumption by wealthy elites whose politico-economic strangehold over the nation ensures the continuation of this growth pattern, which thereby becomes self-reinforcing, since their consumption requirements make for greater capital intensity, which in turn aggravates unemployment and keeps wages depressed.[113]

This argument is plainly incorrect for the Third World countries that include the vast majority of the populations of

113. 'The internal market is thus *mainly* based on the demand for "luxury" goods from these social classes...latifundiaries in some places, kulaks in others, comprador commercial bourgeoisie, state bureaucracy, etc.' Samir Amin, 'The Theoretical Model of Capital Accumulation and of the Economic and Social Development of the World of Today', *Review of African Political Economy*, Volume 1, 1974, p. 12.

Africa and Asia, where the market for 'luxury goods' is too small to sustain profitable production[114] and where the manufacturing sector is based on a mass market catering to lower- and middle-income consumers.[115]

In some countries with relatively high per capita income levels and a substantial degree of industrialization,

114. That is, the higher range of durable consumer goods. (Amin simply defines *all* durable consumer goods as luxury goods.)

115. This is notably the case for West and North Africa, the two regions in which Amin specializes. Cf., for West Africa, Anthony Hopkins, *An Economic History of West Africa* and IMF *Surveys of African Economies,* Vol. VI, Washington DC, 1975. The same is true for India. South Asia, including India, is one of the areas with a comparatively low degree of inequality and great poverty, yet it accounts for 55% of the total non-communist Third World population (Ahluwalia, p. 7). This situation clearly favours manufacturing based on a mass market and producer and intermediate goods, especially where the non-integrated character of the market limits the potential demand of the wealthier classes. In fact, the annual average percentage increase in total industrial production in India between 1960 and 1975 was very much higher than the annual average percentage increase in consumer goods industries production over the same period. By the same measure over the same period, the growth rate of basic industries in India (electricity, mining, fertilizers, heavy chemicals, cement, and basic metals) easily outstripped the growth rate of consumer goods industries. In general the growth rates of the intermediate and capital goods industries during this period were superior to those in the consumer goods industries. (Deepak Nayyar, 'Industrial Development in India: Some Reflections on Growth and Stagnation', *Economic and Political Weekly,* Special Number, 1978, Table 3, p. 1269.) The manufacturing sector in East and Central Africa in the 1970s typically contained industries producing chemicals, fertilizers, textiles, beer, sugar, and cigarettes, which apart from having strong linkages to the agricultural sectors of the economies concerned, were clearly industries producing goods for the consumption of *millions* of Africans. (See R.H. Green, *Toward Ujamaa and Kujitegemea; Income Distribution and Absolute Poverty Eradication Aspects of the Tanzanian Transition to Socialism,* Institute of Development Studies, Sussex, Discussion Paper, No. 66, December 1974, p. 30); Central Statistical Office Lusaka, *National Income and Input Output Tables 1971* and *Ministry of Development Planning Economic Report, 1976,* Lusaka, January, 1977. About 25% of all enumerated industrial units in Sri Lanka depend on rural household demand for their output. (ILO, *Rural Small-Scale Industries and Employment in Sri Lanka,* Part I, p. 23). In the developing countries as a whole the average annual rate of growth of production between 1971 and 1976 for 'heavy manufacturing' (chemicals, basic metals, and metal products) was almost 3 percentage points higher than the corresponding rate of growth of production for 'light manufacturing'. (UN, *World Economic Survey,* 1977).

production of durable consumer goods has been rising rather rapidly (especially in Latin America). An important and detailed study of consumption patterns in Brazil as revealed by household expenditure surveys[116] has seriously under-mined the conventional picture of demand profiles for durable consumer goods in a country that has come to be regarded as the outstanding instance of 'distorted' income distribution. This study shows that the diffusion of a wide range of durable consumer goods was not at all confined to a small minority; the market extended to at least 60 per cent of all Brazilian households. Althouh there is a marked discontinuity in the profile of demand (excluding house-holds in the rural sector and the poorer regions), there was no such discontinuity for *urban* households, even in the poorer Northeastern cities — and Brazil is now predominantly an urbanized country, as are, to an even greater extent, all the other major countries of Latin America. A very wide market diffusion of durable consumer goods[117] was found, reaching well into the lower-income urban groups. In the late 1960s the household goods and appliances sector grew rapidly despite an income redistribution that favoured the rich, owing to the saturation of the market of rich households, the large size of the average Brazilian household, the relatively limited proportion of public consumption, and the ability of the financial system to ensure that the savings of the rich help finance the purchases of the poor. Wells concludes: 'Provided the process of urbanization continues, there appear to be few limits to the process of market-deepening. The data reviewed are not consistent with the pessimistic views of writers, such as Furtado, concerning the possibility of generalizing this pattern of consumption.'[118]

116. J.R. Wells, *Consumption, Market Size and Expenditure Patterns in Brazil*, Centre of Latin American Studies, University of Cambridge, Working Papers, No. 24, 1976.

117. Including sewing machines, refrigerators, televisions, gas and electric stoves, electric irons, table radios, portable radios, gramophones, fans, liquifiers, cake-mixers, floor-polishers, vacuum cleaners, washing machines, air conditioners, motor cars, bicycles, and motor cycles. Ibid., p. 13.

118. Ibid. pp. 51-53.

If this sort of demand profile for durable consumer goods becomes characteristic of other LDCs as their industrial sectors grow[119] (and there have been too few detailed studies to permit any firm judgement on the matter), then the growth of the durable consumer goods industry must be considered likely to benefit substantially increasing sections of the lower-income groups, and not merely a small elite plus limited sections of the middle-income groups.[120]

The fact that purchase of consumer durables by low-income households occurs at the expense of public and perhaps other forms of consumption may be regarded as a distortion of resource allocation consequent to Western influence. But when did the poor ever know what was good for them? Would they actually opt for more collective (public) consumption if given the choice? No one knows, but it cannot be denied that most durable consumer goods — such as bicycles, sewing machines, motorbikes, radios, and even television sets and refrigerators — significantly enhance the quality of life of poor households. It is only those who already possess such goods in abundance who feel it appropriate to suggest that it is undesirable for others to have them.[121]

6. The Spread of Capitalism

The survey in this chapter was inevitably impressionistic. It

119. For survey data suggesting a surprisingly wide distribution of consumption of relatively sophisticated consumer goods in a rather poor African economy, see F.C. Wright, *African Consumers in Nyasaland and Tanganyika,* Colonial Research Studies, HMSO (1955); I. Livingstone, *Results of a Rural Survey: The Ownership of Durable Goods in Tanzanian Households and Some Implications for Rural Industry,* Economics Research Bureau, University of Dar es Salaam, Paper No. 70. I; and Sender, Table 3.15.

120. The much maligned 'trickle-down' theory has something to it after all. Newton was right.

121. Wilfred Beckerman has made this point in connection with the propaganda about pollution in *In Defence of Economic Growth,* p. 24. For an analysis of the ideology of the middle class anti-consumerist/ecological lobby see also H.M. Enzensberger, 'A Critique of Political Ecology', *New Left Review* (March-April, 1974), pp. 9-10.

does, however, seem justifiable to draw the following conclusions.

1. Economic progress as measured in conventional terms by GNP per capita was rapid and fairly generalized throughout the Third World (although very uneven between countries) during the postwar period as compared both with the prewar period for the same group of countries and with the presently industrialized countries during their period of development in the eighteenth and nineteenth centuries, and even, although to a lesser extent, as compared with the DMEs today.

2. There is at least a prima facie case that GNP per capita, although a highly imperfect measure either of progress towards greater material welfare for the majority of the population or of development conceived as movement towards the present central characteristics of the advanced countries, is nevertheless a closer approximation than has generally been believed. Moreover, movement towards the present characteristics of advanced countries does imply a measure of progress towards such widely accepted normative goals as greater equality and reduction of poverty and unemployment.

3. This last point, together with the patchy available evidence of physical indicators measuring fulfilment of the basic needs of the population in health, education, nutrition, and housing, and with fairly definite aggregate evidence that the proportions of those falling below various poverty lines is declining, strongly suggests that major advances in the material welfare of the population have been registered in the Third World postwar. Despite their unevenness, the effects of these advances have reached down to the lower-income groups. Moreover, there is some evidence that in some countries, especially in Latin America, the rise in production of durable consumer goods by no means benefits solely the wealthy or even the middle classes, but penetrates

downwards to the lower-income groups in the urban areas, which now include the majority of the population of Latin America.

4. The widespread belief that the rise in the average availability of goods and services per capita has been largely or completely nullified for the poor majority of the Third World by a general trend towards more uneven distribution is not borne out by the admittedly scanty time-series or cross-section data. The available evidence suggests that trends towards *more even* income distribution have been at least equally important, and are certainly more important in the long run. The aggravation of income inequality that frequently afflicts the earliest stages of growth cannot be regarded automatically as negative, since there are strong, though not yet conclusive, reasons to believe that this rising inequality is as much a cause as a consequence of growth and thereby benefits the poorest sections of the population absolutely, if not relatively.

5. An important dimension of the view that per capita income growth has not contributed substantially to general welfare is encapsulated in the concept of 'marginalization'. But the relevant, non-tautological indicators, such as open unemployment and underemployment as measured by 'short hours', show very little evidence of marginalization (practically none in the case of short hours) and possibly declining unemployment rates in the majority of countries (although the evidence here is slender). Underemployment as measured in relatively low average productivity or levels of remuneration is a tautological concept and cannot by itself suggest deterioration over time in either of these respects. In any case, there is no direct evidence for such deterioration. Nor is there clear evidence that the size of the informal sector is rising significantly relative to the urban population. On the other hand, there is mounting evidence that the informal or unenumerated sector, generally taken to include the bulk of the underemployed, provides a wide range of necessary goods and services for a substantial

section of the urban population. Moreover, it appears to possess not insignificant dynamic features permitting the advance of accumulation, innovation, productivity, earnings, and entrepreneurship. The underemployment concept appears to be a misnomer expressing the important fact of much wider ranges of productivity and remuneration between and within sectors than in the developed countries, particularly at the lower end of the scale.

Evidence for underemployment in agriculture is even more imperfect, but seems to show that it is not as great as has been commonly assumed.

More generally, it can be argued that apparent 'marginalization' in urban areas is actually a progressive phenomenon reflecting the fuller *integration* of the population into the economy as the market widens and activities become more interdependent through increasing specialization.

6. Thus, contrary to widespread populist-liberal opinion, the Third World has not been marked by stagnation, relative or absolute, in the postwar period. On the contrary, significant progress in material welfare and the development of the productive forces has been made, in an acceleration of prewar trends. This fact also runs counter to current Marxist views, which have stressed the alleged impossibility of vigorous national development in the Third World within a capitalist framework.

The period since the Second World War has seen titanic strides forward in the establishment, consolidation, and growth of capitalism in the Third World, with corresponding advances in material welfare and the expansion of the productive forces. Development has been highly uneven, as is entirely characteristic of capitalism (and perhaps of every type of human progress); many countries were still afflicted by significant remnants of subsistence after the war, whilst others, such as Argentina and Uruguay, were already mainly capitalist. Although the capitalist system was introduced largely externally and often by force, its intrinsic dynamic, *superior to that of precapitalist societies,* is even more marked now than it was when capitalism succeeded feudalism in Europe and Japan. What was initially an external force quickly struck deep indigenous roots and manifested a vigorous internal momentum. The reality of this picture of vibrant, 'grass roots' capitalist development in the Third World is attested to by the abundant evidence of rapidly rising commercialization and the resulting social differentiation (especially in the rural areas of Asia and Africa), coupled with the relative expansion of wage-labour at the expense of family or self-employment (including feudal-type tenurial relationships). An exclusive focus on manufacturing industry (especially heavy industry) and the role of foreign capital therein can divert attention from the underlying force of the spread of capitalism from below,[122] quite apart from the fact that the growth of modern industry has been remarkably vigorous and shows every sign of continuing to become integrated into the national economies of the LDCs. The attention now correctly being focused on the relatively poor performance of agriculture should not obscure the profound underlying changes in agrarian social structure gradually gathering momentum. Sooner or later major advances will result, as agrarian capitalism becomes sufficiently developed to use more productive methods and inputs.

The squandering of many of the benefits of Third World postwar economic development due to major policy blunders has failed to halt the gathering momentum of capitalist advance and associated material progress. Many of these blunders are now widely recognized by all schools of thought (including those ideological trends in development economics that promoted them in the first place), for example the

---

122. Partly because the growth of manufacturing has generally owed a good deal to foreign enterprise and government, the impression has been given that capitalism is still very much a mode of production whose advance depends on external action 'from above', rather than any internal dynamic from below.

neglect of agriculture in favour of industrialization and the pessimistic bias against the development of an exporting manufacturing sector and the over-valuation of exchange rates. The character of these errors (and their origin) suggests the nature of the underlying problem. Development economics in the 1950s and 1960s was rent by conflicting trends, and the one that favoured rapid industrialization primarily for the home market as the first priority (Prebisch and Mahalanobis) became extremely influential. This approach was strongly influenced by the Soviet example of development through rapid industrialization, by Western liberal-egalitarian ideals, and by an anti-imperialist bent related to both Leninism and liberalism (of the Hobson variety), which tended to regard underdevelopment as caused largely by the character of international economic relations between wealthy capitalist centres and the countries of Latin America, Asia, and Africa. For obvious reasons, this liberal-populist trend in development economics met with a warm response from the governments of many underdeveloped states.

But the main problem with the liberal-populist approach, which its proponents did not always face squarely, was that the economies with which they were concerned were developing in a *capitalist* direction, in most if not all cases irreversibly so, barring communist revolution. Explicit recognition of this fact would have permitted the promotion of a more efficient and humane capitalist development instead of the inappropriate imposition of a welfare approach and a Soviet-type model on countries lacking both the requisite advanced economic basis for the welfare state and the communist leadership required for the Soviet model.

Failure to recognize that the social realities for which policy was formulated were the realities of *capitalist* development caused neglect of the elementary requirements of promoting such development, especially the expansion of commercialization in agriculture, crucial both to the spread of growth-conducive attitudes and habits and to the expansion of the agricultural surplus essential for successful industrialization. The persistent relative slowness of economic advance in South Asia abundantly testifies to the crucial importance of this aspect of the failure of the liberal-populist school of development economics.[123] Instead, in most of the Third World, development has been held below its potential by the failure adequately to promote rural commercialization and the consequent expansion of the agricultural surplus.

Whatever the new world being created in Latin America, Asia, and Africa is to be, nothing can be gained from a refusal to recognize the existence of the developing capitalist societies already there.

123. It is significant that an explicitly pro-capitalist development economist, P.T. Bauer, was able early on to identify precisely this fundamental weakness in Indian planning. He emphasized not only the neglect of agriculture in resource allocation, but also crucial obstacles to the spread of commercialization such as excessive neglect of road building and elementary education, as well as restricted internal mobility.

Bibliography

Acharya, P., 'Indigenous Vernacular Education in the Pre-British Era: Traditions and Problems', in *Economic and Political Weekly* (December 1978).

Adelman, I. and Morris, C. T., *Economic Growth and Social Equity in Developing Countries,* Stanford, Stanford University Press, 1973.

Agosin, M.R., 'On the Third World's Narrowing Trade Gap: A Comment', Oxford Economic Papers, Vol. 23 (1971).

Aldcroft, D. H., and Richardson, H. W., *The British Economy, 1870-1939,* London, Macmillan, 1969.

Allen, G. C., *A Short Economic History of Modern Japan 1867-1937,* London, Unwin University Books, 1962.

Amin, S., *Accumulation on a World Scale,* New York, Monthly Review Press, 1974.

——, 'The Theoretical Model of Capital Accumulation and of the Economic and Social Development of the World Today', in *Review of African Political Economy,* Vol. 1 (1974).

Amsden, A.H., 'Trade in Manufactures Between Developing Countries', in *Economic Journal* (December 1976).

Anderson, P., *Lineages of the Absolutist State,* London, NLB, 1974.

——, *Passages From Antiquity to Feudalism,* London, NLB, 1974.

Arendt, H., *The Origins of Totalitarianism,* New York, Meridian Books, 1963.

Arrighi, G., *The Geometry of Imperialism. The Limits of Hobson's Paradigm,* London, NLB, 1978.

Aston, T., ed., *Crisis in Europe 1560-1660,* London, Routledge and Kegan Paul, 1965.

Avineri, S., ed., *Karl Marx on Colonialism and Modernization,* New York, Anchor Books, 1969.

Bairoch, P., *The Economic Development of the Third World Since 1900,* London, 1975.

Balogh, T., 'Oxbridge Rampant', in *The Economics of Poverty,* London, Weidenfeld and Nicolson, 1955.

Banaji, J., 'Modes of Production in a Materialist Conception of History', mimeo, n.d.

Baran, P., *The Political Economy of Growth,* New York, Monthly Review Press, 1956.

Barraclough, G., *An Introduction to Contemporary History,* London, Watts, 1964.

Bauer, P., *Dissent on Development,* London, Weidenfeld and Nicolson, 1976.

——, *West African Trade,* London, 1963.

Beckerman, W., *In Defence of Economic Growth,* London, Jonathan Cape, 1972.

Bell, C.L.G., and Dulay, J.H., 'Rural Target Groups', in Chenery.

Berg, A., *The Nutrition Factor,* Washington, Brookings, 1973.

Berry, A. and Sabot, R.H., 'Labour Market Performance in Developing Countries: A Survey', in *World Development,* Vol. 6 (1978).

Berry, S. S., *Cocoa, Custom and Socio-Economic Change in Rural Western Nigeria,* Oxford, 1975.

Bienefeld, M.A., 'Special Gains From Trade With Socialist Countries: The Case of Tanzania', in *World Development,* Vol. 3, No. 5 (May 1975).

——, 'The Self-Employed of Urban Tanzania', IDS Sussex Discussion Paper, No. 54 (May 1974).

Bodenheimer, S., 'Dependency and Imperialism', in *Politics and Society* (May 1970).

Borchardt, K., 'The Industrial Revolution in Germany, 1700-1914', in Cipolla.

Bose, A.N., *The Informal Sector in the Calcutta Metropolitan Economy,* World Employment Programme Research, ILO, Geneva, 1974.

Brenner, R., 'The Origins of Capitalist Development: A Critique of Neo-Smithian Marxism', in *New Left Review* (July-August 1977).

Brown, M. B., *After Imperialism,* London, Heinemann, 1963.

——, *Essays on Imperialism,* Nottingham, Spokesman Books, 1972.

Cafagna, L., 'The Industrial Revolution in Italy, 1830-1914', in Cipolla.

Caldwell, J.C., *African Rural-Urban Migration,* Canberra, 1969.

Cardoso, F.H., 'Some New Mistaken Theses on Latin American Development and Dependency', mimeo (October 1973).

——, 'The Consumption of Dependency Theory in the United States', revised version of lecture to LASA, mimeo, 1976.

259

Carr, E.H., *Nationalism and After,* London, Macmillan, 1945.
———, *The Bolshevik Revolution, 1917-1923,* Vol. 1, Harmondsworth, Penguin Books, 1966.
Chaudhri, D.P., *Education, Innovations and Agricultural Development: A Study of North India, 1961-1972,* London, Croom Helm, 1979.
Chaudhuri, K. N., 'India's Economy in the Nineteenth Century', in *Modern Asian Studies,* Vol. 2, No. 1 (1968).
Chenery, H. B., et al., *Redistribution With Growth,* London, Oxford University Press, 1974.
Chenery, H. B., and Syrquin, M., *Patterns of Development, 1950-1970,* London, Oxford University Press, 1975.
Chilcote, R. H., and Edelstein, J. C., *Latin America: The Struggle With Dependency and Beyond,* Halstead Press, New York, 1974.
Cipolla, C. M., *The Fontana Economic History of Europe: The Emergence of Industrial Societies — 1,* London, Fontana, 1973.
Clapham, J.H., *The Economic Development of France and Germany, 1815-1914,* Cambridge, Cambridge University Press, 1936.
Claudín, F., *The Communist Movement: From Comintern to Cominform,* Harmondsworth, Penguin Books, 1975.
Cleave, J. H., *African Farmers: Labour Use in the Development of Smallholder Agriculture,* London, Praeger, 1974.
Clifton, J. A., 'Competition and the Evolution of the Capitalist Mode of Production', in *Cambridge Journal of Economics,* Vol. 1, No. 2 (1977).
Cohen, S. F., *Bukharin and the Bolshevik Revolution, A Political Biography,* New York, Vintage Books, 1975.
Colletti, L., 'The Question of Stalin', in Blackburn, R., ed., *Revolution and Class Struggle: A Reader in Marxist Politics,* London, Fontana, 1977.
Cowen, M. P., 'Capital and Household Production: The Case of Wattle in Kenya's Central Province, 1903-1964', unpublished Ph. D. dissertation, Cambridge University, (October 1978).
Cripps, F., 'Causes of Growth and Recession in World Trade', in *Economic Policy Review* No. 4 (March 1978).
Dantwala, M.L., 'Future of Institutional Reform and Technological Change in Indian Agricultural Development', in *Economic and Political Weekly,* special issue (August 1978).
Das Gupta, B., 'Calcutta's Informal Sector', in *Institute of Development Studies Bulletin* (October 1973).
———'Agrarian Change and the New Technology in India', UNRISD, Geneva, 1976.
Dewey, L., and Hopkins, A. G., *The Imperial Impact: Studies in the Economic History of Africa and India,* London, Athlone Press,

1978.

Dobb, M., *Studies in the Development of Capitalism,* London, Routledge and Kegan Paul, 1963.

Dodd, W.A.,' "Education for Self-Reliance" in Tanzania, A Study of its Vocational Aspects', Centre for Education in Africa, Institute of International Studies, Columbia University, New York (1969).

Drewnowski, J., and Scott, W., *The Level of Living Index,* UNRISD, Geneva, 1966.

Ducan, K., Rutledge, I., Harding, C., eds., *Land and Labour in Latin America. Essays on the Development of Agrarian Capitalism in the 19th and 20th Centuries,* Cambridge, Cambridge Univeristy Press, 1977.

Emerson, R., *From Empire to Nation,* Cambridge, Massachusetts, Harvard University Press, 1967.

Emmerij, L., 'A New Look at Some Strategies for Increasing Productive Employment in Africa', in *International Labour Review* (September 1974).

Enzensberger, H. M., 'A Critique of Political Ecology', in *New Left Review* (March-April 1974).

Ewusi, K., *The Distribution of Monetary Incomes in Ghana,* Technical Publication Series, No. 18, Institute of Statistical, Social, and Economic Research, University of Ghana, Legon, 1971.

Fapohunda, C.J., *Development of Urban Infrastructure in Greater Lagos,* World Employment Programme Research, ILO, Geneva, 1974.

Feis, H., *Europe: The World's Banker, 1870-1914,* New Haven, Connecticut, 1930.

Fieldhouse, D. K., 'Imperialism: A Historiographical Revision', in *Economics History Review,* Vol. 14, No. 2, 1961.

———, *The Theory of Capitalist Imperialism,* London, Longmans, 1975.

Figueroa, A., 'Income Distribution, Demand Structure and Employment: The Case of Peru', in *Journal of Development Studies,* January 1975.

Fohlen, C., 'The Industrial Revolution in France, 1700-1914', in Cipolla.

Ford, A. G., 'Overseas Lending and Internal Fluctuations, 1870-1914', in Hall.

Foster-Carter, A., 'The Modes of Production Controversy', in *New Left Review,* No. 107 (January-February 1978).

Foxley, A., ed., *Income Distribution in Latin America,* Cambridge, Cambridge University Press, 1976.

Frank, A. G., *Capitalism and Underdevelopment in Latin America,* Harmondsworth, Penguin Books, 1971.

Frank, C.R., and Webb, R.C., eds., *Income Distribution and Growth in Less Developed Countries*, Washington, Brookings, 1978.

Furtado, C., *Political Obstacles to Economic Growth in Brazil*, London, 1965.

Fyfe, C., ed., *African Studies Since 1945*, London, Longmans, 1976.

Gann, L.H., and Duignan, P., *Burden of Empire*, London, Pall Mall Press, 1968.

GATT, 'Adjustment, Trade and Growth in Developed and Developing Countries', Studies in International Trade, No. 6, Geneva, September 1978.

George, S., *How the Other Half Dies. The Real Reasons for World Hunger*, Harmondsworth, Penguin Books, 1976.

Gerschenkron, A., *Economic Backwardness in Historical Perspective*, Cambridge, Massachusetts, 1962.

Gerth, H. H., and Wright Mills, C., eds., *From Max Weber*, London, Routledge and Kegan Paul, 1974.

Ginneken, G. van, 'Mexican Income Distribution Within and Between Rural Areas', World Employment Programme Research, Working Papers, ILO, Geneva, 1974.

Gollwitzer, H., *Europe in the Age of Imperialism, 1880-1919*, London, Thames and Hudson, 1969.

Gramsci, A., *Selections From the Prison Notebooks*, London, Lawrence and Wishart, 1971.

Green, R.H., 'Towards Ujamaa and Kujitegemea: Income Distribution and Absolute Poverty Eradication Aspects of the Tanzanian Transition to Socialism', IDS Sussex, Discussion Paper No. 66 (December 1974).

Grey, R.H., 'The Decline of Mortality in Ceylon and the Demographic Effects of Malaria Control', in *Population Studies*, Vol. 28, No. 2, July 1974.

Hall, A.R., ed., *The Export of Capital From Britain, 1870-1914*, London, Methuen, 1968.

Hancock, W.K., *Survey of British Commonwealth Affairs, Vo. 2, Problems of Economic Policy, 1918-1939*, Oxford University Press, 1940.

——, *Argument of Empire*, Harmondsworth, Penguin Books, 1943.

——, *Wealth of Colonies*, Cambridge, Cambridge University Press, 1950.

Hayter, T., *Aid as Imperialism*, Harmondsworth, Penguin Books, 1971.

Henderson, W. O., *The Industrial Revolution on the Continent: Germany, France, Russia, 1800-1914*, London, F. Cass, 1961.

Hirschman, A. O., *The Strategy of Economic Development,* New Haven, Connecticut, Yale University Press, 1958.

——, 'The Political Economy of Import Substituting in Latin America', in *Quarterly Journal of Economics* (February 1968).

——, 'A Generalized Linkage Approach to Development, With Special Reference to Staples', in *Economic Development and Cultural Change,* Supplement, 25 (1977).

Hobsbawm, E., *The Age of Revolution, 1789-1849,* New York, Mentor Books, 1972.

——, *Industry and Empire,* Harmondsworth, Penguin Books, 1969.

——, 'The Crisis of the 17th Century', in Aston, T., ed.

Hodgkin, T., 'Where the Paths Began', in Fyfe, ed.

Hoogvelt, *The Sociology of the Developing Countries,* London, 1974.

Hopkins, A. G., *An Economic History of West Africa,* London, Longmans, 1973.

——, 'Clio-Antics: A Horoscope for African Economic History', in Fyfe, ed.

Hymer, S. H., and Resnick, S. A., 'International Trade and Uneven Development', in Bhagwati, J. R., et al., *Trade, Balance of Payments and Growth,* Amsterdam, 1971.

Illiffe, J., *A Modern History of Tanganyika,* Cambridge, Cambridge University Press, 1979.

ILO, *Employment and Equality: A Strategy for Increasing Productive Employment in Kenya,* Geneva, 1972.

——, *Report of the Director-General to the Tripartite World Conference on Employment, Income Distribution, and Social Progress and the International Division of Labour,* Geneva, 1976.

——, *Rural Small-Scale Industries and Employment in Sri Lanka,* World Employment Programme, Geneva, October 1978.

IMF, *Finance and Development,* No. 1 (1972).

——, *Surveys of African Economies,* Vol. 6, Washington, D. C., 1975.

Insurgent Sociologist, special issue (spring 1977), 'Imperialism and the State'.

Isaacs, H. R., *The Tragedy of the Chinese Revolution,* revised edition, Stanford, 1951.

Jeffries, R., 'Political Radicalism in Africa: "The Second Independence"', in *African Affairs,* Vol. 77 (July 1978).

Jenks, L. H., *The Migration of British Capital, to 1875,* London, Nelson, 1971.

Jones, G. S., 'The Specificity of US Imperialism', in *New Left Review,* No. 60 (March-April 1970).

Joshi, Lubell, and Mouly, *Urban Development and Employment in Abidjan,* World Employment Programme Research, ILO, Geneva, 1974.

Journal of Development Studies, 'Symposium on the Distribution of Income', April 1978.

Kahl, J. A. *Modernization, Exploitation and Dependency in Latin America,* Transaction Books, New Jersey, 1976.

Kalmanovitz, S., 'Théorie de la Dépendance ou Théorie de l'Impérialisme?', in *Sociologie du Travail* (January-March 1975).

Kautsky, K., *Socialism and Colonial Policy,* Belfast, Athol Books, 1975.

Kemp, T., *Theories of Imperialism,* London, 1967.

Kiernan, V. G., 'State and Nation in Western Europe', in *Past and Present,* No. 31 (July 1965).

———, *Marxism and Imperialism,* London, Edward Arnold, 1974.

King, K., 'Skill Acquisition in the Informal Sector of an African Economy: The Kenya Case', in *Journal of Development Studies,* January 1975.

Kjekshus, H., *Ecology Control and Economic Development in East African History, The Case of Tanganyika, 1850-1950,* London, Heineman, 1977.

Kleiman, E., 'Trade and the Decline of Colonialism', in *Economic Journal,* September 1976.

Knudsen, O., and Barnes, A., *Trade Instability and Economic Development: An Empirical Study,* Lexington, Massachusetts, D. C. Heath, 1975.

Krishnamurty, J., 'Some Aspects of Unemployment in Urban India', in *Journal of Development Studies,* January 1975.

Kuznets, S., 'Economic Growth and Income Inequality', in *American Economic Review,* March 1955.

———, *Modern Economic Growth — Rate, Structure and Spread,* New Haven, Connecticut, Yale University Press, 1967.

———, *Economic Growth of Nations: Total Output and Production Statistics,* Cambridge, Massachusetts, Harvard University Press, 1971.

Laclau, E., 'Argentina: Imperialist Strategy and the May Crisis', in *New Left Review,* No. 62 (July-August 1970).

———, 'Feudalism and Capitalism in Latin America', in *New Left Review,* No. 67 (May-June 1971).

Lall, S., 'Multinationals and Development: A New Look', in *National Westminster Bank Quarterly Review,* February 1975.

Landes, D. S., *The Unbound Prometheus: Technological Change and Industrial Development in Western Europe From 1750 to the Present,* Cambridge, Cambridge University Press, 1969.

Langer, W. L., *The Diplomacy of Imperialism, 1890-1902,* New York, A. A. Knopf, 1935.

Legassick, M., and Wolpe, H., 'The Bantustans and Capital Accumulation in South Africa', in *Review of African Political Economy,* No. 7 (1976).

Lehmann, D., 'A Theory of Agrarian Structure: Typology and Paths of Transformation in Latin America', Centre of Latin American Studies, University of Cambridge Working Papers, No. 25.

Lenin, V. I., 'On the So-Called Market Question', *Collected Works,* Vol. 1, Moscow, 1963.

———, 'The Agrarian Programme of Social Democracy in the First Russian Revolution, 1905-1907', *Collected Works,* Vol. 13, London, 1962.

———, 'The Economic Content of Narodism and the Criticism of It in Mr. Struve's Book' (1894), *Collected Works,* Vol. 7, London, 1963.

———, *Imperialism: The Highest Stage of Capitalism,* London, Lawrence and Wishart, 1948.

———, 'The Essence of the Agrarian Problem of Russia', *Collected Works,* Vol. 18, London, 1963.

———, *Marxism and the State: Preparatory Material for the Book 'The State and Revolution',* Moscow, Progress Publishers, 1972.

Leontieff, W., et al., *The Future of the World Economy, A United Nations Study,* New York, Oxford University Press, 1977.

Lewis, W. A., 'Economic Development with Unlimited Supplies of Labour', Manchester School (May 1954).

———, *Growth and Fluctuations 1870-1913,* London, Cambridge University Press, 1978.

Leys, C., 'Capital Accumulation, Class Formation and Dependency — The Significance of the Kenyan Case', in *The Socialist Register 1978,* London, 1979.

———, 'Interpreting African Underdevelopment: Reflections on the ILO Report on Kenya', Manpower and Unemployment Research in Africa (November 1974).

Lichtheim, G., *A Short History of Socialism,* London, Fontana, 1975.

Lim, R., 'The Philippines and the "Dependency Debate": A Preliminary Case Study', in *Journal of Contemporary Asia,* Vol. 8, No. 2, 1978.

Linn, L. L., 'The Pattern of Income Distribution in West Malaysia 1957-70', World Employment Programme Research, ILO, Geneva, 1976.

Little, I. M. D., 'Economic Relations With the Third World — Old

Myths and New Prospects', in *Scottish Journal of Political Economy* (November 1975).

Livingstone, I., 'The Ownership of Durable Goods in Tanzanian Households and Some Implications for Rural Industry', Economic Research Bureau, University of Dar Es Salaam, Paper No. 70. 1.

MacPherson, W. T., 'Economic Development in India Under the British Crown, 1858-1947', in Youngson, A. J., ed., *Economic Development in the Long Run*, London, Unwin, 1972.

McEachern,D., 'The Mode of Production in India', in *Journal of Contemporary Asia*, Vol. 6, No. 4, 1976.

McFarlane, B., 'Imperialism in the 1980s',· in *Journal of Contemporary Asia*, Vol. 7, No. 4 (1977).

McKeown, T., *The Modern Rise of Population*, London, Edward Arnold, 1976.

Maddison, A., *Economic Growth in the West: Comparative Experience in Europe and North America*, London, Allen and Unwin, 1964.

——, 'Long Run Dynamics of Productivity Growth', Banca Nazionale del Lavoro, 30 (1978).

Maizels, A., *Growth and Trade*, London, NIESR (1970).

Marshall, P. J., *East Indian Fortunes, The British in Bengal in the Eighteenth Century*, Oxford, Oxford University Press, 1976.

Marx, K., *Pre-Capitalist Economic Formations*, London, Lawrence and Wishart, 1964.

Mazumdar, D., 'The Urban Informal Sector', in *World Development*, Vol. 4, 1976.

Meillasoux, 'From Reproduction to Production', in *Economy and Society*, Vol. 1, No. 1 (February 1972).

Melotti, U., *Marx and the Third World*, London, Macmillan, 1977.

Mera, K., 'On the Urban Agglomeration and Economic Efficiency', in *Economic Development and Cultural Change*, January 1973.

Mikesell, R., ed., *Foreign Investment in the Petroleum and Mineral Industries*, Baltimore, 1971.

Minchington, W., 'Patterns of Demand, 1950-1914', in Cipolla.

Mori, K., 'Marx and "Underdevelopment": His Thesis on the "Historical Roles of British Free Trade" Revisited', in *Annals of the Institute of Social Science*, No. 19, University of Tokyo (1978).

Mukherjee, A., 'Indian Capitalist Class and Congress on National Planning and Public Sector, 1930-1947', in *Economic and Political Weekly*, Vol. XIII, No. 35.

Myrdal, G., *An International Economy*, New York, 1956.

——, *Economic Theory and Under-Developed Regions*, London, Duckworth, 1957.

——, *Asian Drama*, London, Pelican Books, 1968.

266

Nairn, T., 'The Modern Janus', in *New Left Review*, No. 94 (November-December 1975).

Nathan, A. J., 'Imperialism's Effects on China', in *Bulletin of Concerned Asian Scholars*, Vol. 4, No. 4 (December 1972).

Nayyar, D., 'Transnational Corporations and Manufactured Exports From Poor Countries', in *The Economic Journal*, 88 (March 1978).

O'Brien, P.K., 'A Critique of Latin American Theories of Dependency', in *Latin American Review of Books*, 1973.

Okhawa, K., and Rosovsky, M., 'The Role of Agriculture in Modern Japanese Economic Development', in *Economic Development and Cultural Change*, Vol. 9 (1960).

Onselen, C. van, *Chibaro: African Mine Labour in Southern Rhodesia, 1900-1933*, London, Pluto Press, 1976.

OECD, *Development Cooperation: 1978 Review*, Paris (November 1978).

Oshima, H. T., 'The International Comparison of Size Distribution of Family Incomes With Special Reference to Asia', in *Review of Economics and Statistics*, Vol. 44 (1962).

Owen, L., *The Russian Peasant Movement, 1906-1917*, New York, 1963, cited in Anderson, *Lineages*.

Owen, R., and Sutcliffe, B., eds., *Studies in the Theory of Imperialism*, London, Longman, 1972.

Padmore, G., *Africa and World Peace*, London, Frank Cass, 1972.

Paige, D. C., Blackaby, F., and Freund, S., 'Economic Growth — The Last Hundred Years', in *National Institute Economic Review*, No. 16 (July 1961).

Paish, F. R., 'British Economic Fluctuations', in *Lloyd's Bank Review*, July 1970.

Palma, G., 'Dependency: A Formal Theory of Underdevelopment or a Methodology for the Analysis of Concrete Situations of Underdevelopment?', in *World Development*, Vol. 6 (1978).

Patnaik, U., 'Neo-Populism and Marxism: The Chayanovian View of the Agrarian Question and its Fundamental Fallacy', in *Journal of Peasant Studies*, 4 (1979).

Patel, S. J., 'Transfer of Technology and Developing Countries', in *Foreign Trade Review*, Annual No., Indian Institute of Foreign Trade (January-March 1972).

Planungsgruppe Ritter, *Project on Urbanization, Employment and Development in Ghana: Report on Two Surveys*, World Employment Programme Research, ILO, Geneva, 1974.

Platt, D. C. M., ed., *Business Imperialism, 1840-1930. An Inquiry Based on British Experience in Latin America*, Oxford, 1977.

———, *Finance, Trade and British Foreign Policy, 1815-1915*, Oxford, 1968.

Polyani, K., *The Great Transformation: The Political and Social Origins of Our Time,* Boston, Beacon, 1957.

Pollard, S., *The Idea of Progress: History and Society,* Harmondsworth, Pelican Books, 1971.

Pollard, S., and Holmes, C., eds., *Documents of European History. Volume 2, Industrial Power and National Rivalry, 1870-1914,* London, 1972.

Poulantzas, N., 'Internationalization of Capitalist Relations and the Nation State', in *Economy and Society,* Vol. III, No. 2 (May 1974).

——, *Fascism and Dictatorship. The Third International and the Problem of Fascism,* London, NLB, 1974.

Raj, K. N., 'Trends in Rural Unemployment', in *Economic and Political Weekly,* special issue, August 1976.

Ramos, J., 'A Heterodoxical Interpretation of the Employment Problem in Latin America', in *World Development,* Vol. 2 (July 1974).

Ray, C. F., 'The "Real" Price Rise of Primary Commodities', in *National Institute Economic Review* (1977).

Rey, P.P., *Les alliances de classes,* Paris, 1973.

Roberts, B., *Cities of Peasants, The Political Economy of Urbanization in the Third World,* London, Edward Arnold, 1978.

Robinson, J., *Essays in the Theory of Employment,* London, Macmillan, 1937.

——, *Aspects of Development and Underdevelopment,* Cambridge, 1979.

Robinson, R. E. and Gallagher, J. E, with Denny, A., *Africa and the Victorians,* London, Macmillan 1961.

Rosovsky, H., *Capital Formation in Japan, 1868-1940,* New York, Glencoe, 1961.

Rothstein, A., *A History of the USSR,* Harmondsworth, Penguin Books, 1950.

Runciman, W.G., *Relative Deprivation and Social Justice,* Harmondsworth, Penguin Books, 1973.

Sampson, A., *The Seven Sisters. The Great Oil Companies and the World They Made,* Seven Oaks, Coronet, 1976.

Schaefer, K., and Spindel, C. R., 'Urban Development and Employment in São Paulo', World Employment Programme Research, ILO, Geneva, 1974.

Schram, S., and Carrère d'Encausse, H., *Marxism and Asia,* London, Allen Lane, 1969.

Schumpeter, J.A., *Capitalism, Socialism and Democracy,* London, Allen and Unwin, 1942.

Sender, J. B., 'The Development of a Capitalist Agriculture in Tanzania: A Case Study with Detailed Reference to the West

268

Usambaras', unpublished Ph. D. dissertation, University of
London, 1975.

Sethuraman, S. V., 'Urbanization and Employment in Jakarta',
World Employment Programme Research, ILO, Geneva, 1974.

Shanin, T., *The Awkward Class. Political Sociology of
Peasantry in a Developing Society: Russia 1910-1925*, Oxford,
Oxford University Press, 1972.

Sinclair, S. W., 'The Intermediate Sector in the Economy', Manpower and Unemployment Research in Africa (November 1976).

Singer, H., 'Brief Note on Unemployment Rates in Developing
Countries', Manpower and Unemployment Research in Africa,
April 1970.

Sinha, R., 'Agricultural Productivity in Meiji Japan', paper
presented at Seventh International Economic History Congress,
Edinburgh (1978).

Spraos, J., 'The Statistical Debate on the Net Barter Terms
of Trade Between Primary Commodities and Manufactures', in
The Economic Journal, 90 (March 1980).

Steel, W. J., 'Empirical Measurement of the Relative Size and
Productivity of Intermediate Sector Employment: Some
Estimates from Ghana', Manpower and Unemployment
Research in Africa (April 1976).

Stokes, E., 'Late Nineteenth Century Colonial Expansion and the
Attack on the Theory of Economic Imperialism: A Case of
Mistaken Identity', in *The Historical Journal,* XII, 2 (1969).

Sukhatme, P. V., 'Assessment of Adequacy of Diets and Different
Income Levels', in *Economic and Political Weekly,* special
issue (1978).

Sunkel, O., 'National Development Policy and External
Dependence in Latin America', in *Journal of Development
Studies* (October 1969).

Sutcliffe, R. B., 'Imperialism and Industrialization in the Third
World', in Owen and Sutcliffe, eds.

Swainson, N., 'State and Economy in Post-Colonial Kenya, 1963-
78', in *Canadian Journal of African Studies,* Vol. XII (1978).

Swamy, S., 'Structural Changes and the Distribution of Income by
Size: The Case of India', in *Review of Income and Wealth*
(June 1967).

Turnham D., and Jaeger, I., *The Employment Problem in Less
Developed Countries: A Review of Evidence,* OECD, Paris, 1971.

UNCTAD, *Handbook of International Trade and Development
Statistics. Supplement 1977,* New York, 1978.

UN, *Demographic Trends in the World and the Major Regions,
1950-1970,* New York (E/Conf. 60/BP/1).

——, *The Developing Countries in the 1960s: The Problem of*

269

Appraising Progress, New York, 1971.

——, *Economic Survey of Latin America,* New York, 1972.

——, Department of Economic and Social Affairs, *1974 Report on the World Social Situation,* New York, 1975.

——, Department of Economic and Social Affairs, *Yearbook of Industrial Statistics 1975,* New York, 1977.

——, *World Economic Survey 1975,* New York, 1976.

——, *World Economic Survey 1976. Current Trends in the World Economy,* New York, 1977.

UNESCO, *Statistical Yearbook 1976,* Paris, 1977.

UNFAO, *The State of Food and Agriculture,* (1970) to (1976), Rome.

——, *1976 Trade Yearbook,* Rome, 1977.

——, *Production Yearbook, 1977,* Rome, 1978.

UNIDO, *Industrial Development Survey: Special Issue for the Second General Conference of* UNIDO, New York, 1974.

UNRISD, *Contents and Measurement of Socio-Economic Development: An Empirical Enquiry,* prepared by D. McGranahan, C. Richard-Proust, N. V. Sovani, M. Subramamian, Report No. 70.10, Geneva, 1970.

Veliz, C., ed., *The Politics of Conformity in Latin America,* RIIA, London, Oxford University Press, 1967.

Vengroff, R., 'Dependency and Underdevelopment in Black Africa: An Empirical Test', in *Journal of Modern African Studies,* 15, 4 (1979).

Vernon, R., *Restrictive Business Practices: The Operations of United States Enterprise in Developing Countries: Their Role in Trade and Development,* UNCTAD, New York, 1972.

Walicki, A., *The Controversy Over Capitalism: Studies in the Social Philosophy of the Russian Populists,* Oxford, 1969.

Wallerstein, I., *The Modern World System: Capitalist Agriculture and the Origins of European World Economy in the Sixteenth Century,* New York, Academic Press, 1974.

Wanatabe, S., 'Exports and Employment: The Case of the Republic of Korea', in *International Labour Review* (December 1972).

Warren, W., 'Imperialism and Capitalist Industrialization', in *New Left Review* (1973).

——, *Imperialism and Neo-Colonialism,* British and Irish Communist Organization (March 1977).

——, 'Nations and Corporations', in *Times Literary Supplement,* 1 November 1977.

——, 'Poverty and Prosperity', in *Times Literary Supplement,* 12 December 1975.

Weeks, J., 'Introduction', Manpower and Unemployment Research in Africa (November 1973).

——, 'An Exploration into the Nature of the Problem of Urban

Imbalance in Africa', Manpower and Unemployment Research in Africa (November 1973).

Wells, J., 'The Diffusion of Durables in Brazil and Its Implications for Recent Controversies Concerning Brazil and Development', in *Cambridge Journal of Economics,* September 1977.

——, 'Consumption, Market Size, and Expenditure Patterns in Brazil', Centre of Latin American Studies, University of Cambridge, Working Papers, No. 24, 1976.

Williams, G., 'Economy and Society', in *Nigeria,* London, Rex Collings, 1976.

——, 'Colonialism and Capitalism: The Nigerian Case. A Review', Paper presented to ASAUK Conference, Liverpool (September 1974), mimeo.

Williams, W. A., *The Tragedy of American Diplomacy,* New York, Delta, 1963.

——, *The Contours of American History,* Chicago, Quadrangle, 1966.

Woodruff, W., *Impact of Western Man: A Study of Europe's Role in the World Economy, 1750-1960,* London, Macmillan, 1956.

World Bank, 'World Economic and Social Indicators', Report No. 700/78/02, Washington, April 1978.

——, 'Commodity Trade and Price Trends', Report No. E.C.-166/78, Washington, August 1978.

——, *Annual Report 1978,* Washington, August 1978.

——, *World Tables 1976,* Johns Hopkins Press, 1976.

Wright, F. C., 'African Consumers in Nyasaland and Tanganyika', Colonial Research Studies, HMSO, 1955.

Zambia, Republic of, *National Income and Input-Output Tables 1971,* Central Statistical Office, Lusaka, 1975.

——, Ministry of Development Planning, *Economic Report, 1976,* Lusaka, 1977.

Index